A MANUAL OF
HOTEL RECEPTION

A MANUAL OF
HOTEL RECEPTION

J. R. S. Beavis
B.A. (Econ.), F.C.A., F.H.C.I.M.A.

Scottish Hotel School
University of Strathclyde

and

S. Medlik
M.A., B.Com., F.H.C.I.M.A.

Department of Hotel and Catering Management
University of Surrey

HEINEMANN : LONDON

William Heinemann Ltd
LONDON MELBOURNE TORONTO
JOHANNESBURG AUCKLAND

© J. R. S. Beavis and S. Medlik, 1967, 1969

First published 1967
Second (decimal currency) edition 1969
Reprinted 1972

434 91243 3

Printed Offset Litho in Great Britain
by Cox & Wyman Ltd,
London, Fakenham and Reading

Preface

IT has become customary for authors of textbooks to state in the Preface their justifications for what they have, and their apologies for what they have not, done. In many ways we find it appropriate to follow their example.

This book has been written with several groups of reader in mind. First, for the increasing number of students entering colleges to take a course in hotel reception or a broader course in hotel and catering subjects, which usually includes a study of hotel reception.

Secondly, for the many thousands of hotel receptionists who have learnt their work 'on the job' and who have to be employed in a number of hotels before they become aware of different methods and procedures.

Thirdly, for the large body of hotelmen who are always interested in different ideas in hotel reception and in having a handy book of reference.

We had to be restrictive, both in defining the field, and in the amount of detail included. On the first point, we had to ignore such instances as, for example, the fairly common practice of dealing in the reception office with other clerical activities such as wages and suppliers' invoices. This occurs particularly in the smaller units where the reception office is the one and only office of the hotel. Our concern here is with hotel reception, which deals with the arrival and departure of guests, their accounts, and many of their problems before, during, and after their stay.

On the second point, we wish to apologize for the many omissions, which the specialist will discover. Not only have we refrained from giving useful hints on how to get round the law and how to dispose of an unwanted guest. We have also often failed to connect the steps and actions taken by the receptionist on every occasion, as we do not believe that hotel reception can be learnt completely by reading a textbook. The specialist will also miss some favourite procedures and aspects of hotel reception dear to him. We would appreciate comments on such points and suggestions from readers, which would improve the usefulness of the book. But we would stress that it is not our aim to describe all the individual procedures which may be used in only a few hotels: rather we deal with the principles and with the reception methods most commonly employed. This approach should be particularly helpful to students who may be engaged in many different reception offices.

The teacher of the subject is likely to find something of interest, but will soon realize that the order in which the subject-matter is treated does not indicate the sequence in which the teaching is to be done. In any case, the teacher's scheme of work and the order of treatment is something no good teacher would accept blindly.

Our terminology follows English practice; thus we speak of the 'reception office', 'reception board', 'alphabetical index', and so on throughout, instead of the American 'front office', 'room rack', 'information-rack'. We are aware that in this field, as in others, American terminology is finding its way into this country, but as yet it has not reached many hotels. Should this book appeal to an American reader, we are confident that he will find no difficulty in understanding it, if he substitutes a few words here and there.

Over the last few years we have studied reception systems and procedures in many hotels, read what has been written on the subject, talked to many hotelmen, travel agents, business equipment specialists, and others. To all these we owe much. We have taught the subject to quite a few students. Lastly, we had arrived at some conclusions, only to find that what we had considered to be original methods had been previously arrived at by others. The following pages are the outcome of all this. By and large they provide an outline of the principles underlying hotel reception and the basic methods which, we hope, will promote further thought and research into an important aspect of the hotel business. In our view there is always a better method, and the best one will never be achieved.

London 1967
J. R. S. Beavis
S. Medlik

PREFACE TO SECOND EDITION

THIS Edition reproduces with some alterations the text of the First Edition but all amounts of money have been expressed in decimal currency, which replaces the existing currency in the United Kingdom on 15 February 1971.

London 1969
J. R. S. Beavis
S. Medlik

Contents

Appendixes

Acknowledgments

WE wish to thank those who helped us in the preparation of this book by allowing us to reproduce copyright material and in particular to:

Anker Cash Registers and Accounting Machines Ltd., for permission to reproduce a photograph;

American Express Company, for permission to reproduce a specimen credit card;

Battersea College of Technology, for permission to include questions from past examination papers;

British Hotels and Restaurants Association, for permission to reproduce their registration form;

Grand Metropolitan Hotels Ltd., for permission to reproduce a photograph and to adapt their instructions to staff;

Hotel and Catering Institute, for permission to reproduce questions from past examination papers in their original or amended form;

Lloyds Bank Ltd., for permission to reproduce a specimen cheque and a paying-in slip;

National Cash Register Co. Ltd., for permission to reproduce forms and photographs;

Shannon Ltd., for permission to reproduce illustrations of their equipment;

The Oddenino Organisation, for permission to reproduce a photograph;

Sweda Ltd., for permission to reproduce photographs;

Trust Houses Forte Group, for permission to reproduce photographs.

Plates

Introduction

THROUGHOUT the world more people than ever travel – on business, for pleasure, and for other reasons. More people than ever stay at hotels. They get their first impressions of an hotel from the way they are received. These first impressions are often the most lasting ones. Therefore, it is difficult to exaggerate the importance of good hotel reception.

In the great majority of hotels most of the income is derived from rooms. Two hotel activities are responsible for earning it: housekeeping, which prepares the rooms and looks after the guest's comfort during his stay, and reception, which sells the rooms. Looking at it in this way, hotel reception is the main sales outlet of the hotel.

But hotel reception is not confined to selling the bedrooms. The reception office supplies others with information, maintains liaison with them, and contributes to the co-ordination of hotel hospitality – reception is, therefore, the nerve centre of the whole hotel.

The men and women who receive guests – the receptionists – are not only salesmen or clerks but also key employees whose position is second only to management; for many of them hotel reception is a stepping stone to hotel management.

What Is Expected of Receptionists?

Their personality matters. They must be smart in appearance, pleasant in manner, tactful, and possess the ability to convey to the guest that they are there solely to serve him. Other people's pleasure is their business.

They need intelligence and a great deal of knowledge – not only about hotels – but also about people and places. They should have the ability and desire to solve other people's problems, to act independently, and to make decisions.

They must be efficient. Good hotel reception is based on a system and on procedures which must be operated smoothly and effectively. This requires an alert mind, a methodical approach to work, and attention to detail.

Men and women who possess these and several other desirable qualities operate reception offices in hotels in every country of the world. But these offices are far from alike.

Variations in Hotel Reception

Each reception office is different from every other reception office, and there are many reasons for this.

In the first place, hotel reception is influenced by the size of the hotel (Figure I.1). In a small hotel of up to thirty or forty bedrooms

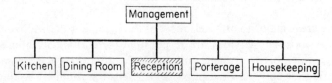

In a small unlicensed hotel

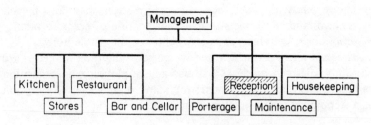

In a medium-sized licensed hotel

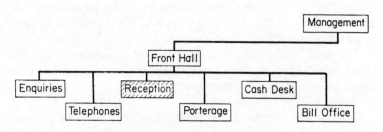

In a large hotel (section only shown)

Fig. I.1 Reception in hotel activity

only one or two receptionists may be employed. There the reception office may be the only office in the hotel and may deal with wages, suppliers' invoices, and many other clerical tasks. In the smallest of them the proprietor or manager may do much of the work himself. In such circumstances a simple system fulfils all the requirements.

As the hotel increases in size, specialization steps in. This may not be very apparent in a medium-sized hotel (in Britain this would be up to about 100 bedrooms), but once the hotel exceeds that size and, especially, if it is one of several hundred bedrooms, there are not just book-keeper/receptionists who cover the whole range of duties, but receptionists, book-keepers or bill office clerks, cashiers, inquiry clerks.

Hotel reception also varies according to the type of hotel. In a highly transient hotel where most guests stay only for one or two nights, a high proportion of them depart each morning, only to be replaced by a rapid succession of new arrivals in the late afternoon and evening. There the average cycle of the guest's stay is short and its effect on hotel reception organization and methods is in sharp contrast to the predominantly residential hotel where most guests stay for longer and often for such regular periods as a week or a fortnight; in many seaside resort hotels most arrivals and departures are concentrated between Friday and Sunday, with a distinct peak on Saturday.

Last but not least, the character of hotel reception is also determined by the standard of the hotel. This is not to say that good reception can only exist in a luxury hotel, but it is obvious that there is a close relationship between the price paid and the range and quality of services and amenities provided, including those within the scope of reception.

In this book hotel reception is viewed as an important hotel activity, which varies in its methods from one hotel to another but which has, nevertheless, much in common in all of them. The whole approach has been so designed as to recognize the common features as well as the differences. The validity of each chapter for different hotels derives from this approach.

1. *General*

PRICES of hotel services are usually incorporated in a list known as the hotel tariff. A description of the various types of charges which may be incurred by a guest in an hotel appears later in the part of this book dealing with visitors' accounts. But it is desirable to outline here the principal tariff structures to be found in hotels, as they are fundamental to a further consideration of hotel reception.

'Per room' or 'per person'

In the first place, prices of accommodation and of some other hotel services may be formulated either 'per room' or 'per person'. In the former case the bedroom is the unit of pricing, and the hotel tariff gives prices for a single room, twin-bedded room, double-bedded room, and suites. These categories may be further subdivided for bedrooms with and without private bathrooms, and also according to position and other criteria.

Where a 'per person' tariff is in operation, the guest forms the unit of pricing, and not only meal prices, but also accommodation prices, are formulated and charged per guest. There may be differential pricing for children of different ages and also for different standards of accommodation, but as distinct from the room tariff, prices are in the first instance fixed for an individual guest as a unit of sale.

Separate Charges and Inclusive Terms

Prices for accommodation and individual hotel services may be either fixed and charged separately or, to a greater or lesser extent, combined under inclusive terms.

Separate Charges

The simplest method is to establish separate rates for accommodation and other services and to charge them individually. Thus under a room tariff the price of a single room with bath may be fixed at £3·50 per night; this would normally be charged on the day of arrival for the first night of the guest's stay and each day subsequently for the coming night's stay. Breakfast and other charges would be debited to the guest as and when he incurs them. Similarly with a 'per person' tariff, the price of accommodation would represent a separate and distinct item both in the tariff and on the guest's bill.

This method lends itself to accurate pricing as the price of each item of hotel sale is arrived at separately; even breakfast may be *à la carte* and individual guests may be charged different amounts according to their choice. Whilst this is a fair method, a complete separation of accommodation and all other charges normally increases book-keeping work and may, in some instances, produce less revenue than combined charges; thus guests may go without breakfast or have breakfast and other meals outside the hotel. In this respect separate charges also add to difficulties in forecasting the demand for the various hotel services. For these reasons, this method is mainly used for transient guests in the larger luxury and first-class hotels.

Accommodation and Breakfast Charges

The tariff of most transient hotels includes a combined accommodation and breakfast charge, which may be stated either as an inclusive room and breakfast charge or as an inclusive bed and breakfast charge. Under this method the two items appear as one on the guest's bill, although an estimated breakdown may be made in internal records; normally no reduction is allowed to guests not taking breakfasts. Sometimes a combined charge includes only a Continental breakfast; a full English breakfast, if chosen, is charged separately.

Where a breakdown of the combined charge is made in internal records, it is done with a view to obtaining separate estimates of the revenue from accommodation and from breakfasts. Thus a price of £3·00 per person, which includes breakfast, may be apportioned as £2·50 for accommodation and £0·50 for breakfast, and a similar apportionment may be made in the case of a room tariff for a single-room rate, which includes breakfast. An inclusive price of £5·00 for a twin-bedded room may be apportioned as £4.00 for accommodation and £1·00 for breakfasts, i.e. two breakfasts at £0·50 each.

It is important to realize that the apportionment is intended to provide separate estimates of revenue from accommodation and from breakfasts and not estimates of their respective costs; thus it would be wrong to include merely the cost of breakfast under one heading and the remainder of the combined charge under accommodation.

If it is desired to record inclusive bed and breakfast terms accurately, the room charge is debited to the guest on the day of arrival and the breakfast on the following day. In this way the recorded revenue relates accurately to the day on which the charge is incurred. But it is far more common to record both charges in advance. This is quite acceptable provided that it is borne in mind that each day's breakfast revenue, as debited, relates to the following day. This latter method saves time and lessens the risk of the breakfast charge being overlooked on departure. The practice of debiting the combined charge both on the day of arrival and on the day of departure, and making an allowance on departure, is a bad accounting practice, as it may provide misleading figures, both of the value of business done and of allowances.

It is apparent that in most hotels a combined room (or bed) and breakfast charge increases revenue. It usually also facilitates the forecasting of the volume of breakfasts to be served on a particular day.

'En Pension' Terms

In many residential hotels the tariff is based on more or less fully inclusive terms; in others some guests may stay on inclusive terms and others not. The inclusive terms, also known as 'en pension', usually indicate a high proportion of residential guests who stay for longer periods, as distinct from the highly transient guests, for whom fully inclusive terms would be inappropriate.

Inclusive terms may be daily or weekly; sometimes a special tariff is introduced for Christmas or Easter, covering three or four days. Whichever is the case, it is important to define and state clearly what the inclusive terms cover: often they cover afternoon tea, but not early morning tea nor coffee after lunch and dinner.

It is customary to attempt an apportionment of the inclusive charge in internal records, at least between accommodation and meals; sometimes a further breakdown is made of meals. This is particularly important where, as is often the case, some guests stay on inclusive terms and others not. Only in that way can the revenue from inclusive terms be integrated into a detailed analysis of the hotel revenue. Whilst it is very common to apportion one-third of the revenue to accommodation and two-thirds to meals, it is obvious that the appropriate basis can only be arrived at after a careful consideration of the particular circumstances of each hotel.

'En pension' terms enable an accurate forecasting of the volume of business and may, in particular cases, produce a higher revenue than would be the case otherwise, especially if, as is usual, no reduction is made to guests not taking a meal.

Demi-pension Terms

A particular type of an inclusive tariff is known as demi-pension. As the name suggests, the terms include some food but not all. The normal demi-pension arrangement covers accommodation, breakfast, and one main meal, which may, but need not, be specified. Considerations similar to those discussed above in connection with the 'en pension' tariff apply, both as regards its effects and charging.

It should be pointed out at this stage that there is much to be said for a few well-defined tariff categories with a standard price in each, rather than a wide variation. Not only is the receptionist's work simplified, but it also simplifies forecasting and budgeting and avoids unpleasantness with price-conscious guests.

ROOM NUMBERS

In all but the smallest hotels the work of receptionists (and of others) is greatly facilitated if rooms are numbered by floors, the first digit indicating the floor on which the room is situated. In an hotel in which the number of rooms on each floor does not exceed nine, the room number may consist of only two digits: thus room 23 would be a second-floor room and room 41 a fourth-floor one. Where there are between ten and ninety-nine rooms per floor, the room number would consist of three digits: thus room 234 would be a second-floor room and room 412 a fourth-floor one.

It is interesting to note in this connection that in modern hotels, built with a view to efficient operation, the layout of floors is standardized, so that the same floor plan is followed for all bedroom floors in the building. Apart from obvious advantages and saving in the actual construction and maintenance of such buildings, reception work is greatly helped, as the room numbers also follow a standard pattern on each floor.

Coding of Room Numbers

In some hotels a system of coding is used for room numbers. This usually consists of a letter code, which is only intelligible to the staff, and which is used for example, on key tags and in the hotel register. If a code is adopted, a room key found by an unauthorized person is of little use to him. Below is an example of such a code:

$$
\begin{array}{cccccccccc}
1 & 2 & 3 & 4 & 5 & 6 & 7 & 8 & 9 & 0 \\
C & V & K & P & B & Z & D & M & R & H
\end{array}
$$

Thus room number 234 would appear as VKP while PCV would stand for room number 412. Sometimes, to help the staff remember the code, the ten letters form a recognizable word, e.g. *hydraulics* or *profitable*.

ROOM KEYS

In addition to master keys in the possession of certain members of staff, there should be two keys available for each letting bedroom.

The first set is the one in current use, and each key of this set must be either on the key board (if the room is not let or if the guest is out) or in the possession of the particular guest who occupies the room at the time.

The second set is on a duplicate key board, which is usually under the personal supervision of the head receptionist or another senior member of staff. Whenever a duplicate key is removed from the duplicate key board, a tag should be put in its place, indicating when, by whom, and for what purpose the key was removed (Figure 1.1). A regular daily

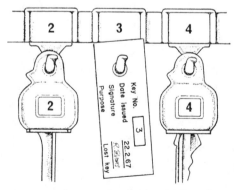

Fig. 1.1 Section of key board for duplicate keys

check then ensures that the duplicate key board is only depleted for a good reason and that keys are returned to it without delay.

Hotel keys should be supplied by a reputable specialist firm or by the hotel locksmith. They are normally securely fastened to a large tag bearing the name and address of the hotel; it is preferable that the room number be engraved on the key. A note on the tag to the effect that 'if this key is found a stamp should be affixed and the key posted' may help the hotel in recovering keys which have unintentionally been taken out of the hotel by departing guests. In some hotels neither the keys nor the tags give a clue to the identity of the hotel; where this is a conscious decision, it is usually on the grounds that the key may be lost and found outside the hotel by a person who might put it to unauthorized use.

WRITING OF NAMES

It is absolutely essential that records of guests' names are correctly spelt and legible. When names are not typed, it should be the normal practice to print them in BLOCK LETTERS. When looking for a name in a list, it is convenient to have names arranged underneath each other with surnames first, and to follow always the same order.

Below are a few illustrations of a simple arrangement to secure legibility and quick reference; it is suitable for all internal records, but for communications intended for guests, the order and form should, of course, be the normal ones as used, for example, in correspondence.

BROWN	Mr	S.
DANIEL	Mrs	F.
EDWARDS	Miss	L.D.
HAWLEY	Capt	D.H.
JAMES	Rev	L.A.
JONES	Mr/s	A.B.
LAWLEY	Rev & Mrs	B.C.
MATHEWS	Mesds	S. & D.
NOLAN	Messrs	L.K. & D.F.
PAGE & SMITH	Messrs	T.D. & F.C.
SIMON	Mr/s & Miss	C.D. & L.
SMITH & PAGE	Messrs	F.C. & T.D.
THOMPSON	Mrs & Master	J.K. & B.A.

Note the abbreviation Mr/s, which means 'Mr and Mrs'.

USE OF SYMBOLS AND ABBREVIATIONS

In order to save time and space in records, a number of symbols and abbreviations are in use in most reception offices. Sometimes their use also prevents guests from acquiring information not intended for them. It must, however, be stressed that the symbols are for internal use by members of staff, to whom they should be explained; they are not used in dealing with guests, for whom they are mostly meaningless. The short list below gives some of the more general symbols and abbreviations and is by no means exhaustive. In many hotels further ones are adopted, and others may be used instead to denote the same information.

Rooms		*Others*	
—	single room (or S)	A	adult
=	twin-bedded room (or T)	C	child(ren)
+	double-bedded room (or D)	N	night(s)
B	bath	WK	week
SR	sitting-room	MTH	month

Example

SMITH   Mr/s   J.A.   1 = B   3N from 21.3.71

A reservation received by telephone of a twin-bedded room with bath from 21 to 24 March 1971 for Mr and Mrs J. A. Smith may thus be simply and quickly taken down as shown above.

2. *Basic Aids and Records*

THE hotel register is one of the most important hotel records. It has two main functions: to satisfy the legislation relating to the registration of guests in hotels, and to provide a record of guests, from which information is obtained for other reception records and for other departments of the hotel. The rules of law relating to hotel registration are summarized in Appendix D and should be read before the different types of hotel register are studied.

Types of Hotel Register

There are three basic types of hotel register: book, loose leaves, and individual forms. These three are described and compared below.

Book

The hotel register in book form is the oldest and probably still the most common type. It is a bound volume of suitably ruled pages, in which each guest's particulars are entered in chronological order of arrival. A specimen ruling appears in Figure 2.1.

Date	Full Name	Nationality	Address	

Fig. 2.1 Hotel register: specimen ruling

There is little justification for including in this type of register any other particulars, such as room numbers or prices, which may be seen by other guests. Where it is deemed essential, a code should be used for all such information. The principal merits of this type of register are several:

(*a*) COMPACTNESS. It provides in a compact form a chronological record of all guests in their order of arrival, and if the date of arrival is known, a guest's registration can be easily located for some time back.

(*b*) SAFETY. The risk of loss, or of unauthorized removal of an entry, or of a whole page, is negligible.

(*c*) COST. It is a relatively cheap method as each entry occupies only one line of space.

But the register in book form suffers from a number of drawbacks, some of which apply generally, others in particular circumstances:

(*a*) INDISCREETNESS. This is an indiscreet method of registration as previous entries can be seen by subsequent guests.

(*b*) APPEARANCE. Its appearance tends to deteriorate with use, and the bulkier the volume the more thumbed and defaced it is likely to become.

(*c*) SPEED OF REGISTRATION. Where a number of arrivals occur at the same time, some may have to wait for their turn to register, and the transfer of information to other records is also delayed.

(*d*) FLEXIBILITY IN USE. It cannot be removed from the office during the day for such purposes as audits of the day's business, and its size often precludes its use in different parts of the office.

Loose Leaves

Where the loose-leaf method is adopted, a loose sheet of the same ruling as in Figure 2.1 is used and usually placed on a blotting pad; it is either removed and filed in a fixed binder at the end of each day and replaced by a new blank page, or used as long as space permits, and then replaced.

This method mitigates some of the worst drawbacks of the book form of register and has a number of advantages over it:

(*a*) APPEARANCE. If the sheet and blotter are replaced often enough, the register remains clean.

(*b*) SPEED OF REGISTRATION. More than one sheet may be in use at a time to enable more than one guest to register concurrently.

(*c*) FLEXIBILITY IN USE. If the register is required in another place it can be transferred easily, and it need not be missed in the office as another sheet can be used in the meantime.

The principal drawbacks are:

(*a*) DISCREETNESS. Although not to the same extent as the book, the loose-leaf form of register is still indiscreet, as a number of entries may be seen by subsequent guests.

(*b*) SAFETY. Loose sheets may be mislaid, lost, or removed from the file without the fact being immediately noticed.

(*c*) COST. If all available space on each sheet is not utilized, some wastage occurs.

The 'Alien' Form

With both of the above types of register it is customary to use a separate 'alien' form to secure the additional information required by

```
┌──────────────────────────────────────────────────────────────┐
│                                                                │
│            SUPPLEMENTARY              Date of arrival          │
│          REGISTRATION  FORM           ──────────────           │
│                                                                │
│                                                                │
│   Surname _____       Other names _____       │
│   Passport or Registration Certificate                         │
│   Number _____      Place of issue _____    │
│                                                                │
│                                                                │
│   Next destination (full address if known)   Date of departure │
│   ─────────────────────────────────────      ──────────────   │
│                                                                │
└──────────────────────────────────────────────────────────────┘
```

Fig. 2.2 Specimen 'alien' form

law from aliens. Where the details of the next destination are not known on arrival, it is desirable to attach the form to the guest's bill so as to ensure that it is completed when the guest's bill is being settled on departure. A specimen of an alien form is given in Figure 2.2.

It is, of course, possible to provide additional columns, which are completed only by aliens, on the above types of hotel register and so dispense with separate aliens' forms.

Individual Registration Form

The individual registration form is a more recent development in hotel registration and is meeting with increasing acceptance as a modern method suitable for any hotel. A specimen of such a form, as supplied to its members by a trade association, is reproduced in Figure 2.3.

REGISTRATION FORM

A separate form to be completed for each guest of 16 years of age and over

SURNAME ....   DATE OF ARRIVAL.......................................
(in capitals)

CHRISTIAN NAMES ....   The following information to be given by a guest who is NOT a British subject:

HOME ADDRESS ....   NUMBER OF PASSPORT.........................

....   ISSUED AT ....

NATIONALITY ....   NEXT DESTINATION, and full address there, if known. . . .

ROOM No..   ....

CAR REGISTRATION No..   ....

SIGNATURE..

This form has been prepared by the British Hotels and Restaurants Association for the use of members

Fig. 2.3 Individual registration form

The numerous advantages of the individual form over the other methods may be summarized as follows:

(*a*) DISCREETNESS. Absolute discreetness is assured as each guest only sees his own form.

(*b*) APPEARANCE. There is no difficulty in ensuring a clean and tidy appearance.

(*c*) SPEED. Any number of arriving guests can register at the same time and information can be quickly transferred to other records.

(*d*) FLEXIBILITY IN USE. This form may be used subsequently in different places, if required. It also facilitates allocation of rooms to guests who cannot be accommodated immediately, as their forms may be kept separately in one place until rooms become available. The forms may be filed alphabetically at the end of the day to enable a particular form to be easily located subsequently, even if the date of arrival is not known.

(*e*) SIMPLICITY. No separate 'alien' form need be used; a separate section is incorporated for completion by aliens only, and other useful information may also be included in the form.

There are only two major drawbacks, which should be mentioned:

(*a*) SAFETY. An individual form may be easily lost, mislaid or removed without it being noticed.

(*b*) COST. The cost of this method of registration is likely to be higher than with other methods.

Summary

The type of register to be used is within the hotelier's discretion, and should be chosen after a careful consideration of the relative advantages and drawbacks of the three methods outlined above. The choice will be to some extent influenced by the number of arrivals, their distribution throughout the day, the standard of the establishment, and other factors.

Whichever type is adopted, several points should be observed as regards hotel registration:

(*a*) A secure inkstand with a good pen should be provided, and the receptionist should hand the pen to the guest when asking him to register.

(*b*) The receptionist should establish at the time of receiving the guest the exact spelling of the name and other particulars; if there is any doubt about the legibility of an entry, the receptionist should print the word(s) above the guest's own handwriting.

(*c*) If there is any doubt about such matters as whether a particular alien is required to supply further particulars, advice should be obtained from the police.

RECEPTION BOARD

In all but the smallest hotels a variety of devices is adopted to provide a visual indication of room occupation. This is often combined with other objectives, such as a visual guide to the position and particulars of letting bedrooms and, in some instances, also to advance reservations.

Methods

The common feature of most of these devices is a board divided into a number of slots corresponding to the number of letting bedrooms, in which cards or slips are placed when rooms become occupied.

The slots, one for each room, should be arranged by floors for easy location, so that in a horizontal arrangement each tier represents one floor, and the layout of the board corresponds to that of the key board; in a vertical arrangement room slots for bedrooms on the same floor are underneath each other, and there is one column to a floor. The room numbers on the board should follow the floor plan so that communicating doors between rooms may be indicated.

The room cards, which are placed in the slots on arrival of the guest(s) to indicate that the room is occupied, and removed on departure as rooms become vacant, should have a standard ruling. This enables a uniform set of information to be displayed as regards the occupation of

SURNAME Title INITIALS	
Date of Arrival	Date of Departure
Number of guests	Terms

SMITH Mr. J. A.	
12. 1. 72.	14. 1. 72.
1	£2·75

Horizontal layout

SURNAME	Title	Number	INITIALS
Date of Arrival	Date of Departure	Number of guests	Terms

SMITH Mr. J. A.			
12. 1. 72.	14. 1. 72.	1	£2·75

Vertical layout

Fig. 2.4 Reception board: specimen room cards

each room, and a particular piece of information is always found in the same part of the card. Information usually included on the room card consists of the guest's name(s), the arrival and departure dates, the number of guests occupying the room, and the terms per room. Figure 2.4 shows two examples of room cards, one for each main type of reception board layout.

Sections of the horizontally and vertically arranged reception boards are illustrated in Figure 2.5. In both cases the rooms are arranged by floors, and an indication of the type of room is given underneath or alongside the room slot in abbreviated form. Where the room rates do not vary between different times of year, they can also be permanently displayed with the description of the room, and need not be repeated on each room card.

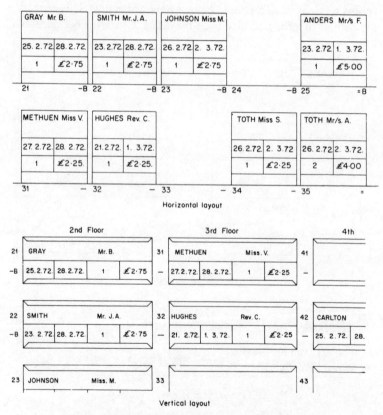

Fig. 2.5 Reception boards: alternative layouts

Plate 1.1 Reception area at the Eastgate Hotel, Lincoln, an hotel in the
Trust Houses Forte Group

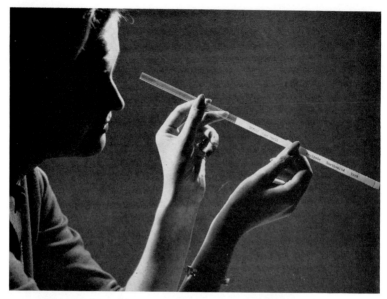

Plate 2.1 Inserting a typewritten strip into transparent tube

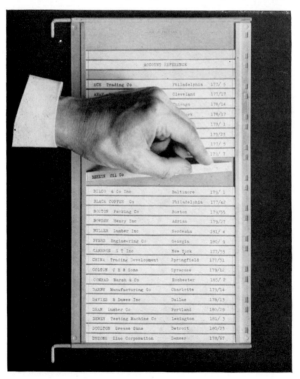

Plate 2.2. Fitting the strips into a panel

Position of Reception Board

It is undesirable that the reception board be visible from outside the office but it should be so situated that the receptionist can see it and refer to it conveniently without moving away from the counter. The board need not be suspended from the wall. Often it may be more convenient to set it into a high reception counter, sloping at a sharp angle towards the receptionist, who can then refer to the board whilst dealing with customers in front of him.

Board Operation

As mentioned, a room card is inserted in the appropriate slot on the guest's arrival and removed on his departure. When a room is vacant, the corresponding pocket of the reception board is empty. It is often impossible to prepare the room card immediately after the guest has registered; this may happen for example when a number of arrivals register at the same time or in quick succession. In order to prevent selling the same room twice, before the room card is inserted, a simple signalling device can be used to indicate that the room is sold and awaiting the room card. In any case it is important to bear in mind in operating this type of board, that it only provides an indication of room occupation at any given moment, and that it shows that the room is either vacant *now*, or that it is occupied *now*, and when it will be vacated. It does not enable letting of rooms to be done without reference to advance bookings. The use of a reception board which will also indicate advance reservations is described in the next chapter.

Furnishing Card

In some smaller hotels where the furniture, furnishings, and other facilities of rooms vary widely, not only between the main categories of rooms but also within the same category, it may be useful to include on the board a more detailed description of each room. This may either provide a full list of the above items, or only those which deviate from the standard. A simple method is to insert in each slot a permanent 'furnishing card'. The receptionist is then able to refer to it quickly on occasions when a particular item is requested by a guest; the cards can also serve as a simple inventory of all letting bedrooms. Two specimen cards are illustrated in Figure 2.6; the first lists the whole contents, the second only 'abnormal' items.

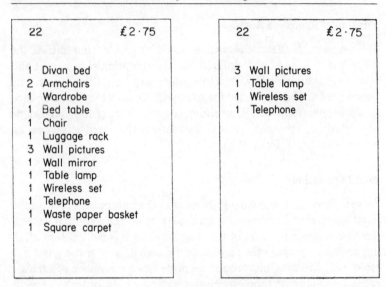

22	£2·75
1	Divan bed
2	Armchairs
1	Wardrobe
1	Bed table
1	Chair
1	Luggage rack
3	Wall pictures
1	Wall mirror
1	Table lamp
1	Wireless set
1	Telephone
1	Waste paper basket
1	Square carpet

22	£2·75
3	Wall pictures
1	Table lamp
1	Wireless set
1	Telephone

Fig. 2.6. Specimen furnishing cards

ALPHABETICAL GUEST INDEX

Function

In nearly all but the small hotels, especially where the guests are changing daily, the names of all the guests and their room numbers cannot easily be memorized. As this information is often required for directing mail and telephone messages to guests, for putting telephone calls through to their rooms, and for answering visitors' enquiries, it is advisable to have a visible index of all the guests arranged in alphabetical order, to which reference can be made, and from which the room number of any particular resident, or whether a particular person is staying at the hotel at all, can be ascertained at a glance.

Method

The most common type of index consists of one or more metal panels, in which strips of uniform length and width, bearing the required details, are inserted in alphabetical order on arrival. It is advisable to adopt a standard way of entering the details on the strip to facilitate a quick reference, and the examples in Figure 2.7 illustrate how this can be done. They may be written out by hand in block letters, or typed if there is a typewriter available, which can be devoted entirely to the purpose. The strips are supplied in continuous sheets so that they can be inserted in the typewriter and left there to be used as and when desired: only completed strips are detached from the sheet and inserted in a panel. Plate 2.1 shows a strip guarded by a transparent tube and ready for insertion; the panel itself appears in Plate 2.2. Where two persons of different names share a room, a strip should be inserted under each name as indicated in Figure 2.7. In addition to the name, title, and room

| SMITH | Mr. J.B. | R.A.F. | 126 |

| SMITH | Mr/s F. | Leeds | 194 |

| BROWN & SMITH | Messrs. K. & L. | U.S. | 76 |

| SMITH & BROWN | Messrs. L. & K. | U.S. | 76 |

| CARTER | Rev. & Mrs. A. | | 243 |

Fig. 2.7. Alphabetical guest index: specimen strips

number it may be useful to insert further information on the strip, which would assist the receptionist in identifying the guest where, as is often the case in large hotels, there are two or more guests of the same name; such particulars as the guest's home town or other background information will often help in deciding for whom the mail is intended.

The size of the panel installation will be determined by the size of the hotel. Whereas one panel may be sufficient for an hotel with a capacity of fifty rooms, large hotels will require several panels arranged in a revolving stand (*see* Plate 2.3); an alternative installation is a wall bracket, in which panels are turned like leaves in a book. Where many hundreds of names have to be indexed each panel may be devoted to one or two letters of the alphabet only.

Procedure

A strip is made out and inserted in the panel on arrival, and there it remains unaltered for the whole length of stay, unless the guest has changed his room, or has been joined by another guest; changes such as these necessitate a correction on the strip to keep the index up-to-date.

Procedure on departure may vary considerably. In some hotels strips of departed guests are removed and destroyed immediately. In others they are merely marked with a coloured pencil and are all removed at the end of the day. Yet a third, and probably the best method, is to stamp the strips of departing guests with a date stamp, and to transfer them immediately to a separate panel, where they are kept for a little time before they are destroyed. The latter two methods, and particularly the last one, thus preserve a visible record of all recently departed guests until the end of the day, or even longer, so that enquirers, for example, may also be given concrete information as to the guest's departure.

In large hotels several indexes of the type described may be used by different departments: in the reception office, by the enquiry clerks, by the switchboard operators, etc. Where this is the case, their co-ordination may be achieved by means of the integrated system.

Alphabetical Order

Where several hundred names have to be sorted alphabetically it is important that a consistent system is adopted, so that the strips are always placed in the correct position. There are well established rules in secretarial practice dealing with such matters as where to file names prefixed by Mc and Mac, names prefixed by De and De la, hyphenated names, and so on. Where more than one person uses or compiles an index they must all adhere to the same order, otherwise names will unaccountably become 'lost'.

If a hotel has a high percentage of foreign guests, staff must expect also to meet unusual and complicated names. Some rules might usefully be formulated to avoid perpetrating elementary mistakes; it should be known, for example, that a Chinese family name is placed first (Chiang Kai-shek is Mr *Chiang*; the strip is filed under 'C' not 'S').

KEY AND MAIL RACK

A combined key and mail rack is a standard item of the equipment of an hotel and is often kept in the reception office. It consists of numbered pigeon holes, one for each room, over which the key hangs on a hook, or in which the key is placed; guests' mail is arranged in the pigeon holes.

Each opening should be large enough to hold mail of ordinary size and to allow the room key to hang over it without covering the space below and next to it. In practice pigeon holes with an opening of between 4 × 2 in. and 5 × 3 in. in area and with holes from 8 to 10 in. in depth are adequate. They should be arranged for quick location and it is common to divide the rack by floors so that each tier represents one floor. Plate 2.4 shows a typical rack.

The position of the key and letter rack within the office deserves attention. The number of hotels where it is placed outside the office for guests 'to help themselves' both to keys and to mail is fortunately diminishing and the undesirability of such practice need not be emphasized. The rack should be so situated within the office as to obviate unnecessary walking by the receptionist; this is particularly important in a large hotel where the handing out of keys and mail and the receiving of keys is a time-consuming activity. In any case it is useful to place the rack in such a position that a receptionist standing at the counter can see the rack and inside the pigeon holes without having to walk to them. Its position in relation to the guest is more problematic and opinion on this is divided. Some hoteliers prefer to expose the rack to view from outside the office; thus the guest can see for himself whether there is any mail in his pigeon hole and does not have to ask each time. On the other hand such an arrangement also enables others to see the whereabouts of a particular guest: a key in place indicates that the guest is out of the hotel. This information may be positively dangerous.

Experiments have been made with other than the conventional types of key and mail racks in order to save space and effort. For instance, a rack arranged on a revolving stand has been used to replace one stretching over some 10 ft along the wall; it was found that a drum-shaped stand with a radius of less than 1½ ft and with pigeon holes around its circumference saved a great deal of walking by being situated by the counter, but it necessitated turning the stand into position when it was desired to refer to a particular room number for key or mail.

Key Procedure

Receptionists receive keys from guests and in large hotels they also take them from receptacles provided for use by guests in the reception and cashier's counters. They must be careful to place the keys in their correct position on the rack. When handing out a key, they should always check the number on it to make certain that the wrong key has not been placed on or taken from the wrong hook. The fury of a guest on reaching the door of his room and finding that he has been given the wrong key should be a sufficiently unpleasant prospect for every receptionist!

Guests' attention should be drawn by notices to the desirability of handing in their keys to the reception desk when going out of the hotel. If this procedure is followed, a glance at the key and letter rack indicates at once not only whether there is any mail for a particular room number, but also whether a guest is in or out:

> KEY IN   —   Room Unoccupied
> or
> Guest Out
> KEY OUT   —   Guest In

Duplicate keys and keys of connecting rooms are best kept on a separate duplicate key board and should be only handed out when absolutely necessary. Each time this is done, a small paper tag should be put in their place, stating to whom the key has been issued and for what purpose.

Both the combined key and letter rack and the duplicate key board should be checked at standard times, e.g. at 6 a.m., and at other specified times. Any cases of keys missing, which should be there, and vice versa, should be investigated promptly: a key should not be missing if the room is vacant, and there should not normally be a key for an occupied room at 6 a.m.

ROOM RECORD

In some hotels it is considered desirable to have a separate record of the occupation of each room over a period of time, so that it can be ascertained at a glance who stayed in a particular room on a particular date in the past.

The common feature of this record is a room card and most systems have two aspects in common:

(a) the room card provides a chronological record of the occupation of each room;

(b) the room card is kept in some form of cabinet in which the cards are arranged in room number order.

The Room Card

The room card is not in use for one occupation only, as is the case with the reception board, but continually; the last entry indicates the present or last occupation of the room (*see* Figure 2.8).

234.   —B

Date of arrival	Date of departure	Name(s)	No. of guests	Terms	Remarks
12–1–72	14–1–72	SMITH Mr. J.A.	1	£2·75	
14–1–72	15–1–72	JONES Miss M.D.	1	£2·75	
20-1-72	24-1-72	JAMES Mrs. A.B.	1	£2·75	

Fig. 2.8 Room record: specimen room card

The Cabinet

The cabinet provides a convenient means of storing the room cards for easy reference. They are preferably arranged by floors and by room number, so that the record of any room can be easily located. The state of occupation of the whole hotel is not visible at a glance as is the case with the reception board, but each card provides a 'room history' for some time back, in addition to the current occupation. For this reason the record is sometimes kept not in the reception office but maintained by the housekeeper who may have occasion to use it quite frequently, especially where she is responsible for lost-and-found property. But in large hotels the room record has also been used as a substitute for the reception board in the reception office, as the space required for a board to hold several hundred rooms is considerable. Two kinds of cabinet for holding the room cards are illustrated in Figure 2.9.

VISITORS' RECORD

Function

It is often considered desirable to have a permanent record of each guest's previous stays at the hotel. It enables the receptionist to see at a glance whether a particular person has stayed at the hotel before, and if so, when and for how long, which room he occupied, and any other particulars relating to his previous stays such as his special wishes. Each guest's record can then be regarded as his 'case history', containing an account of his association with the hotel. This is a counterpart of the room record, described above, in which room occupation is entered

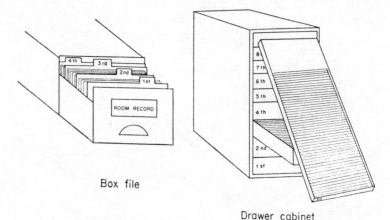

Box file

Drawer cabinet

Fig. 2.9. File and cabinet for room records

chronologically on room cards, providing the 'room history'. The two records thus contain similar information, differently arranged, and can be cross-checked at any time.

Methods

The method adopted to secure this information depends primarily on the amount of detail which it is considered advisable to retain for future reference.

Method A

Where the main objective is to have only a record of past stays and where no other details are required, individual registration forms may be filed alphabetically under guests' names for the purpose. This means that each time a particular guest stays at the hotel, his registration form is attached to the set of registration forms relating to his previous stays, and all are kept in a box file. The registration form of the guest who has not stayed before will be filed in the box in alphabetical order to form the basis of his set.

This method enables the receptionist to ascertain at any time whether a person stayed before, and if so, his address, dates of arrival, and any other information which is found on the particular registration form. The simplicity of the method is obvious; it does not involve additional work beyond correct filing.

Method B

In some hotels information secured by the above form of visitors' record may not be found adequate. It is contained on separate forms so that it is necessary to compare several forms if a comprehensive view of any one 'case history' is required. The method also requires alphabetical filing of registration forms, whilst in some cases it may be preferable to file registration forms of departed guests chronologically under dates of arrival. Where any of these factors apply, a more appropriate method of keeping a visitors' record is a separate card index.

A separate card is kept for each guest who has stayed at the hotel, on which details of stays are recorded as they occur. The card can thus contain a more detailed 'case history' of a guest, all of which is available on one card. The type of information recorded varies with circumstances and in many cases it is much more than a mere record of previous stays. In addition to this the card often contains valuable information about the guest, such as his credit-worthiness, and his worth to the hotel as expressed in terms of his spending. If used intelligently, it helps the receptionist to anticipate his requests, to decide on allocation of rooms and acceptance of bookings when accommodation is scarce, and in many other ways. To the management such a record may serve as a basis for market research. A specimen guest card is reproduced in Figure 2.10.

Method C

Alternatively a registration form may be used for more than one stay; in this case it is in the form of a card and the visitors' record appears on the reverse of the registration card. This means that for a guest who has stayed at the hotel before, only the date of arrival need be inserted to fulfil the registration requirements; the guest does not have to supply any further information and other data about his stay can be entered as appropriate.

JOHNSON			Mr. A.B.			Name
43 Old Avenue, Huddersfield, Yorks						Address
						Change of
Textile merchant, unlimited credit						Other particulars

Date of Arrival	Date of Departure	No. of Nights	Room No.	Terms	Remarks	Total Bill
6-10-71	17-10-71	11	78	£3·50		£64
28-11-71	30-11-71	2	44	£6·00	+ Mrs Johnson	£18
3-1-72			112	£3·50		

Fig. 2.10 Visitors' record: specimen guest card

Operation

The card index usually consists of two sections – 'past' and 'current' guests. At any time the former contains cards of all persons who have stayed at the hotel but are not staying at present, and the latter contains cards of present guests. In both sections the cards are usually filed alphabetically, although present guests may be filed under room numbers.

When a new guest arrives, he should have a card in the 'past' section if he has stayed at the hotel before; this is taken out, entered, and transferred to the 'current' section. For a person who has not stayed before, a new card is made out, and inserted in the 'current' section. It is customary not to complete the 'departure' and 'nights' columns until departure takes place, when remarks and the bill total are inserted, and the card is transferred to the 'past' section. Alternatively, the 'departure' and 'nights' columns are filled in on arrival in pencil only. Both methods serve the same purpose, namely to obviate crossing out if the guest, for example, extends his stay, and to distinguish a card of a 'past' guest from a 'current' one.

The card transfer from the 'past' to the 'current' section on arrival, and vice versa on departure, may be effected individually as each occurs, but more often it is possible only once a day; arrivals are then handled all together by reference to the hotel register and to such other records as the arrivals and departures book. Departures are entered and transferred collectively by reference to one of a number of records which show departures.

Note. The use of a visitors' record for black-listed customers is considered separately below.

BLACK-LIST

The hotelier's duty to receive and to accommodate guests, and his right of refusal, are in some cases regulated by law. An outline of the relevant rules of law is given in Appendix A and should be studied before this section. It will be seen that the hotelier can in some cases exercise absolute discretion in the choice of his guests, but in certain circumstances his right of refusal is restricted. Subject to the observance of the legal rules, where applicable, after a few years of operation there will be in almost every hotel a number of guests who will become undesirable and black-listed. This may happen for a number of reasons: for example, they might have been objectionable to other guests during a previous stay or they did not pay their bill. In all but the smallest establishments, it becomes necessary to keep a record for the reference of receptionists.

Methods

The record of guests placed on the black-list should be in a form facilitating quick reference to it by the receptionist when dealing with a customer, whether in person or by telephone, or when dealing with guest correspondence. Three basic methods are described below.

Book Form

When the black-list is in the form of a book, undesirable guests are usually entered in an alphabetically indexed book, with details and reasons for their inclusion; notes are also made on whether they must not be admitted under any circumstances, whether the manager should be informed on arrival, and whether special observation of the guest is required if admitted.

A book has, however, disadvantages. It can be mislaid, it cannot be seen at a glance whether a particular name is included, and reference to it tends to become spasmodic, rather than a matter of routine, as it should be. If a name is removed from the list, it continues to take up the space, even if crossed out. For these reasons two other methods are preferable.

Visitors' Record

The visitors' record may include a record of black-listed customers by marking their cards prominently with such warnings as 'Do not admit' or 'N.T.B.T.A.' (Not to be taken again); the reasons are stated on the card, too.

The cards of black-listed customers may be
    either   left in the 'past' section together with other cards;
    or   transferred to a separate section marked 'black', containing only cards of black-listed guests.

If this method is adopted, the visitors' record is, therefore, divided into three sections: past, current, and black. Whilst preferable to the first method, this procedure, like the first, if used alone still does not enable the receptionist to see at a glance whether a particular name is included.

A List

By far the most efficient method makes use of one or more copies of a list, strategically placed in the office, on which names of black-listed customers are arranged underneath each other in alphabetical order, with spaces for additions. If a separate visitors' record index is used, the list need not contain any details, as these should be given on the guest's card, or alternatively in a special book. The mere insertion of a guest's name on the list should, however, be sufficient to remind the receptionist to refer to these for further details. A section of a specimen list is reproduced in Figure 2.11.

ARRIVALS AND DEPARTURES RECORD

A specimen ruling of this record, which is sometimes also described as the Visitors Journal or the Terms Book, is given in Figure 2.12.

Operation

Each day's arrivals and departures are entered as they occur on two or more facing pages, the arrivals on the left-hand page and the departures on the right-hand page. The information relating to both is identical: room number, name, time, number of guests, terms per night. One line

		H	
HOWARD	Mr.K.		No
HORNSBY	Mr/s J.F.		Inform manager after admitting
HALLIDAY	Miss E.		No
		I	
		J	
JAMES	Mr.A.		No
		K	
KEMP	Mr.J.B.		Inform manager before admitting

Fig. 2.11 Specimen black-list

is used per room, irrespective of the number of persons occupying the room. Entries of arrivals are normally made from the hotel register, and entries of departures from the room cards removed from the reception board.

When a guest changes his room during the stay, the change is treated as a departure from one room and an arrival in another. As such a change does not affect the total number of guests in the hotel, the number of visitors is not inserted on either side of the record; to enter the same number of guests on both sides of the record would only inflate the number of arrivals and departures and the entries would cancel each other out.

ARRIVALS							
ROOM No.	NAME	TIME OF ARRIVAL	No. OF VISITORS			TERMS	
			A	C	S	£	p
	LEFT—HAND PAGE						

DEPARTURES		...................19............					
ROOM No.	NAME	TIME OF DEPART	No. OF VISITORS			TERMS	
			A	C	S	£	p
	RIGHT—HAND PAGE						

Fig. 2.12 Arrivals and departures record: specimen ruling

The treatment of a room change in the 'terms' column depends on the relative prices of the rooms. Where the prices of both rooms are the same, no entry is made in the 'terms' columns on either side, because such entries would only inflate the income derived from arrivals and the loss caused by departures, and would cancel each other out. Where a guest moves to a higher priced room, only the difference in price is entered on the arrivals page, as the daily revenue of the hotel from rooms has been increased only by this amount by the move; when the guest moves to a lower priced room, the difference in terms is entered on the departures page, as the daily revenue of the hotel has been decreased by the move by this amount. These situations can be illustrated by the following changes of rooms:

12.15 p.m. Mr & Mrs L. G. Lancet
    from room 17 (£5·00) *to* 18 (£5·00).

3.20 p.m. Capt J. K. Merryman
    from room 4 (£2·75) *to* 12 (£2·25).

4.30 p.m. Mesds S. Jones and H. F. Smith
    from room 20 (£5·00) *to* 15 (£6·00).

The consequent entries in the record are shown in Figure 2.13.

ARRIVALS

ROOM No.	NAME		TIME OF ARRIVAL	No. OF VISITORS			TERMS	
				A	C	S	£	p
18	LANCET	Mr/s L.G.	12·15 P.M.	CHANGE	OF	ROOM		
12	MERRYMAN	Capt J. K.	3·20	CHANGE	OF	ROOM		
15	JONES & SMITH	Mesds S.& H.F.	4·30	CHANGE			1	OO

DEPARTURES   17th March 19 71

ROOM No.	NAME		TIME OF DEPART	No. OF VISITORS			TERMS	
				A	C	S	£	p
17	LANCET	Mr/s L.G.	12·15 P.M.	CHANGE	OF	ROOM		
4	MERRYMAN	Capt J. K.	3·20	CHANGE		O		50
20	JONES & SMITH	Mesds S. & H.F	4·30	CHANGE	OF	ROOM		

Fig. 2.13 Arrivals and departures record: change of room

Daily Summary

The balancing of the Arrivals and Departures Record is done daily in a summary statement at the bottom of the departures pages, after the columns on both sides of the book have been added up. Departures are first subtracted from last night's balance to ascertain the number of rooms remaining occupied, the number of guests staying on from the previous night, and the income from the rooms derived from them. The day's arrivals are then added to this sub-total to ascertain the number of rooms occupied, the number of guests staying, and the income from accommodation for tonight. This balance then forms the opening balance of the next day's statement (*see* Figure 2.14).

ROOM No.	NAME		TIME OF DEPART	No. OF VISITORS			TERMS	
				A	C	S	£	p
	DEPARTURES	11th March 19 71						
27	JAMES	Mr K.	11·10	1	–	–	2	75
14	PAYNE	Miss C.	11·20	1	–	–	2	75
		D.		1				
	DAILY SUMMARY							
56	IN RESIDENCE LAST NIGHT		B/F	72	5	–	243	75
15	– DEPARTURES			21	1	–	67	50
41				51	4	–	176	25
22	+ ARRIVALS			27	–	–	81	75
63	IN RESIDENCE TO–NIGHT		C/F	78	4	–	258	00

Fig. 2.14 Arrivals and departures record: specimen daily summary

Functions

Most of the information derived from the Arrivals and Departures Book is apparent from the above description and its functions and value may be summarized as follows:

(*a*) It serves as a chronological record of all arrivals and departures on a particular day, with their times, rooms allocated and vacated, numbers of guests, and their terms.

(*b*) It provides a running record of the number of rooms occupied, number of persons staying in the hotel, and of the daily income from accommodation. (This information emerges from the daily summary statement but may also be extracted at any time whenever desired.)

(c) It provides a useful check for other records, e.g. for the reception board, alphabetical index, current section of the visitors' record, reservation chart, tabular ledger, and others.

(d) It facilitates calculations of occupancy and of room sales.

(e) In some hotels it serves as a basis and authority for opening visitors' accounts by the book-keeper who at intervals opens the accounts of newly arrived guests from the arrivals page.

In spite of the obvious advantages of this book, its compilation and balancing is a time-consuming activity, which is often not warranted, particularly in the smaller hotel and one with a long average stay of guests.

3. *Advance Bookings*

IN most hotels a proportion of guests reserve their rooms from a few hours to several months before they actually arrive. These reservations create a multitude of contractual relationships between the hotel proprietors and their guests, which exist from the time each reservation is made until the departure of the guests at the end of their stay or until they settle their accounts after departure. Whether the guests are 'chance', i.e. arriving without a prior reservation, or whether they had reserved their accommodation in advance, does not necessarily affect the basic aids and records described in Chapter 2. But advance bookings constitute an important responsibility on the part of the hotel, both in the legal and in the business sense, and call for additional records, which owe their existence entirely to reservations made in advance of guests' arrival.

These records should satisfy three requirements:

(*a*) The receptionist should be able to refer quickly to any individual reservation and to ascertain its particulars.

(*b*) All reservations should be classified by date of arrival so that all arrivals on a particular day should be available at a glance.

(*c*) There should be an accurate indication of all accommodation reserved in advance for any day, week, or month, which would enable the receptionist to see at a glance rooms reserved and those remaining free to be sold.

These requirements are met in all but the smallest hotels with three main records: (*a*) reservation form; (*b*) bookings diary; (*c*) booking chart.

RESERVATION FORM

Each reservation should be treated as a separate case, and all correspondence and other documents relating to that case joined together to form a separate set. When a reservation is made by telephone or in person, there need not be, initially at least, any documents to form the basis of the booking. A suitably ruled reservation form is then particularly useful, because it forms the basis of a booking. In some hotels its use is restricted to personal and telephone bookings, but it may be extended to all reservations, i.e. even those made by letter. This procedure has the merit of making the details of a booking, contained perhaps in several letters, available at a glance. Two specimens of reservation forms are shown in Figures 3.1 and 3.2.

Reservation Form

PERSONAL - TELEPHONE - LETTER - TELEGRAM

Name_____ Address _____

Date_____

Accommodation required:

Number of rooms - Type - Terms - From - Till   Other details

Booked by _____

If to be confirmed by Hotel _____

If to be confirmed by Guest _____

Dealt with by _____

Fig. 3.1 Duplicated reservation form

The benefits to be secured from the use of a reservation form may therefore be summarized as follows:

(*a*) The form standardizes the details of each reservation. It forms the top sheet of the set of documents relating to it, and thus facilitates quick reference without the necessity of reading through several letters.

(*b*) It assists in securing all the necessary information when a reservation is being accepted. (This applies particularly on the telephone when it is very easy to omit asking an important point.)

BOOKINGS DIARY

The second requirement of a good system, to provide a record of advance reservations arranged by date of arrival, is met by the introduction of a bookings diary; a possible ruling of this record with a few specimen entries is shown in Figure 3.3.

The principal characteristics are:

(*a*) One or more pages are used for each day, with the date promi-

```
NAME ........................................................
     (BLOCK LETTERS)

RESERVED BY...............................................

ADDRESS.....................................................

...................................................TEL...................

REQUIREMENTS ............................................

ARRIVAL DATE................ LENGTH OF STAY................

ARRIVAL DATE................ LENGTH OF STAY................

TERMS .......................................................

REMARKS .....................................................

............................................................

............................................................

DATE.................... SIGNATURE....................
```

Fig. 3.2. Printed reservation form

nently displayed at the top of the page. The pages are usually contained in a binder, from which past days' pages are continually removed so that the current page is always the first. New pages are inserted at the end, usually for at least a month ahead. The range of dates covered in the diary is determined by the maximum period for which reservations in advance are received.

(b) Each reservation is entered in the diary when it is made, on the page devoted to the date of arrival. The amount of detail entered against each name varies; in hotels where a reservation form is in operation in respect of every booking, the number of columns in the

11th March 1972

Date of booking	Name(s)	No. of persons	Length of stay	Accommodation required	Terms	Remarks	Room allocated
27-1-72	JAMES Mr K	1	3N	1 – B	£3·25	arriving late	11
7-2-72	BROWN Mr/s G	2	1N	1 =	£5·00		23
13-2-72	SMITH Messrs J&I	2	7N	1 = B	£6·00	garage	18

Fig. 3.3. Bookings diary

diary may be reduced, as the details of any booking can be readily ascertained from the form.

BOOKING CHARTS

The design and operation of a visual record, which would enable the receptionist to see at a glance the overall booking position of the hotel, gives much scope for ingenuity. There are two types of chart in use for the purpose, each being more appropriate in different circumstances, and these are described below.

The Conventional Chart

A conventional chart with a few specimen entries is reproduced in Figure 3.4. The reservation of a room for a given period is indicated in the chart by an entry of the name of the guest against the room number and over the dates for which the room is reserved. Entries are made in pencil to allow for alterations to be made in the case of cancellations or when a re-allocation of rooms becomes necessary subsequently.

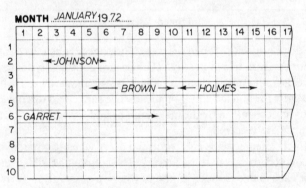

Fig. 3.4. Conventional booking chart

The main characteristics of this type of chart are:

(*a*) Normally a separate sheet is used for each calendar month, and the number of months covered in advance and, therefore, the number of sheets in use at any one time, is determined by the maximum period for which reservations are received.

(*b*) A reservation is usually recorded in the chart at the same time as the entry is made in the bookings diary. Because this is normally done when the booking is accepted, allocation of guests to particular rooms must also take place at the time.

(*c*) In addition to advance reservations, entries must also be made on the chart in respect of each 'chance' letting, because the chart must provide at any time the present and future room occupation.

(*d*) Any extension or reduction of the length of stay, not envisaged at the time of the original entry but decided upon subsequently, must be shown immediately and the chart adjusted accordingly.

The conventional type of chart, although used by the majority of hotels, and appropriate for many of them, suffers from several drawbacks in particular circumstances. Its operation becomes increasingly difficult, and its usefulness limited, if some or all of the following conditions apply in a particular hotel:

(*a*) Where many guests stay for one or two nights only, the entries on the chart are made difficult by limitations of space.

(*b*) Where it is often necessary to alter the allocation of rooms because of cancellations and in an effort to secure continuous occupation of rooms, maintaining the chart involves erasures, which are conducive to errors.

(*c*) A difficulty arises particularly where guests stay for short periods; then it often happens that the room originally allocated to them is not ready for occupation when they arrive. This may arise when the previous occupant has not departed in time, or when the room has not yet been prepared for the new occupation by the housekeeping department. In such circumstances the guest has to wait or be given another room which is ready, but this again involves an alteration of the chart.

(*d*) Generally the use of this type of chart is not conducive to maximum occupancy in hotels where the length of stay of guests varies; its operation becomes increasingly inflexible as occupancy increases.

To sum up, the conventional type of chart is mainly suitable for a resort hotel, where guests' stay tends to be longer, and for such regular periods as a week or a fortnight. In such circumstances the changes of guests and of rooms are not so frequent; arrivals and departures are mainly concentrated in one day, and the allocation of rooms can usually be arranged in such a way as to obviate waiting or changes on arrival. Few difficulties are experienced in the operation of this type of chart in these circumstances.

The Density Chart

The booking chart described previously may be found rather cumbersome in certain circumstances. In larger hotels with a short average length of stay, allocation of rooms has drawbacks if it is done when reservations are received.

For these reasons a different type of chart has to be adopted, which is described here under the title 'density chart'. Its main feature is that it merely records the number of rooms of a particular kind booked for each night as bookings come in. Individual reservations are not identified with particular room numbers until the date of arrival, when new arrivals are allocated to their rooms.

A prerequisite of this method is the standardization of hotel bedrooms into several main types, which are grouped together on the chart; alternatively a separate chart may be used for each type of room. In the simplified example in Figure 3.5 there are three types of room:

13 single with bath
8 single
6 double with bath

The total room capacity of twenty-seven is broken down on the chart into the three categories, and the example shows the appearance of the chart with some entries for the month of May. The numbers on the sides are not actual room numbers but represent a scale, against which can be seen the total number of rooms of each type, and the number remaining free to be sold – for this reason the scale runs from bottom to top. The dates of the month run across the top from left to right as on the conventional chart; the shading or colouring of certain dates indicates Sundays and facilitates reference.

The operation of the density chart is next discussed under separate headings.

BOOKING

On receipt of a request to reserve, a glance at the chart immediately reveals whether there is a room of the required type available for the stated night(s). If this is the case, the booking is recorded on the chart simply by filling in the next available space from the top under the particular date(s). The booking may be also recorded on the reservation form and must be recorded in the bookings diary. In fact, the diary assumes an even greater importance with this chart, because recorded bookings of rooms are not identified with any name in the chart.

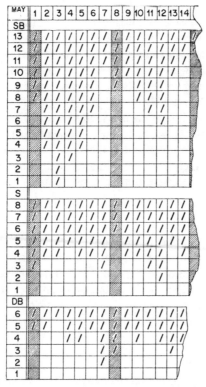

Fig. 3.5. Section of density chart

ALLOCATION OF ROOMS

Allocation of rooms takes place daily. On any one day the reception board or the room record indicate which rooms will continue to be occupied and which rooms will be vacant, either because they are vacant now or because the guest(s) occupying them will depart on that day. If all records are correct, the following check should be easily accomplished:

Number of rooms required for = Number of rooms occupied by
the night (as per booking chart)   guests staying on (as per recep-
                                    tion board or room record)
                                              plus
                                    Number of rooms required by
                                    new arrivals (as per bookings
                                    diary)

What is true of the total number of rooms required, is also true of any particular type: some of them will continue to be occupied by guests staying on, others will be required by new arrivals. When rooms are allocated, existing guests are, therefore, left in the rooms occupied by them already, and new arrivals are allocated to vacant rooms. This is done daily, either first thing in the morning or last thing at night for the coming day. The allocation is usually recorded on an arrival list, described at a later stage, or on the reception board, adjusted for the purpose, which is also dealt with below. This is the basic principle of the density chart, namely, that room allocation does not take place when the bookings are received, but from day to day.

CHANCE ARRIVALS

Chance arrivals must be recorded on the density chart in the same way as reservations in advance, in order to maintain an accurate record of the number of rooms of each type booked, and of the number of rooms remaining free to sell; but this is not different from the conventional chart, which also contains all room occupation, whether booked in advance or chance.

CANCELLATIONS

Cancellations are effected on the density chart by simply erasing the lowest filled-in space under the particular date(s) for the type of room cancelled, so that the number of rooms available for each night continually corresponds to the 'scale' on the sides of the chart. Care must also be taken to adjust the chart in respect of reduced or extended lengths of stay of present guests. To facilitate these corrections and adjustments, it is necessary to record bookings on the density chart in pencil, as is the case with the conventional chart.

The advantages of the density chart may be summarized as follows:
(*a*) No re-allocation of rooms arises between the time a booking is

received and the time of arrival, because bookings are not allocated to particular room numbers until the day of their arrival. This saves a great deal of time and reduces the risk of mistakes being made.

(*b*) The chart helps in ensuring that arriving guests can be quickly shown to available rooms without waiting. Even if a room allocated to them in the morning is not ready for occupation, they can be given another available room by simply altering the arrival list or the reception board but not the chart.

(*c*) The chart assists in achieving maximum occupancy by eliminating 'gaps' in continuous lettings, which arise when allocations of rooms are made a long time before the actual arrivals take place.

The Density Chart on Visual Boards

It is now easy to see that the principle of the density chart can be used with visual boards, thus replacing the printed chart and pencil entries. This requires little explanation; instead of filling in spaces for bookings in pencil, the recording of bookings takes place by inserting plastic plugs, one for each night, in the next available space under the appropriate date. When a reservation is cancelled, the plugs are removed. The elimination of pencil entries contributes to a better and clearer appearance of the chart, and may reduce mistakes.

RECEPTION BOARD AND ADVANCE BOOKINGS

It is apparent that the type of reception board, described in Chapter 2, is of little help in indicating to the receptionist whether a room is available for letting, even if the absence of a room card indicates that it is not occupied at the time. The receptionist must refer to the booking chart to establish how many rooms are free to be let, and for what period.

However, it is possible to adapt a reception board in such a way as to enable the selling of rooms to be done, particularly to chance guests, without reference to the chart; a variety of methods are used to achieve this in practice. Some of them also have the merit of speeding up the procedure on arrival by allowing the receptionist to prepare room cards in advance.

First method – the horizontal board

With the horizontal board the most common method is to prepare a room card for each reservation and insert it in the appropriate slot behind the current room card. Such a room card is sometimes in a contrasting colour from the current one to distinguish easily between current and future occupation. Sometimes only the next letting is represented by a coloured room card; in other cases room cards are inserted for some time ahead, in the order in which the room will be occupied. Figure 3.6 indicates this approach.

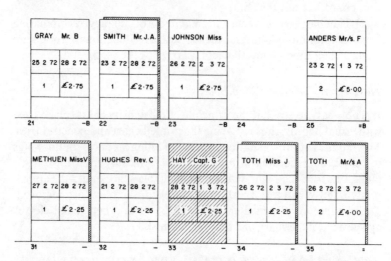

Fig. 3.6 Section of horizontal reception board with indication of advance bookings

The receptionist may be faced with one of several possibilities as regards any one room when consulting the reception board:

White room card	Room now occupied (*with dates*)
(*no coloured card behind*)	Not reserved for future (*21,23,25,32*)
White room card	Room now occupied (*with dates*)
(*coloured card behind*)	Reserved from date on coloured card (*22, 31,34,35*)
Coloured room card	Room now empty
	Reserved from date on coloured card (*33*)
No card	Room now empty
	Not reserved for future (*24*)

In the system described here the coloured room card is replaced by a white one on guest's arrival.

Second method – the vertical board

A somewhat simpler method is sometimes used with a vertical reception board, on which room slots are arranged in columns by floors. A duplicate column of slots is provided for each column, so that there are two slots next to one another for each room number. The first column of slots holds current room cards, the second reservations. All room cards are of the same colour, so that there is no necessity for replacing the card when the guest arrives – the card merely changes position, being moved from the reserved column to the current column. The distinction between current and future occupation is, therefore, made not by different colours of cards as with the first method, but by their positioning in one or other of the two columns.

2nd Floor								3rd Floor		
21	GRAY Mr. B							31	METHUEN	
−B	25 2.72	28.2.72	1	£2·75				—	27.2.72	28.2.72
22	SMITH Mr. J.A.				COULTON Mr. A.			32	HUGHES	
−B	23.2.72	28.2.72	1	£2·75	28.2.72	1.3.72	1 £2·75	—	21.2.72	28.2.72
23	JOHNSON Miss M							33		
−B	26.2.72	2.3.72	1	£2·75				—		
24								34	TOTH	
−B								—	26.2.72	2.3.72
25	ANDERS Mr/s F							35	TOTH	
=B	23.2.72	1.3.72	2	£5·00				=	26.2.72	2.3.72

Fig. 3.7. Section of vertical reception board with indication of advance booking

Besides sharing the advantage of the first method in providing the receptionist with an indication of immediate future bookings without reference to the chart, this method has an additional merit in speeding up the arrival procedure; a new card has to be made out when the arrival occurs only for chance arrivals. Arrivals who have reserved in advance should have their room cards in position in the second column before arrival. No particular difficulty arises when a change of room allocation has to be made, only the position of cards has to be altered.

Figure 3.7 is an illustration of this second method; the position represented above on a horizontal board is in part reproduced on a vertical board as on 28 February 1972.

It should be realized that neither of these two methods is a complete substitute for a chart; they do not provide a visual indication of the whole reservation position for the future at a glance, and should preferably be used in conjunction with a chart. The second method is particularly useful in conjunction with the density chart, as the room allocation is done at the most for a day ahead, and the room cards for the day's arrivals can be made out in advance and placed into position in the second column. The only major drawback may be the limitation of space; the reception board illustrated above occupies almost twice as much space as the simple board dealt with in Chapter 2.

BEDROOM BOOK

Many hotels use as one of their principal reception records a bedroom book. The name is applied to a variety of records, which perform different functions in different hotels. In its simplest form a bedroom book consists of suitably ruled separate pages for each day, with room numbers on the left-hand side and names of guests entered against the numbers of the rooms which they occupy; sometimes other details may also be entered. In this form the bedroom book replaces the reception board or room record, described in Chapter 2, in providing a visual indication of room occupation.

But its use may be extended to the recording of advance bookings and, according to the form it takes, it replaces the diary and even the booking chart. It is the use of this type of record in connection with advance bookings that deserves particular attention in this chapter as it represents one of the three main methods of recording advance bookings and as it may be adapted for this purpose in hotels of almost any size. It is particularly suitable where the length of stay of guests is short.

If it is desired to obtain the maximum advantage and to eliminate the need for a chart, the principles of the density chart are incorporated and the main features and operation may be summarized as follows:

(*a*) Separate pages are provided for each day (or night).

(*b*) All bedrooms are standardized into several main types and grouped together on each day's page; alternatively a separate page may be used for each type of room for each day or, in fact, rooms of different type may be recorded in separate books.

(*c*) The number of lines provided for each type of room for each day corresponds to the total number of rooms of that type and the lines are numbered from bottom to top. (These line numbers provide a scale against which can be seen the total number of rooms of each type and the number remaining free to be sold.)

(*d*) The essential information to be recorded is the name and the length of stay.

(*e*) When a room is booked, whether in advance or by a chance guest, his name and length of stay in nights is recorded on the page devoted to his day of arrival on the first free line from the top; at the same time, if his length of stay is more than one night, his name is also entered in the first free line on all subsequent day's pages but the length of stay is shown as the unexpired number of nights, not the total length of stay.

(*f*) When the room is allocated, the room number is also shown against the guest's name.

(*g*) Unless it is desired to change a guest's room, the room numbers of guests staying on are repeated on all pages covering his stay; only new arrivals are allocated new rooms each day.

Figure 3.8 illustrates the approach in showing sections of three days' pages side by side. It is evident that this method incorporates the advantages of a density chart, described on pp. 36-9, but it also identifies each booking by name.

It is possible to retain some features of this method even if room numbers are printed on the left hand side of the page and names are entered against particular room numbers when bookings are received. Establishing who is staying in a particular room is quicker; but it is then necessary to allocate rooms when bookings are made and it is not possible to see at a glance how much accommodation of a particular type is available at any time.

FILING

So far little reference has been made to the filing system to be adopted in connection with advance bookings. Yet the efficiency of a reception office may be greatly improved or reduced by the method of filing adopted. The main requirement is that the system should enable easy and quick reference to any particular reservation.

The first principle to be followed is to treat each reservation as a separate case and to keep any documents relating to it together in the chronological order in which they accumulated. Where a reservation form is used, it should constitute the top sheet of each set of documents, providing in a summary form a standard set of details about each

	5th MAY				6th MAY				7th MAY		
	NAME	N	ROOM		NAME	N	ROOM		NAME	N	ROOM
SB				SB				SB			
13	JOHNSON Mr B	1	27	13	BRIDGE Mr F	1	37	13	HASSEL Mr C	2	26
12	LACEY Mr/s C	1	38	12	HASSEL Mr C	3	26	12	JAMES Miss W	1	29
11	BRIDGE Mr F	2	37	11	JAMES Miss W	2	29	11	McKAY Mr L	1	
10	HASSEL Mr C	4	26	10	HARTLEY Rev G	1		10			
9	JAMES Miss W	3	29	9	McKAY Mr L	2		9			
8	PARRY Miss P	1	28	8	JOHN Miss F	1		8			
7	HARTLEY Rev G	2		7	WALTER Col R	1		7			
6	McKAY Mr L	3		6				6			
5	JOHN Miss F	2		5				5			
4	WALTER Col R	2		4				4			
3				3				3			
2				2				2			
1				1				1			
S				S				S			
8	PORTER Mr F	2	34	8	PORTER Mr F	1	34	8	ALDER Mrs C	1	
7	SUGARS Mr B	1	44	7	ALDER Mrs C	2		7	ALDER Miss M	1	
6	ALDER Mrs C	3		6	ALDER Miss M	2		6	MARTER Mr F	3	
5	ALDER Miss M	3		5	MARTER Mr F	4		5	FRANK Dr J	1	
4	THOMAS Miss T	1		4	FRANK Dr J	2		4	SIMON Mrs M	1	
3				3				3	TOBIN Mr K	2	
2				2				2			
1				1				1			
DB				DB				DB			
6	FRANKLIN Mr/s T	2	25	6	FRANKLIN Mr/s T	1	25	6	ANDREWS Mr/s D	2	
5	BOND Misses T&D	1	33	5	ANDREWS Mr/s D	3		5	JEREMY Misses T&K	1	
4	THOMAS Mr/s J	1		4				4	KAY & FAY Misses B&D	3	
3				3				3	HALL Rev & Mrs A	1	
2				2				2	PUGH Mr/s L	2	
1				1				1			

Fig. 3.8. Bedroom book used as a record of advance bookings (on 5 May, showing entries for three days)

reservation. It is preferable to staple the documents together rather than use paper clips, which slip off easily.

There are two basic alternatives in filing the sets of documents: alphabetically or by date of arrival.

In alphabetical filing any particular set can be referred to, if the name is known. This is also useful in connection with enquiries about future arrivals, since there is usually no other record containing future arrivals arranged in alphabetical order. The drawback is that sets of documents relating to arrivals on a particular date are not together.

If filing is arranged by date of arrival, sets of documents relating to a day's arrivals are together, and are arranged alphabetically under each date. Any particular set can be quickly located only if the arrival date is known.

In most cases alphabetical filing has a balance of advantages. The bookings diary forms a record of arrivals by date, and sets of documents relating to a particular date can be easily extracted from the filing cabinet by reference to the diary. But without a separate record of future arrivals arranged in alphabetical order reference to any set is often cumbersome.

In small hotels the filing system need not consist of more than two sections:

1 Advance reservations	containing all sets until the guest has departed, and
2 Past reservations	into which all sets are transferred after departure.

In a larger hotel it is advisable to divide the filing system into as many as five sections, which closely correspond to the natural stages through which a reservation usually passes:

1 Enquiries	contains enquiries and any preliminary documents as long as the arrangements remain provisional – usually the first letters from guests and copies of replies by the hotel
2 Bookings	contains sets of documents, which constitute definite bookings, before the guest has arrived – usually the first letters from guests, copies of hotel replies, guests' replies, and hotel confirmations

3 Day's arrivals	contains sets of documents as above but only those relating to the day's arrivals
4 Present guests	contains sets of documents in respect of guests who have arrived and are resident
5 Past reservations	contains sets of documents of guests after their departure

The sets within each section are filed alphabetically, and transfers from one section to another take place as follows:

```
1
↓  Individually  when the booking becomes definite
2
|  Collectively   all sets relating to the day's arrivals according to
↓                 the bookings diary or arrival list
3
↓  Collectively   all sets from previous sections, daily
4
↓  Collectively   sets relating to the day's departures, daily
5
```

It is obvious that not all reservations necessarily pass through all the stages and sections. For example, where a definite request is received by the hotel to reserve accommodation (whether a confirmation is sent or not) it is placed immediately with 'bookings', or if it relates to today, with the day's arrivals. All reservations do, however, pass through the last three stages.

It is sometimes argued that this system creates difficulties in reference, as a particular booking may have to be looked for in two different sections. This is rarely a valid argument: when it is desired to locate a particular reservation, the receptionist knows on most occasions what stage the booking has reached by the wording of the letter with which he is dealing, and for the sake of which he is referring to the filing cabinet, or by some other indication. The occasions when he has to look in more than one section for a particular set are not frequent.

On the other hand the sectional filing splits the large number of sets of documents relating to reservations into manageable sections, which, in most instances, in itself makes location speedier. In some instances as many as five sections would hardly be justified, and then it is desirable to simplify the sub-division of filing by combining the first two sections,

Plate 2.3. Shannostrip revolving stand

Plate 2.4. Key and mail rack at the Hertford Hotel (Trust Houses Forte Group), London

Plate 4.1. Section of bill office at the Europa Hotel (Grand Metropolitan Hotels Ltd.), London

or sections 3 and 4, or both; the following alternative arrangements of sections then offer themselves:

A	B	C
1 Enquiries and Bookings	1 Enquiries	1 Enquiries and Bookings
	2 Bookings	
2 Day's arrivals	3 Day's arrivals and present guests	2 Day's arrivals and present guests
3 Present guests		
4 Past reservations	4 Past reservations	3 Past reservations

This is one of the aspects of hotel reception where no dogmatic rules can be laid down. The individual circumstances of each hotel should determine the filing arrangements, of which the above are only illustrations. But it is important that there should be a system in the first place; secondly, that it should be designed after due consideration of the needs prevailing there, and not one perpetuated just because no alternatives are known or admissible; and, thirdly, that the system is efficiently operated by those who understand it.

The above arrangements should be considered merely as simple illustrations of procedure, which may require adaption in particular circumstances. Such matters as the type and location of the hotel, the identity of the prospective guest and his requirements, do necessarily influence the procedure in individual circumstances.

CANCELLATIONS

The Legal Position

A reservation of accommodation at an hotel creates a contract between the hotel proprietor and the guest, and as such is enforceable at law. It imposes an obligation on the proprietor to hold a room (or rooms) at the disposal of the guest for an agreed period, and on the guest to pay for the accommodation so reserved. If either the hotel proprietor or the guest wish to alter or cancel the reservation, they can do so only by mutual agreement, or, if they do not mutually agree, subject to a liability to compensate the other party for any loss occasioned by the alteration or cancellation of the reservation.

From the point of view of the hotel proprietor, cancellation of a booking by a guest, without the proprietor's consent, or failure to arrive on the due date, whatever the reason, entitles the proprietor to claim compensation subject to the following conditions:

(*a*) He must take all reasonable steps to attempt to re-let the accommodation and, if successful even for part of the period, must reduce his claim accordingly.

(*b*) As re-letting is possible up to the last day of the booked period, no claim should be made until that period has expired.

(*c*) Any claims for compensation must exclude items, such as food, which have not been supplied; extra expenses incurred in an attempt to re-let (such as advertising, telegrams, telephone calls, etc.) may, however, be added to the claim.

(*d*) If the guest has paid a deposit, it is not returnable, unless the proprietor's claim is less than the deposit, in which case any balance must be refunded.

In cases in which claims for compensation have been decided by courts of law, hotel proprietors have been normally awarded damages on the basis of two-thirds of a booking with full board, and the remaining one-third has been regarded as the value of food not supplied and of other costs not incurred. It has also been held that illness does not entitle a guest to cancel the contract without compensating the proprietor.

Although a valid contract may exist without any of its terms being in writing, it is sensible to secure at least some evidence of the arrangements in writing, if it is desired to pursue a claim in a court of law. The most important point to bear in mind is that there must be a definite agreement as to the booking; a mere offer of accommodation by the hotel, which is not accepted by the guest, does not amount to a contract. Similarly, a request by a guest to the hotel to reserve accommodation does not constitute a contract until the hotel has agreed to do so, and the guest has been notified.

Most claims by hoteliers for losses occasioned by cancellations are settled out of court, and only in extreme circumstances, when the guest refuses to compensate the hotelier, does the latter consider suing the guest for a breach of contract.

Policies

The above statement summarizes the legal position in case of cancellations. The steps taken by a hotelier in practice when reserved accommodation is not taken up by the guest do not necessarily follow his legal rights in any one case. The course to be adopted is rarely left to the receptionist's discretion; it should form a part of the sales policy of the hotel, and standard procedures ought to be laid down by the management for the guidance of receptionists. The policies in existence fall broadly into three categories:

(*a*) One possible approach is to take advantage of the legal rights and to claim compensation for any loss suffered. This approach is rarely adopted without modification for special cases. It is taken by some resort hotels, when a cancellation of a stay of one or two weeks represents a substantial loss to the business, but even in these establishments the proprietors usually do not assert their rights with old-established customers and in other special cases.

(*b*) An opposite approach is adopted by many other hotels, which never claim for any cancellations. This is normally on the ground that to do so would be damaging to the goodwill of the hotel. In this category fall many resort and transient hotels, and the latter are, no doubt, influenced in their policy also by the relatively small amounts involved owing to short lengths of stay, and by the possibility of re-letting cancelled rooms, especially in cities.

(*c*) In order to facilitate the re-letting of cancelled rooms, a third approach is often adopted by many transient hotels, which is really a modification of the non-claiming approach above. When the booking is accepted, guests are informed that rooms are normally held only up to a certain time, say 6 p.m. or 7 p.m., unless they advise the hotel of a later arrival. This means that the receptionists are free to re-let the rooms not taken up by the stated time, if the guests do not notify the hotel of their later arrival. This approach is sometimes adopted as regards all bookings, in other cases only for verbal or telephone bookings. Legally, the reservation is then made conditional on the guest's taking up the accommodation by the stated time.

Procedure

CLAIMS

Claims are rarely handled by the reception office. When a cancellation occurs, it is customary for the head receptionist to extract the set of documents relating to the reservation from the file, list all cancellations once a day, and to submit the list with remarks and with supporting sets of documents to the manager. He then formulates the claim, or may delegate this matter to the accountant or to a person in a similar position. The documents remain in this person's possession until the case is closed, when they are either filed in his office, or returned to the head receptionist who files them under 'past bookings' or in a separate section of the filing system under 'cancellations'.

NON-CLAIMING

Non-claiming is certainly the simpler procedure from the clerical point of view. Guests who inform the hotel by correspondence of their cancellation, have their letter acknowledged; if they do not take up the accommodation without informing the hotel, or if they do so verbally or by telephone, the cancellation is noted on the reservation form or the top sheet of their set of documents. The sets of documents are then filed away under 'past bookings' or under 'cancellations'.

ADJUSTMENT OF RECORDS

Whether claims for losses occasioned by cancellations are made or not, the records, in which the reservations are entered, must be adjusted immediately when it becomes known that the guest will not be arriving as arranged.

If the reservation is cancelled entirely:

(*a*) The entry in the bookings diary is crossed out, a note made and initialled.

(*b*) The record of the reservation in the booking chart is removed.

(*c*) Any indication of the reservation on the reception board is also removed.

If the reservation is altered as to any of its aspects, such as date of arrival, length of stay, and so on, the above records must also be immediately amended, if any of the information recorded in them is affected.

RESERVATION PROCEDURE

There are four basic ways in which accommodation may be reserved: in person, by telephone, by telegram, and by correspondence. Some aspects of the reservation procedure are common to most or all of them; in other respects they differ. Figures 3.9 to 3.12 provide a simple outline of the basic procedures for each of the four methods.

Personal Reservations

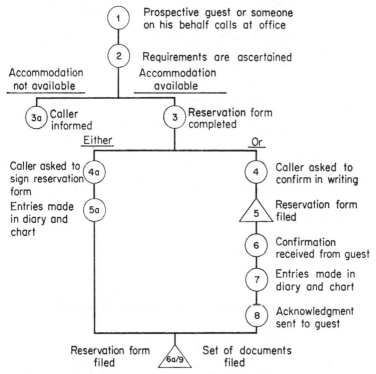

Fig. 3.9 Reservation procedure: personal reservations

Telephone Reservations

Telephone reservations are often made for the same day or for a date only a short time ahead. Confirmations may, therefore, have to be dispensed with in certain cases. This possibility is illustrated in Figure 3.10, as well as the possibility of the reservation not being confirmed.

Telegram (Cable) Reservations

Telegrams are normally used for reserving accommodation for the same day or for a short period ahead, and are in the nature of requests to book and not inquiries. For this reason the guest is not asked to confirm; indeed, the desirability of a written confirmation is hardly there: if someone goes to the trouble of sending a telegram, which the hotel retains, a confirmation would be superfluous. Whether a confirmation is sent by the hotel depends on the time available before the actual arrival.

In case of telegram requests there is also the possibility that the accommodation will not be available. If the guest's address is known, and if there is time to do so, he must be informed. If the address is not

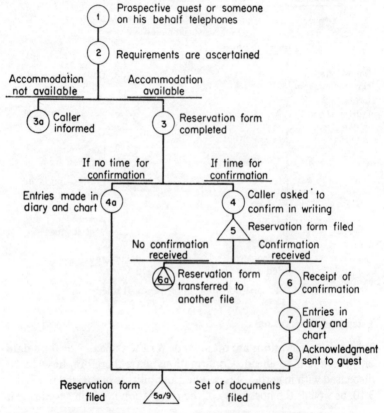

Fig. 3.10 Reservation procedure: telephone reservations

known or if there is no time, the hotel will normally endeavour to reserve accommodation for him elsewhere. Often this step is taken with all requests which cannot be accommodated, whether it would be possible to inform the guest or not.

The above possibilities are illustrated in Figure 3.11.

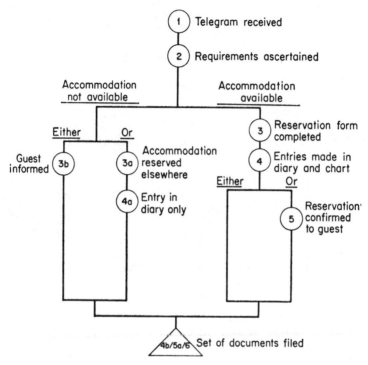

Figure 3.11 Reservation procedure: telegram reservations

Correspondence Reservations

Reservations by correspondence probably create the greatest variety in procedure. The first letter from a prospective guest may be in the nature of inquiry or request, and the procedure for dealing with it varies accordingly.

If the first letter from the guest is a request to reserve accommodation, the procedure is very similar to that for telegram bookings. But many letters are merely enquiries, which the guest might have sent to more than one hotel; in that case the procedure might be as shown in Figure 3.12.

The reservation form has been omitted from this diagram for the sake of simplicity. If a reservation form is used with correspondence bookings to provide a summary of each booking, it is normally started when the guest accepts the offer of accommodation.

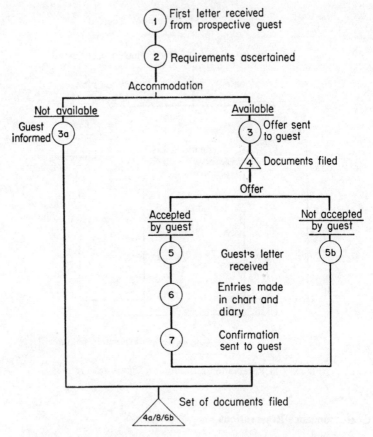

Fig. 3.12 Reservation procedure: correspondence reservations

4. *Visitors' Accounts*

IN a large number of British hotels visitors' accounts form a part of the records and activities of the reception office. In larger hotels specialization is carried out and a separate bill office takes visitors' accounts out of the realm of hotel reception. However, this is by far not the most common arrangement and in any case a close liaison between the two departments is essential even where they are separated. For these reasons visitors' accounts have been included within the scope of this book.

Several features of hotel operation influence the methods of dealing with visitors' accounts:

(*a*) Credit sales to residents take place continuously throughout their stay and comprise a large number of relatively small transactions.

(*b*) The sales take place in various parts of the hotel from the time a guest arrives to the time he departs.

(*c*) In most instances credit is extended to guests for the period of their stay and the majority of accounts are settled on departure.

These characteristics call for a system, which enables the multitude and variety of transactions to be speedily recorded and paid for. A normal sales ledger, containing the personal accounts of guests, would be unwieldy and a special form of tabular ledger is, therefore, adopted in hotels which, together with the guest bills, forms the basis of the system of visitors' accounts.

SOURCES AND ANALYSIS OF CHARGES

In the first chapter an outline is given of hotel tariff structures. Here an attempt is made to indicate the types of charge which may be incurred by the guest during his stay in an hotel, where they originate, and how they find their way to the guest's account. In most hotels these charges may be divided into six main groups: accommodation, food, drink, sundry sales, visitors' disbursements, and service charges (Figure 4.1).

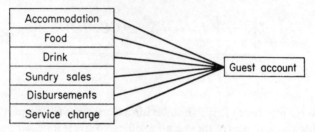

Fig. 4.1. Analysis of guest charges

Accommodation

This is the basic charge incurred by all guests who stay at least one night. It originates in the reception office which, as the sales outlet responsible for selling rooms, also provides the authority for the charge. The guest's account is opened as soon as possible after his arrival either from the register, the terms book or, in larger hotels, from the arrival notification, which must clearly indicate the terms on which the guest is staying. The accommodation charge is then debited to the guest's account for the first night's stay. On subsequent days the accommodation charge is usually debited to the guest each evening for the coming night's stay.

In some hotels the receptionist, in fact, opens the guest's bill by completing the bill heading and inserting the required particulars. Whilst this is normal in a small hotel where the same person may not only receive the guest but also look after his account, it is also an acceptable method even in larger hotels where the duties of the receptionist and of the book-keeper are separated. In those circumstances the guest's bill, started by the receptionist, serves as an arrival notification for the bill office, without the necessity of transferring the details from an arrival notification on to the bill.

Food

The charges in this category normally include breakfast, lunch, afternoon tea, dinner, non-alcoholic beverages other than minerals, and other light refreshments. They may be served in the restaurant, the lounge, or in the guest's bedroom by a floor waiter, chambermaid or possibly a night porter.

It is important both that these charges are notified to the book-keeper as soon as they are incurred, and also that each charge is supported by documentary evidence in the form of a voucher.

The first rule may not apply in hotels where guests stay for longer periods and on more or less inclusive terms, as there is less risk of a guest departing without payment immediately after a meal. Similarly, there may be no need for individual vouchers for each guest or room, and a list of charges incurred may be sent to the book-keeper for debiting to the guests' accounts after each meal.

However, the importance of these rules cannot be exaggerated in transient hotels. Vouchers with details of charges must be forwarded for posting to guests' accounts as soon as they are incurred, and retained by the book-keeper, in case the charges are later queried by guests, and also for checking purposes.

If the book-keeper also checks that each charge is in accordance with the menu or tariff, before posting it to the guest's account, he contributes to an early discovery of mistakes and reduces the amount and detail of subsequent control.

Drink

Under this heading are normally included charges for alcoholic beverages and minerals. They are dealt with in a similar way to meals in that vouchers are used to communicate the charges to the book-keeper for posting to guests' accounts. Drink charges may originate in several parts of the hotel – the dispense bar, the cocktail bar, the lounge, on the floors – but wherever a drink is sold without cash payment, the selling department must notify the charge to the book-keeper. It is usual for waiters to insert the price on the voucher, but in some hotels the pricing of drink is left to the book-keeper before he enters the charge in the guest's account.

In order to discourage guests from consuming their own drinks in a licensed hotel, a charge is often imposed, known as 'corkage'. This is a payment per bottle and it is the responsibility of the department, in which the guest consumes his own drink, to originate the charge.

Sundry Sales

There are a number of charges a guest may incur in addition to those in respect of accommodation, meals, and drink. They may include such items as telephone calls, telegrams, laundry, valeting, car hire, garage, hairdressing, newspapers. In all these cases a voucher is made out and sent to the book-keeper for posting to the guest's account by the department in which the guest has incurred the charge.

Visitors' Disbursements

An hotel employee may make a payment on behalf of the guest, for example when receiving C.O.D. mail delivered for the guest, for taxis, theatre tickets, flowers or such special services as repairs to guests' belongings. Even some of the items included above under sundry sales may rank as visitors' disbursements in particular circumstances; what would be a sundry charge in one hotel may be a guest's disbursement in another. For example, in an hotel where the porter actually goes out and buys newspapers for residents out of petty cash, the payments would be treated as disbursements on behalf of guests, if guests do not pay for them in cash and the hotel does not make a profit out of their sale. But in an hotel where there is a bookstall, or where an order is placed with newsagents and paid periodically, guests' newspapers would represent a sundry charge.

It is essential that all payments made on behalf of guests (sometimes also described as 'visitors' paid out') are both recovered from the guests and that the employee who made the payment is reimbursed for the amount paid out. This is achieved by the use of vouchers, which are sent to the book-keeper by the paying departments for posting to the guest's account, and of petty cash books. It is important to realize that visitors' disbursements are not a part of hotel revenue, but merely represent a recovery of payments made by the hotel on behalf of guests.

Service Charges

A service charge may be regarded as a partial or a complete substitute for individual gratuities. As opposed to a 'tronc' system, whereby employees pool the gratuities received by them individually, a service charge is levied on the guest's account by the hotel. Sometimes all charges incurred by the guest are subject to a service charge and this is calculated as a percentage of his total bill. Sometimes a service charge is levied on some items and not on others, e.g. on accommodation, meals, or on meals served in guests' rooms; in other cases the amount of the service charge varies as between these services.

An overall or accommodation service charge is normally added to the guest's bill by the book-keeper before it is presented for settlement; but in some cases a waiter may be made responsible for adding the service charge to the bill or voucher for meals before it is sent to the book-keeper. In any case a service charge must be brought to the guest's attention before he has entered into a contract with the hotel, e.g. in a brochure, on the menu, or in some such way, before he incurs the charge. Otherwise it is not enforceable in Britain as it is neither 'a custom of the trade, which is generally known and accepted', nor is it provided for by legislation, as in some other countries.

VISITORS' LEDGER

This is a columnar ledger, also known as the tabular ledger, which is often considered the most characteristic feature of hotel book-keeping. Yet it is merely a particular application to personal accounts of hotel guests of columnar book-keeping, a system very common in other businesses; it has grown out of the special needs of the hotel business and is a part of the double entry system of book-keeping.

The main features of the ledger are:

(*a*) A number of personal accounts of guests are arranged on the same sheet in tabular form for easy reference.

(*b*) Narration is reduced to the minimum through the use of printed descriptions applicable to all accounts on the sheet.

(*c*) As the cycle of hotel operation is repeated daily, the guests' accounts are balanced daily and one or more sheets of the ledger relate to a day's business.

	Horizontal	*Vertical*
Derives its name from	the arrangement of individual guests' accounts in horizontal lines running from left to right across the page	the arrangement of individual guests' accounts in vertical columns running from top to bottom of page
Guests' names and room numbers	appear underneath each other on left-hand side	appear at the top of columns across the page
Descriptions of charges and credits	appear at the top of columns across the page	appear underneath each other on left-hand side
Debit entries	appear on left-hand side of page	appear in upper part of page
Credit entries	appear on right-hand side of page	appear in lower part of page

There is a great variation in the forms of visitors' tabular ledger used in practice and designed to meet particular needs, but they all fall in one or the other of two basic categories: horizontal or vertical. Their main features are summarized above.

The relative merits of the two basic forms of layout may be compared as follows:

Horizontal

Vertical

(*a*) The layout of the sheet and of each individual personal account corresponds closely to that of an ordinary personal account in double entry book-keeping, with the debit part on the left and the credit part on the right. This may secure a quicker appreciation of the double entry aspects of the individual transactions and of the records.

The layout of the sheet and of each individual account corresponds closely to that of the guests' bills, which are invariably laid out in vertical columns. The comparison between a ledger account and the corresponding bill is thus facilitated.

(*b*) As different types of charges and credits are arranged in columns, the adding of a day's totals is speeded up. Where charges and credits are numerous, this arrangement, therefore, helps in daily balancing.

As individual personal accounts are arranged in columns, adding of amounts due is speeded up. Speed is most important in settling accounts on departure, and this arrangement, therefore, contributes to quicker balancing of individual accounts both on departure and in daily balancing.

(*c*) A larger number of individual guests' accounts may usually be entered underneath each other on the same sheet.

A greater analysis of charges and credits underneath each other may usually be achieved, and several lines may be allowed for one type of charge, if it is a recurring one.

Points to consider

A number of aspects of the visitors' ledger receive different treatment in different hotels. Their importance warrants a careful consideration when the layout of the ledger is being decided.

Horizontal or vertical?

The distinction between the two basic forms has been drawn above, and their relative merits have been considered. The choice should be made after weighing up the extent to which particular requirements prevail in an hotel.

Room numbers – fixed layout?

In some hotels the room numbers in the visitors' ledger are printed. This ensures that the same room number is always found in the same place, and may assist greatly in locating any individual account when entries are to be made, or when it has to be referred to for any other reason.

In hotels where the number of occupied rooms fluctuates widely and may fall considerably short of the maximum, a fixed layout of accounts with preprinted room numbers may prove wasteful, as a constant amount of stationery has to be used for the visitors' ledger each day. In those circumstances, especially if the total number of rooms is not large, room numbers are entered and guests' accounts opened in the next available space on arrival. The occupied room numbers are arranged in their order once a day when the accounts are brought forward to the new day's sheet(s) to ensure quick location; new arrivals are entered as they arrive.

More than one room occupation in a day

The number of lines or columns required for each day's business depends not only on the number of rooms sold, but also on the number of arrivals and departures in a day. There may be an outgoing and an incoming guest for the same room number on the same day. In that case there will be two accounts for the same room number on the day's visitors' ledger: one for the departing guest with charges up to the time of leaving, and another one for the arriving guest with charges from the time of arrival. In hotels where this is a frequent occurrence, it is advisable to reserve two lines or two columns for each room number.

This approach enables one account to be closed and another one to be opened in the same part of the ledger; it focuses the book-keeper's attention on the possibility of a charge being incurred by a departing guest after the new guest's account has been opened.

In order to highlight new arrivals and to distinguish them easily in the ledger, their accounts are frequently entered in a distinctive colour on the first day. Red is commonly used. This is of particular use where preprinting has not been practicable.

In some hotels the balancing of the day's ledger takes place at midday or early afternoon instead of late evening, with a view to separating, as far as possible, departed guests' accounts from those of new arrivals. By midday all guests departing on that day should have settled their accounts and no new ones will have arrived by then; if they have, their accounts are held over and opened only on the next sheet(s). Thus a day's tabular ledger balanced in this way corresponds more closely to the cycle of the most important hotel activity, the sale of rooms.

Treatment of chance sales

'Chance' guests – guests taking up accommodation without a previous reservation – do not significantly affect the method of hotel book-keeping. The word 'chance' is, however, also commonly applied to the casual business of customers who use hotel facilities without taking up accommodation. Such are mainly restaurant sales to non-residents. These sales may be cash or credit sales. In the former case cash settlement is made at the time of sale, and no need arises for opening an account for the customer; in the latter case the customer usually has a credit account with the hotel.

The treatment of 'chance' credit sales may be arranged in one of two ways:

(*a*) In larger hotels, where they may represent a substantial part of sales, it is advisable to treat them entirely separately from residents' sales and they do not enter the visitors' ledger. Cash takings are paid in by each department to the chief cashier or some such person. Credit sales to non-residents are debited to their personal accounts in the sales ledger. Both are recorded in separate books, usually known as 'chance books', and then posted to the credit of the sales account in the ledger, which completes the double entry aspect of the transaction.

(*b*) In smaller hotels, or in those where chance business does not constitute a large proportion of sales, 'chance' sales are sometimes debited in the tabular ledger, so that each day's tabular ledger represents a summary of the total business done, including chance. In this case cash takings from various departments are paid in and recorded in the tabular ledger in one or more chance columns (vertical form) or lines (horizontal form), headed, for example, 'restaurant chance sales', or 'chance bar sales'. The total cash paid in for the day by each department must equal the total chance cash debited to each department; the chance accounts are closed daily and there cannot be a balance carried forward to the next day.

Chance credit sales to non-residents are debited first to their separate accounts in the tabular ledger, and then transferred to their personal accounts in the sales ledger at the end of the day. Once again, there can be no balance carried forward to the next day in the tabular ledger.

This approach ensures that cash and credit sales to non-residents are daily brought into the tabular ledger in addition to residents' business, so that the tabular ledger provides an analysed summary of the whole day's business of the hotel.

It should be noted that there is an increasing tendency even for residents to be charged cash at the sales points throughout the hotel. It can be seen that this reduces the amount of credit extended to guests and also the volume (and cost) of the related book-keeping. In some hotels, and more particularly motels, guests pay cash for their accommodation on arrival and also for their purchases during the whole stay.

VISITORS' LEDGER
AS PART OF DOUBLE ENTRY SYSTEM

The tabular ledgers enable the visitors' accounts to be kept conveniently grouped together, using one or a few pages for each day's business (*see* Figure 4.2). It should be particularly noted that they do not serve the same function as book-keeping journals, such as purchases day books or sales day books, from which total purchases and sales are posted to the purchases and sales accounts respectively, and also individually to the separate personal accounts on the opposite side of the ledger. As soon as an entry is made in the visitors' tabular ledger, it has automatically been recorded on one side of the ledger. All the charges are debit entries in the individual accounts, each charge being analysed under the visitor's name or room number, and also under the specific heading to which it refers, e.g. drink. At the end of the day, or at some other specified time, the debit entries under each analysis heading are totalled, so

July 14th

The figure is a "Simple vertical tabular ledger" for the date July 14th. Each room/sales column is divided into £ and pence sub‑columns. The middle food rows are broken by wavy omission lines in the original. Values below are given as "£ pence".

	1 Betts F.Mr	2 Smith L.Miss	4 Jones S.Mr/Mrs & Son	5 Phipps L.F/Lt/Mrs	8.2 Smart J.Rev	12 Fortin S.Mr/Mrs	7 Chalk O.Dr	3 Jennings L.Mr/Mrs	Party Johnson S.Mr	Lounge Bar	Chance	Total
Number of visitors	1	1	2	2	1	2	1	2				31
Brought forward	24 50	8 35	37 05	14 00		30 05	5 00	7 50				398 95
Apartments									33 50			158 50
Food: E/M/Tea												2 25
Breakfast	0 75	0 15					0 50					24 75
Luncheon	1 50	0 75		1 50		1 50					8 90	29 70
A/noon tea											2 50	8 50
Dinner		1 50									10 60	75 25
Other food											0 45	4 75
Liquor			6 75				2 10		24 10	39 85		87 15
Sundry sales									4 25	1 93		8 63
Paid outs												9 12
Service charge	2 91	1 08		1 55		3 16		0 95				8 70
TOTAL DEBITS	31 94	11 83	62 05	17 05	27 15	34 71	7 60	8 45	61 85	41 78	22 45	826 25
Cash and cheques	31 94					33 01	7 60			41 78	22 45	198 17
Allowances						1 70						1 70
Transfers to ledger		11 83							61 85			73 68
Carried forward			62 05	17 05	27 15			8 45				552 70
TOTAL CREDITS	31 94	11 83	62 05	17 05	27 15	34 71	7 60	8 45	61 85	41 78	22 45	826 25

L/146   L/121

Fig. 4.2 Simple vertical tabular ledger

Notes on tabular ledger

1. The tabular ledger illustrated does not have preprinted room numbers. Therefore the names and accounts of guests who stayed the previous night are brought forward in room number order. New arrivals are entered in the next vacant column as they arrive. (For reasons of space, the illustration is broken at two places in the centre.)

2. The Rev J. Smart has moved this day from room 8 to room 2, indicated by the neat crossing through at the head of his account.

3. 'Party': here a separate column has been used for an account of a person not staying at the hotel, which is going to be transferred to the sales ledger.

4. A separate column is used to record takings from each area of bar for which a separate record of sales is required. All other chance sales are recorded in the appropriate column.

5. A = Adult and C = Child (in many old-established tabular ledgers an S = Servant section is also included). Here are recorded the number of sleepers for the night, the total of which appears in the total column. Some hotels record the number of all guests for an account even though it may be closed that day and the guest(s) leave. The number of adults and children leaving can then be crossed through, and the total of the uncrossed persons gives the total of sleepers for that night.

6. Where there is more than one voucher for a heading in any one account these will be shown separately. In planning a tabular ledger sufficient room should be left for these, especially when such general headings as 'liquor' or 'sundry sales' are used.

7. Many tabular ledgers have considerably more detail in the number of analysis headings and where these are given, charges must be posted appropriately (for example liquor is often broken down into the headings of 'wines', 'liqueurs and spirits', 'beers', 'minerals', with a heading and two or three lines for each).

8. A catch-all 'miscellaneous' or 'sundry sales' is a useful heading when designing a tabular ledger.

9. The 'paid outs' include any item paid out on the guests' behalf on which there is no profit. Here Mr Jones may have been given, with the manager's permission, £5 cash by the cashier.

10. When a guest leaves, he may settle his account by cash (or cheque) or it may be transferred to the ledger. In either event the account is balanced in the tabular ledger and a line run through his account to stress that it is closed and make the risk of posting a further charge erroneously to that account less likely.
    When the account has been transferred to the sales ledger, the relevant sales ledger folio number may be written on the tabular ledger below the guest's account.

that there is a daily total figure for accommodation, drink, and so on. These global figures are ultimately posted to the credit of the appropriate sales account. They balance the individual debits posted to the tabular ledger during the day.

Apart from the brought forward total and the service charge total, the only other daily debit total figure in the tabular ledger which is *not* posted to the sales account and indeed, in practice, frequently not posted to the ledger at all is the total of disbursements (or 'visitors' paid outs'). This is because the corresponding credit entries have been made in the petty cash book and thus the double entry is already complete and a bulk credit entry is not necessary. However, it is necessary to check frequently that the amounts for disbursements entered in the petty cash book and the amounts charged via the tabular ledger to the guest are in agreement, otherwise there will be a loss on disbursements. Where no entry is made in the ledger for 'visitors' paid outs', one method of control is to reimburse the cashier for the disbursements according to the amount entered on the tabular ledger when the 'float' for disbursements should be fully replenished – and any shortage be apparent (and made good).

There are some hotels which post the total of disbursements from the tabular ledger to the credit side of a 'visitors' paid out' account in the ledger, the debit entries being posted from the V.P.O. column of the petty cash book (or the disbursements book if a separate one is kept). This ledger account should be in balance and the fact that it is so proves that all disbursements have been charged out.

It is not customary to post the analysed daily totals of business done directly to the credit of the appropriate sales accounts in the ledger; they are collected in a summary book and the totals are posted periodically from the summary book to the ledger. This is normally done once a month and gives rise to the name of the daily summary book, an illustration of which is given in Figure 4.3. Apart from its main function – to collect analysed daily sales totals for monthly transfer to sales ledger accounts – the summary book also provides a convenient monthly statistical statement, giving a sales analysis by day and by type of charge.

It will be seen that the total sales figure in the daily summary sheet (£409·48 in the example) equals the total debits in the tabular ledger (£826·25) for that day less the brought-forward figure (here £398·95), the service charges (£8·70), and the 'paid outs' or disbursements total (here £9·12), which are not posted to the summary

	Apartments		E/M/Tea		Breakfast		Luncheon		A/noon tea		Dinner		Other food		Liquor		Sundry Sales		Total	
	£	p	£	p	£	p	£	p	£	p	£	p	£	p	£	p	£	p	£	p
1																				
2																				
3																				
4																				
5																				
6																				
7																				
8																				
9																				
10																				
11																				
12																				
13																				
14	150	50	2	25	24	75	29	70	8	50	75	25	4	75	87	15	18	63	409	48
15																				
16																				
17																				
18																				
19																				
20																				
21																				
22																				
23																				
24																				
25																				
26																				
27																				
28																				
29																				
30																				
31																				
	4531	30	99	15	713	25	981	30	200	50	1601	65	183	70	2281	48	724	13	11,316	71

Fig. 4.3 Daily summary sheet

book. All the remaining items are sales and, through the medium of the daily sales summary, are posted into the sales accounts in the ledger.

Each visitor's account in the tabular ledger is balanced daily. If the visitor is staying on, this is done by crediting his account with the total due to date, and carrying that amount forward to the debit of his account in the tabular ledger for the following day. If the guest departs and pays his bill before departure, his personal account in the tabular ledger is credited with the amount paid and closed; the cash book is debited.

Any allowances given to the guest are also credited and the allowances book (and through this the particular sales or allowances account) are debited.

Where it is known in advance that an allowance is to be given on accommodation, or special rates are to be charged, it is customary to enter the lower rate immediately on the bill and on the tabular ledger. In the case of a reduction of full pension terms, parts of which are entered daily under the various meals, the whole of such a reduction should be made against the amount allocated to accommodation so that the percentage profit on kitchen sales can be correctly calculated. A more correct practice is to charge the full amount and to highlight the reduction by entering it as an allowance. This will be posted to the allowances book and then to the debit side of the ledger where the amount of these special reductions can be seen clearly.

Most allowances given to guests are in respect of overcharges, adjustments for unsatisfactory service, or disputed charges which cannot be proved (mainly local telephone calls). Where it is possible to rectify an overcharge in all records at once, this may be done, but it is usually safer and a better practice to make out an allowance slip as is done when any other form of allowance is given. This slip is completed and passed through all records. The department to be debited is noted as well as the amount, the room number, and the reason for the allowance. The slip must be signed by the person authorized to sanction allowances. The amounts are entered on the credit side of the tabular ledger and also analysed daily in an allowances book, from which the totals are posted to the debit of the various departmental sales accounts.

When a visitor leaves and does not settle his account by paying cash, the account is, nevertheless, balanced and closed. In this instance, instead of being carried forward to the next day, the balance is transferred to a personal account in the sales ledger. When the transfer has been entered in the sales ledger, it is desirable to put the sales ledger folio reference under the amount in the tabular ledger to show both that it has been posted and where.

VISITORS' BILLS

The visitors' tabular ledger described above is the hotel summary of each day's business, and frequently provides the only hotel copy of the guest's bill (*see* Figures 4.4 and 4.5). The particulars concerning any guest or room are summarized for the visitor on his bill, which is opened on his arrival and which is usually presented to him on his departure (or at fixed intervals if the stay is a long one). The bill corresponds to the columns or lines relating to the guest's stay on the appropriate individual day sheets of the tabular ledger. This duplication is shown in Figure 4.6.

	July 12		July 13		July 14			
Brought Forward			11	75	24	40		
Apartment & Breakfast	8	50	9	25	0	75		
Early Morning Tea			0	15				
Luncheon					1	50		
Afternoon Tea								
Dinner	1	60	1	80				
Other food								
Liquors	1	15	0	75	0	60		
			0	60	0	45		
Telephones etc.								
Paid outs	0	30	0	10	1	00		
Else	0	20			0	33		
TOTAL	11	75	24	40	29	03		
DATE					SERVICE %		2	91
					TOTAL DUE		31	94

WELCOMBE HOTEL

To *Mr F Betts*   Room No. *1*

Fig. 4.4. Guest's bill: preprinted headings

Handwritten bills always follow a similar columnar layout, each column being devoted to a day's business. The printed narrative varies as between hotels, but consists of the same analysis of charges as appears in the hotel tabular ledger in the same order. The only transposition that occurs is in the case of a horizontal tabular ledger: the charges are arranged vertically on the guest's bill.

WELCOMBE HOTEL
Newtown

Proprietor. J. Smith   Telephone Newtown 222

Name Mr. F. Betts   Apartment No. 1

19 71	July 12		July 13		July 14		
Brought forward			11	75	24	40	
Apartments	8	50	8	50			
Early morning tea			0	15			
Breakfast			0	75	0	75	
Luncheon					1	50	
Afternoon tea							
Dinner	1	60	1	80			
Other food							
Liquor	1	15	0	75	0	60	
			0	60	0	45	
Sundry sales	0	20			0	33	
Paid outs	0	30	0	10	1	00	
					29	03	
Service 10%					2	91	
Carried forward	11	75	24	40	31	94	

Fig. 4.5. Guest's bill: no preprinted headings

The size of the bill is determined by the average length of stay of visitors. Where it is short, a three- or four-day bill is customary, but in hotels with a longer average stay a seven- or eight-day bill may be more appropriate. For reasons of economy many hotels use both types of bill as appropriate.

Sometimes minor charges of the same type, such as 'telephones' or sundries', are grouped under one heading on the bill without each charge being exactly identified. Where this is the case and experience proves that it is a source of queries by the guests, it may be advisable to provide an explanatory statement on the back of the bill.

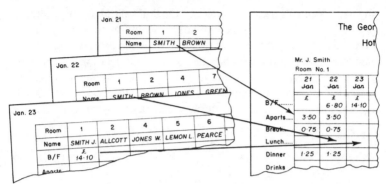

Fig. 4.6 Tabular ledger and guest's bill

Guests' bills are normally arranged for easy reference in order of their room numbers in a folder, binder, box file or ledger tray, with the bill for each room being separated from the next by an interleaf or a holder with an indicator for quick location.

It is normal practice to present a weekly account to a guest staying for longer than a week, and to inform the manager of any outstanding accounts, the balance of which is increasing or which has accumulated. The guest may also be asked to settle his account if it has reached more than a specified amount.

Bill Office

A section of the bill office may be seen in Plate 4.1. The billing machine illustrated is an N.C.R. 42 model. In the foreground is the ledger tray containing the bills of the present guests. On the left are the pneumatic tubes which are used to convey the charge vouchers (Figure 4.7) from the various departments to the bill office.

Duplicate Bills

Some hotels consider that it is desirable to retain a copy of each bill after the guest's departure. This is done by using duplicate bills, which are entered in one writing by using carbon paper; the top copy is presented to the guest and the carbon copy retained by the hotel.

The duplicate bills do not normally replace the tabular ledger as the summary of the day's business, as this is considered of the utmost importance. It is, however, possible to dispense with the tabular ledger in some circumstances and to secure the daily summary by adding up each type of charge from the individual bills using an adding machine and thus arriving at the daily totals. This is the principle underlying several patent methods of simplified hotel book-keeping, which do not require the maintaining of a tabular ledger. As will be seen later, it is also the underlying principle of mechanized billing systems, although the daily totals are produced automatically as a by-product of posting

Fig. 4.7 Charge voucher

charges to the guests' bills on the hotel billing machine. In these circumstances the bottom copy of the bill is also the guest's current account with the hotel. Charges are credited to the individual nominal sales accounts in total daily, or through the medium of a summary book at longer intervals; each individual charge is entered on the guests' bills (top copy) and simultaneously debited on their personal current accounts (the bottom copy of the bill), which is here replacing the tabular ledger.

WRITING UP OF VISITORS' ACCOUNTS

Visitors' accounts may be written up in three different ways.

(*a*) The ideal approach is for two separate persons to make entries in the tabular ledger and in the guests' bills concurrently. This means in the first place that each charge reaching the book-keeper is entered twice at the same time, in the visitors' ledger and in the bill. Secondly, any credit entry is also recorded in both records at the same time. Thirdly, there is an independent check for accuracy.

In this way the guest's account in the ledger can be compared with his bill at any time and the two should correspond exactly. Daily balancing and the presentation of accounts to guests for settlement is facilitated. Alternatively, one person may make both entries concurrently, but this tends to lessen the advantage of an independent check. The uneven distribution of work throughout the day often precludes the above approach and one or other of the records takes precedence.

(*b*) One possibility is to make entries first in the tabular ledger as the charges reach the book-keeper, and to copy the bill entries from the visitors' ledger or from the voucher once a day.

This method enables visitors' accounts to be written up when there is most time to do it and is used particularly in hotels with a longer average stay of guests. Its principal drawback is the divergence between the two records at times, which may slow down the balancing and the presentation of bills called for unexpectedly. If bill entries are made from the visitors' ledger and not from the original voucher, there is also an increased risk of error.

(*c*) In hotels with a short average stay of guests and a large daily number of departures, the bill usually takes precedence and is kept in duplicate. Entries are first made only on the bill, and the tabular ledger is treated only as a summary of the business, to which entries are made from the bills – from the original during the stay, and from the copy retained after departure.

In this way there is no delay in the presentation of bills for settlement but the risk of error in transferring figures from the bills to the ledger remains, unless the original voucher is used.

BALANCING THE TABULAR LEDGER

The handwritten tabular ledgers are balanced each day, usually at the close of business. In order to complete the balance, the debit part of each visitors' account is totalled and agreed with the total credit. As a check that charges have not been omitted or have not been entered in the wrong guest's account, these totals are checked against the totals of the individual guests' bills. This is best accomplished by two persons adding the bills and tabular ledger independently and checking their results. Next, each dissection of the debits and the credits is totalled and entered in the appropriate column. The totals of the debits are then added as are the totals of the credits. These two grand totals must agree.

As a final check the total of the debits and credits of the individual guest accounts' columns should be added and agreed with the grand totals.

The purpose of the checking and cross-checking is to prove the arithmetical accuracy of the additions in the tabular ledger. However, there are several types of error which this balancing does not reveal. Such errors may be grouped under three main headings:

Errors of omission
Errors of commission
Compensating errors

An error of omission will occur when a voucher has gone astray or is not posted for any reason. It will also occur when the brought-forward figure is omitted from a visitor's account in the tabular ledger. This latter error will be revealed when the balances in the ledger are checked against the balances on the bills at the end of the day. The former error may be similarly revealed, but in these instances the omission may have occurred in the bill as well and only come to light when the control or internal audit department carries out its checks against independent sources, as will be seen later.

A check against errors in the brought-forward figures is to enter them in the new day's ledger, total them, and agree this figure with the total of the carry forward from the previous day, as soon as the previous day's tabular ledger has been balanced. The 'labour-saving device' of copying the carry forward total along with the individual balances defeats the check.

An error of commission entails posting a wrong amount (which could be any form of debit, including a brought-forward figure, or any form of credit), or posting the right amount to the wrong visitor's account or under the wrong analysis heading. It may even be a combination of these errors.

The tabular ledger may also balance containing an arithmetical error when another error or errors of the same amount has been made in a compensating manner. For example, one guest's account in the ledger may have been totalled £1·00 too much and another £1·00 too little. The total of outstanding bills will be correct. The comparison with the individual bill totals is a useful check here and will reveal the error. However, a similar mistake in the totalling of the analysis columns could well pass unnoticed as there is no independent check at this stage.

SALES LEDGER

The sales ledger contains all the debtors of the hotel other than those accounts which are still accumulating in the tabular ledger. It functions in the same manner as the sales ledger of any other business. There is a separate account page for each regular customer (Figure 4.8) and these pages are generally arranged in alphabetical order, although they may have account numbers and an index. The total bill, having been credited

				£	p					£	p
									Folio No 16		
Credit Limit £75				James Low, Esq.				16 Able Avenue, Norton			
1971			Tab	£	p	1971				£	p
June	19	To Accommodation	167	18	35	June	30	By Balance	c/d	25	25
"	24	" Dinners	Tab 184	6	90						
				£	25	25			£	25	25
July	1	To Balance	b/d	25	25	July	25	By Allowance		1	30
"	26	" Accommodation	Tab 204	8	50	"	"	" Cheque	CB 76	23	95
"	30	" Returned Cheque	CB 83	23	95	"	31	" Balance	c/d	32	45
				£	57	70			£	57	70
Aug	1	To Balance	b/d	32	45	Aug	4	By Cheque	CB 87	32	45
				£	32	45			£	32	45

Fig. 4.8 Sales ledger example

in the tabular ledger, is debited here to the appropriate personal account; payment received is credited in that account and debited in the cash book.

Each account in the sales ledger is headed with the name and address of the firm or individual, and also any special remarks, such as special discounts, limitation of credit, and how frequently the statement should be sent. Normally, where a balance is outstanding at the end of any month, or other set day, a statement of account is sent to the client as a reminder, so that customarily a batch of statements is rendered to debtors monthly. Where a firm is paying bills of individuals, it usually requires a signed copy of the bill to accompany the first statement on which it occurs. It is, therefore, necessary for the cashier or receptionist booking out those visitors who have arranged to have their bill paid subsequent to their departure, to ensure that the visitors sign the bill acknowledging the indebtedness, and that this signed bill is passed on to the person maintair.ng tl sales ledger. Where only one copy of the hotel bill is made out, the visitor ... ·t be required to leave it behind, so that it can be sent to the paying agen*

5. Cash and Banking

JUST as the billing of guests may be one of the duties of the book-keeper/receptionist or may be undertaken in a separate department so, too, the size of an hotel frequently determines whether there is a separate cashier's department as in the larger hotels or, whether its functions are combined with those of the bill office, or even with reception and billing, as in the smaller establishment. However, the methods, records, and procedures are largely the same, irrespective of the size of the hotel. Cash books and petty cash books are kept, receipts given, deposits dealt with, and cash floats maintained. A guest may wish to settle his account by cash, credit card, cheque, travellers' cheque or in foreign currency in any hotel. The principles underlying the acceptance and handling of all these do not differ merely because a cashier is working solely in that capacity, as distinct from the situation where the settlement of visitors' accounts is only one part of the receptionist's duties.

CASH FLOATS

The main function of the cashier is to accept payment in settlement of accounts. This may be done by any of the methods indicated above and, most commonly, by the payment of cash. In any event, a cashier needs a sum of money of small denomination for the purpose of giving change. This cash float, as it is termed, varies in size from hotel to hotel and from season to season, according to need, but it is desirable to keep the amount fairly constant in the short run to avoid mistakes of over- or under-banking. It is important to ensure that the float is sufficiently large and adequately broken down into notes, silver, and copper, to provide change under all normal circumstances.

It is usually the responsibility of the cashier on duty at the end of the day's business to make up the float and keep it separate before depositing the balance of the day's receipts in the night safe. Where a float is left by one cashier for another, this should be checked by the new cashier when coming on duty and any discrepancy reported immediately. It is of assistance if the cashier going off duty fills in a slip stating the make-up of the float, and dates and signs it. The new cashier can check the float against the list and see more easily where any discrepancy occurs (for example, a £1 note over or £1 of silver short); the new cashier also signs the slip, which signifies that the float has been checked.

In some hotels the time involved in checking floats is felt to be better spent at other work and each cashier maintains an individual float. Where it is the practice to have individual cashiers' floats, management should ensure that spot checks are carried out from time to time to ascertain that there are no misappropriations of the floats.

CASH SETTLEMENT

It is the right of a creditor to receive payment in cash. A visitor at an hotel cannot insist on paying by any other method. A cheque on a banking account is not legal tender, although the majority of business payments are made safely and satisfactorily by this means.

Legal tender is the amount of money which a creditor must legally accept in payment of a debt. In Great Britain and Northern Ireland the Bill before Parliament at the time of going to press proposed:

bronze (copper) coins - up to 20 new pence or 4 shillings
cupro-nickel (silver) coins of 5p and 10p - up to £5
cupro-nickel (silver) coins above 10p - up to £10
Bank of England £1, £5, and £10 notes up to any amount

The old Bank of England £5 and £10 notes, which were large and printed black on white, although not legal tender, may be accepted and honoured by the bank if presented.

Scottish banknotes are similarly acceptable although they are not legal tender outside Scotland. Charges are not made by the banks on changing these Scottish notes so that the practice of only accepting them at a lower value, say 97p for a £1 note, is to be deprecated.

Legally, nobody is compelled to give change, as the exact amount of the debt should be produced in legal tender and offered unconditionally. In practice everybody gives change and many people accept payment by means other than legal tender.

SETTLEMENT BY CHEQUE

Frequently a cashier or receptionist is asked to cash a cheque or to accept payment by cheque. There is no legal obligation to do so. In most hotels there is a house policy covering the acceptance of cheques, and the receptionist, who should be informed of this, simply acts within rules laid down. The two extremes are to accept cheques freely (very few hotels do this) or not to accept cheques at all. It is a very common requirement that a visitor who wishes to settle his bill by cheque is asked to pay his account to the end of his stay three or four days before departure. This may give the hotel time to pay the cheque into their bank and have it presented at the visitor's bank and honoured. Where time is short or the visitor's bank is somewhat inaccessible, the procedure may

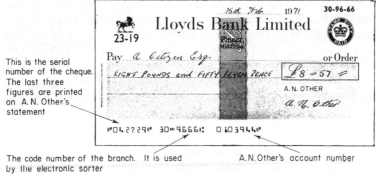

Fig. 5.1 Specimen cheque

be speeded by presenting the cheque for special clearance. This entails the hotel's bank posting it separately and directly to the bank on which the cheque was drawn, and then telephoning there the following day to ascertain whether it has been met. This procedure speeds up one's knowledge that a cheque is valid by two or three days. When a special clearance is used, the bank usually makes a direct charge of a few shillings. The receptionist's instructions should include a clear indication whether the charge is to be passed on to the guest.

It should be noted that the Midland Bank card introduced in 1966 guarantees cheques of its customers up to £30; this alleviates the risk to hoteliers in accepting cheques from Midland Bank customers presenting one of these cards.

A cheque may be defined as a bill of exchange drawn on a banker payable on demand (*see* Figure 5.1). As a bill of exchange it is subject to the Bills of Exchange Act, 1882, as well as to the Cheques Act, 1957. The terminology on a cheque is thus the same as that used on other bills of exchange. In the example above A. N. Other has drawn the cheque and is known as the drawer; the bank on which it is drawn is the drawee. The person or company to be paid, in this case A. Citizen, is the payee.

Whatever the amount for which it is made out, stamp duty is payable on a cheque. A banker supplies his client (against payment for the stamp duty) with a book of cheques already printed and stamped. However, a cheque may be made out on any material provided that it instructs the drawee to pay so much to the payee, is signed by the drawer, dated, and the duty is paid, e.g. the appropriate stamp attached.

Care must be exercised with cheques already prepared with numbers specially printed for use with computers. The account number printed on the cheque is charged with the payment and not specifically the drawer's account. Normally, of course, these are the same but, if a person borrows such a cheque from another, it is the latter's account which is charged.

As a result of the Cheques Act, 1957, cheques need no longer be endorsed, i.e. signed on the back, if they are paid into the account of the payee or one in which he is a partner. However, endorsement is still required on:

(a) Cheques cashed over the bank counter.

(b) Cheques payable to joint payees where they are payable to an account to which all are not parties.

(c) Negotiated cheques.

A negotiated cheque is one which is ultimately paid into an account other than that of the original payee. Negotiation is effected by the payee endorsing the cheque. It should be particularly noted that the endorsement must be exactly the same as the payee's name on the cheque; thus, where the name is Roy S. Seaford, an endorsement 'R. S. Seaford' or 'Roy Seaford' is not a valid endorsement. If the cheque is endorsed, that is signed on the back 'Roy S. Seaford', it can pass freely. If Mr Seaford writes 'Pay L. Black or Order' and then signs, this makes L. Black the payee, and he will have to endorse it similarly before it can be negotiated. Finally, if Mr Seaford writes 'Pay L. Black *only*', this is a restrictive endorsement and no further transfers of the cheque may take place.

Crossing of Cheques

A cheque may be crossed, i.e. have parallel lines drawn across its face (*see* Figure 5.2). In this case the money can only be collected by another bank from the bank on which it is drawn and paid into the ultimate payee's bank account. This is termed a general crossing; the words '& Co' may be added but no special significance attaches to them. 'Not negotiable' may also appear on a cheque. Strangely enough this does not mean that the cheque may not be negotiated or transferred but serves as a warning that a holder of such a cheque may not obtain better title than that of the person from whom he received it. Thus, if it were discovered that the person from whom he received it had stolen it, the holder would have to return the cheque or make good the loss to the genuine owner of the cheque.

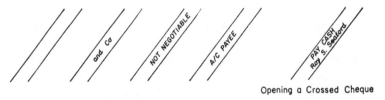

Opening a Crossed Cheque

Fig. 5.2 Types of cheque crossing

There are also special crossings; these may be with or without the parallel lines on the face. One type has the name of a bank across the face. Such a cheque may only be collected through that bank, although this is done by any bank on behalf of its client. A second type of special crossing is 'A/C Payee'. This wording notifies the collecting bank that the cheque must be credited to no other account than the payee's. This is a crossing which is observed by custom by bankers although it has no legal backing.

When a cheque contains no crossing, it is termed an open cheque and may be cashed over the counter of the particular branch of the bank on which it is drawn; it need not be paid into an account. When a cheque is crossed, it may be opened by the drawer writing 'Pay Cash' in the crossing and signing therein, in addition to the normal signature on the cheque.

Returned Cheques

Cheques may be returned to the person presenting them by his bank marked 'N/S' meaning *not sufficient funds* to meet the cheque, or 'R/D', *refer to drawer*. An R/D cheque may mean that there are insufficient funds in the drawer's account, but it may also be to correct some irregularity in the drawing of the cheque. Alterations on a cheque must be initialled by the drawer. Other common irregularities are the omission of the drawer's signature on the cheque, the words and figures of the amount of the cheque not agreeing, errors in the endorsement, or wrongly dated cheques. Commonly a bank returns a cheque that is more than six months old for up-dating. A cheque can be post-dated, i.e. made payable at some date in the future by putting that date on the cheque. In this case the bank will not honour it until that date, and will return it in the interim to the person presenting it.

Where the words and figures of the amount of the cheque do not agree, the bank will return the cheque to the payee so that the drawer can make and initial the appropriate corrections for the two to agree. This action is to protect the bank's client, the drawer, from having a simple fraud perpetrated on him (for which the bank may also be ultimately responsible to reimburse him). It may be easy to insert a figure 1 before 10 to change the figure to £110, whilst the writing remains at 'ten pounds only' as the amount of the cheque. However, the depreciation in the value of money has led to the common practice of writing in words only the amount of pounds followed by pence in figures,

e.g. Eighteen pounds 57 .... | £18 – 57 |

Generally when drawing cheques, the words and figures should be written close to the left-hand printing so that insertions and additions cannot be made.

Where the drawer has closed his account (or indeed never had one), the cheque would be returned marked simply 'No Account'. Should the drawer have died and the bank have had notice of this before the cheque was presented, it will be returned marked 'Drawer deceased'.

FOREIGN CURRENCY

Many overseas visitors prefer to pay their hotel bills in foreign currency and many visitors' accounts are settled in this way, particularly in tourist hotels. The cashiers must know the rates of exchange and also make allowances for any small charge which may be made to the hotel exchanging foreign currency by the bank. Whilst the daily rate of exchange for most currencies can be obtained from many sources, it is best to obtain the rate from one's own bank, as it is there that currency received is ultimately changed for sterling.

It is the practice of some hotels to establish a fixed rate of exchange, slightly more favourable to them than the lowest market rates. By this means the hotel ensures that it never loses on a transaction, that any bank charges will be covered, and that hotel employees handling currencies know the rate of exchange and can deal with such requests quickly and accurately (conversion tables can be drawn up – see Appendix H) For example, 40p might be given for a U.S. dollar. The market exchange rates vary from 41·32p to 42·02p. Should the guest demur, he is tactfully advised that those are the hotel rates, and that the local bank would accommodate him if he wished to obtain a better rate.

When banking the foreign currencies, it is advisable to enter them on a separate paying-in slip. It is then possible to see from the bank statement how much the hotel received from the currency, and it can be ascertained how much profit accrued to the hotel. The amount of this profit should be credited to an exchange account.

Alternatively, the exchange account is debited and cash book or the visitors' ledger credited with the amount the visitor is allowed for his foreign currency. Then the exchange account is credited with the full amount (less charges) given by the bank to the hotel for this currency.

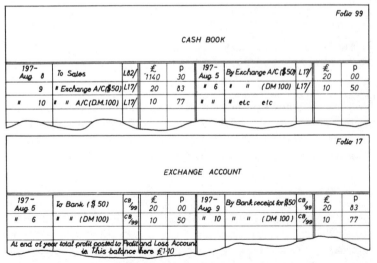

Fig. 5.3 Treatment of foreign currencies

The difference in this account is transferred to the profit and loss account at the end of the period (Figure 5.3).

Any hotel may receive foreign currency but under the foreign exchange regulations it is obliged to pay it into a bank or to an authorized agent. It is not permissible to give change in the foreign currency. For example, if a visitor presents a $50 note for exchange, this can be exchanged for the full amount but he must not be given (or credited with) a part of this sum in sterling and given the balance in dollars.

TRAVELLERS' CHEQUES

Travellers' cheques are used frequently by persons travelling abroad or even in this country as a convenient method of paying their bills or as a financial reserve. They are safer than carrying cash, as they are not as

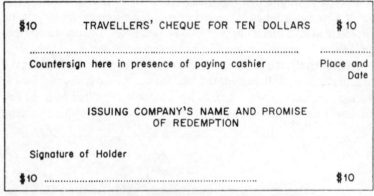

Fig. 5.4 Principal features of a travellers' cheque

easily exchanged as money should they be stolen. Travellers not needing to exchange them on the journey, can encash them on returning home; in the case of travel abroad it is thus possible to avoid a loss in currency exchanges. Travellers' cheques are well known and are issued by many banks and travel agencies. Their principal features are shown in Figure 5.4.

When a visitor wishes to encash a travellers' cheque, he should be requested to countersign it in the space provided on the cheque in the presence of the paying cashier. This person is responsible for checking to see that this counter-signature agrees with the holder's original signature, which he has had to write on the cheque at the time of its purchase. Where the travellers' cheques have been countersigned before being presented to the paying cashier, the holder should be requested to countersign again on the reverse side in his presence. Should there be any difference between the two signatures or any other doubt, a documentary próof of identity, such as the production of a passport, should be requested. Most travellers are, in fact, pleased to find that precautions are being fully observed before their travellers' cheques are accepted. It gives them a feeling of greater security to know that they would not be easily encashed, should they be mislaid or stolen.

If the face value of the travellers' cheque is in sterling, it is customary to encash it free of charge, i.e. to give the holder its face value. If the face value is in some other currency, such as dollars, it is usual to give the holder the same amount of sterling as he would be given, had he presented the same amount in foreign currency. Normally, the rate of exchange for travellers' cheques is fractionally better than that for currency; there is, therefore, in this case a minute margin of profit made by the hotel.

Travellers' cheques which have been altered or mutilated should not be encashed. The holder should be advised to contact the head office of the firm which issued the cheque. These firms also issue stop lists from time to time advising those likely to cash travellers' cheques of the details of the cheques, which (usually through theft or having been mislaid) will no longer be honoured by the company. Such stop lists should be displayed where all cashiers can easily consult them before cashing a travellers' cheque.

TRAVEL AGENTS' COUPONS

With the growth of group travel, travel agents' coupons are increasing in use. They can cause some difficulty when presented in hotels as, unlike travellers' cheques, they vary widely in their size, design, and purpose. The person dealing with them must read them with care to ascertain exactly what the coupon implies. Some are a notice that the travel agent will refund the hotel the charges to a guest for a fixed number of nights' accommodation and for certain meals; these vouchers are expressed in terms of services rather than cash. Others are expressed in terms of cash, which may be shown in a variety of currencies. The vouchers may or may not include an allowance for a service charge. Some are not worth anything, and are merely used by the agent as a method of introducing a client for whom a booking had been arranged by the travel agent. It is clear that some action by the travel agents to obtain uniformity in this sphere would do much to assist in their dealings with the staff of hotels. Until such time these coupons and vouchers must be treated with special care.

In hotels where a number of these vouchers are presented, a tourist account book is frequently kept. In it is posted the name of the client, the travel agency, and details of the voucher. In other hotels the fact that the guest has a voucher is noted in the bookings diary. In either case the guest bill may have some notation entered on it when it is opened on the arrival of the guest. Against the visitor's name on the arrival sheet should be marked the word COUPON so that the receptionist on duty can request these coupons when the guest arrives. It can be seen from these exactly what the agent is reimbursing, and a bill can be started for the other services the hotel provides for the guest. Only this bill will be presented to the guest on his departure.

Frequently two bills are kept for the one guest and, where a hand-written tabular ledger is kept, two columns are used: one (headed by the agency's name) for those services to be paid for by the agency, and the other (bracketed with it and headed by the guest's name) to contain items to be paid for by the guest. On his departure the guest will pay for his extras. That part of the account to be covered by the agency will be posted from the tabular ledger to the agent's account in the ledger. Agents' commissions, normally 10 per cent on all charges other than service charges, are deducted before rendering the final account.

CREDIT CARDS

Some hotels as well as restaurants and other businesses are prepared to give credit facilities to holders of credit cards. These cards are issued by well known organizations, such as American Express, Barclays Bank, Diners Club, and others, who have investigated the credit-worthiness of the holders.

Each card (Figure 5.5) is separately numbered and bears the holder's name and signature. Where it is the policy of the hotel to accept such cards, the staff of the hotel must ensure that any credit card presented is checked to ensure that it is not out of date, and that it is not on any list of invalidated cards. The holder should be requested to sign his bill and the signature checked against that on the credit card. The card number should be printed clearly on the bill together with the holder's name.

Towards the end of each month the retail outlets which accept credit cards send a list to the credit card companies of the amounts spent with them by the holders, together with the corresponding credit card numbers. The companies pay out the retailers the amounts due less a commission, which they retain to cover expenses, risk, and profit. They in turn collect the debts from the card holders. Some large hotel com-

Fig. 5.5 Specimen credit card

panies also issue their own credit cards, the head office arranging the collection of the debt.

RECEIPTS

Often the final step of the cashier in dealing with a visitor, regardless of the manner in which the bill has been paid, is to issue a receipt, which he would normally attach to or stamp on the bill. There is no obligation to give a receipt unless one is requested but should one be given, it must bear a stamp for duty if it is in respect of a credit transaction or for an amount of £2 or over. Most hotel bills fall into this credit category, although a bill for a chance meal payable at the end of the meal is deemed to be a cash transaction and requires no stamping.

Receipt books are generally numbered and close control is kept over them, the duplicates being checked against the tabular ledger and the cash book. In some systems of 'three-in-one posting' the completion of a receipt is an integral part of the book-keeping. These systems use carbon paper extensively and make an entry in more than one set of books at a time by using loose-leaf books and marrying the lines up on patented peg-boards. The amount of each receipt is transferred by carbon paper on to another sheet of paper which is totalled at the end of the day and the total entered in the cash book. The sheets are bound in a loose-leaf folder to form a subsidiary 'cash receipts book'. In these cases all cash received must have a receipt issued for it, including cash received from the bars, lounge waiters, restaurant cashiers, and other sources. It is regarded as good practice to give all persons a receipt regardless of the system used, as it aids internal control and is of great value if there is any dispute about the amount of money paid in by a department. These receipts, of course, need not be stamped.

When receipts are issued for all cash received, whether or not a three-in-one posting system is being employed, there is generally one receipt book or sheet for cash received in payment of ledger accounts, and another for all normal cash receipts, which should be entered in the tabular ledger. The daily total of this latter book or sheet must agree daily with the cash figure in the tabular ledger.

Generally, where a handwritten system is used, cashiers appreciate this extra check on their transactions, especially where there is more than one cashier during the day. It is possible by initialling receipts, or by using separate analysis columns in the cash (received) book for each cashier or by using separate receipt books, to allocate responsibility and for the cashiers to prove their takings independently.

DEPOSITS

The difficulty in accepting cheques in hotels is, firstly, that much less is known about the persons who owe the hotel money, than in many other forms of business and, secondly, that the services have already been rendered. One cannot refuse to complete a sale by withholding tangible goods as in many other transactions, and often one does not know that the visitor does not intend to pay in cash before the services have been rendered. The law recognizes the innkeeper's special risks in this matter and grants him special rights of lien on goods a traveller has brought with him. That is to say, where the visitor is unable to pay in cash and the proprietor is not prepared to accept his cheque, he may hold the visitor's luggage whether or not it is the visitor's own property, until the debt is paid. This right of lien applies only to hotels which are technically inns within the definition of the Hotel Proprietors' Act, 1956. It does not apply to private hotels, guest houses, and similar establishments (*see also* page 190).

The alternative course open to the hotelier is to ask for a cash payment in advance, and this is frequently done in transient hotels when a guest has little luggage. If the visitor is unable or unwilling to pay cash in advance, there is no admission and thus no service rendered. The payment in advance is referred to as a deposit and is calculated to cover not only overnight accommodation and breakfast but also any other likely small charge. Further amounts may be requested, should the visitor seek to stay for a longer period than he first stated and for which he has paid his deposit. Such 'deposits' are treated as payments received and may be entered straight away in the tabular ledger; the guest is given a receipt for his deposit. Alternatively, the cash received may be debited to the cash book and credited to the guest's personal account or to the deposit account in the ledger. On departure the guest's personal account or deposit account (whichever was originally credited) is debited and the tabular ledger is credited with the deposit.

Deposits, in the more accepted sense of an amount sent to the hotel in advance to secure a reservation, are more common and are dealt with by different procedures. One method, against which much can be said, is to keep the deposit in the safe in an envelope marked with the guest's name until the arrival of the guest, noting in the diary and on the reservation form that a deposit of a certain amount has been received. A refinement of this method is to list the amounts in a book, crossing out the names and amounts as the guests arrive. The keeping of deposit cash and cheques in the safe is to be deprecated as there is a risk of loss or theft, the cheques may become outdated, and the hotel is not making use of the money. It is strange that this practice seems to be most prevalent among seasonal hoteliers who are in particular need of liquid resources at the beginning of the season.

There is no reason why the money or cheque received should not be included with other receipts and banked, a record having been made of it. If the accommodation is to be reserved, a receipt for the amount of the deposit should be sent to the guest with the acknowledgment. These receipts should be made out from a separate receipt book used only for deposits. In this way control is kept over the deposits, and the likelihood of defalcations, by sending other receipts and failing to enter the cash, is minimized.

In some hotels receipts for deposits are combined with the acknowledgment of the reservation as illustrated in Figure 5.6.

In its simplest form the deposit is recorded by debiting the cash book and crediting the personal account or a deposit account in the ledger. A note is made in the bookings diary that a deposit has been received to draw the receptionist's attention to it when the guest arrives. When the guest has arrived, the deposit is noted on his bill. It is then transferred to the guest's account in the tabular ledger, either on arrival or on departure, by debiting the personal (or deposit) account and crediting the tabular ledger.

```
                    The Boar Hotel
                       Newtown


                                        1st June 19........



        Dear............................ ,


            Accommodation has been reserved as you

        requested from .............................

            We trust that you will have an enjoyable

        visit.

            The amount of your deposit as recorded

        below will be credited to your bill.


                                Yours sincerely,



                                R. Ford
                                Manager

        6418                            £14·00
```

Fig. 5.6 Receipt with acknowledgment of reservation

PETTY CASH

It is necessary from time to time to pay out small sums of cash for minor transactions. These payments are most conveniently made and recorded by the office staff, who are used to this type of work.

The most common practice is to keep a separate cash float from which to make these payments, and to record the purpose for the payment in a petty cash book. Frequently the petty cash book is in columnar form, an example of which is given in Figure 5.7. Receipts of cash for the purpose of replenishing the float are entered in the receipts column, which constitutes the debit side of the petty cash book (the general cash book being credited). Payments from petty cash are entered first in the total payments column and then in the appropriate analysis column or columns. Each payment should have a supporting voucher which should be numbered in sequence, the number being entered in the

Receipts £	Cash Book Folio	Date	Particulars	Voucher Number	Total Payment £	Provisions £	Cellar £	Postage £	Stationery £	Cleaning £	Repairs £	Sundries £	V.P.O. £	Ledger £	Ledger Folio
		1967													
20·00	24	Jun 1	Cash												
		" 1	Envelopes	1	0·60				0·60						
		" 2	A. Lamb–Meat	2	1·43	1·43									
		" 2	Postage	3	0·27			0·27							
		" 4	G. Green Room 44 C.O.D Parcel	4	0·35							0·35			
		" 4	Cleaning Window	5	0·65					0·65					
		" 5	Office Furniture Chair	6	2·40									2·40	
		" 6	R. Potter – Paint and Travelling	7	1·20						1·10		0·10		
		" 6	L Newcomb dusters & W. pad	8	0·95				0·35	0·60					
		" 7	Postage	9	0·20			0·20							
					8·05	1·43		0·47	0·95	1·25	1·10	0·10	0·35	2·40	
			Balance c/d		11·95	L/62		L/61	L/89	L/14	L/86	L/91		L/101	
20·00					20·00										
11·95		" 8	Balance b/d												
8·05		" 8	Cash												

Fig 5.7 Analysed petty cash book

appointed column. The voucher should be signed by an authorized person, usually the head of the relevant department.

At the end of each period, commonly a week, all the columns are totalled and the total payments column agreed with the grand total of the analysis columns. These analysis columns are ruled off so that the amounts paid out under the different headings may subsequently be posted to their respective expense accounts in the ledger. This form of petty cash book obviates the necessity of posting each payment individually to the ledger.

Whilst the exact division of the analysis headings is a matter of local convenience, they should include a column for sundry expenses (those which cannot be analysed correctly under any other heading), a 'ledger' column for those items for which there is no analysis column but which can be posted directly to a ledger account, and a column for disbursements on behalf of visitors. This latter heading, frequently known as 'visitors' paid outs', should be particularly noted. The total of this column should be checked against the totals charged to the guests in the corresponding V.P.O. column of the tabular ledger (or on the summary cards if mechanized billing is being undertaken) for that period, and the totals agreed. This checking may have to be done more frequently than the balancing of the remainder of the petty cash book, as any errors or omissions should be rectified before a guest's bill is presented. Sometimes a hotel keeps a separate visitors' paid out book. In such case a single total figure may be entered in the petty cash book daily.

The items analysed into the 'visitors paid out' column should be governed by the rule 'does the hotel make any profit out of this transaction?' Thus clearly an advance of cash to a guest (which should, in any case, only be made if properly authorized) would be entered as a disbursement on behalf of the guest, in this case being paid directly to him. So, for example, would a payment for a C.O.D. parcel, received on behalf of a guest, or payments for taxis, and items bought on the guest's behalf detailed in the previous chapter.

Occasionally a guest may query a charge on his bill. Many hotels make a practice of filing vouchers, which have been signed by guests, under their room numbers until they leave. Where this has been done, it is fairly simple to produce the signed vouchers to remind the guest of the source of the charge.

In the case of visitors' disbursements the signed vouchers or other pieces of corroborative evidence are sometimes filed in the order in which they are entered in the petty cash book. Should any query arise, the entry on the bill must be traced back through the visitors' paid out column of the petty cash book on the relevant day, and the prime document found.

Where there is any profit accruing to the hotel for a transaction, the entry should appear in a column other than V.P.O. in the tabular ledger (or its equivalent), so that such receipts can be analysed appropriately in the monthly summary as sales and the relevant profit on them calculated. The cost of such a transaction, should it have been paid for out of petty cash, must on no account be analysed into V.P.O., as it is in the nature of a purchase which has subsequently been re-sold to the guest at a profit.

An analysed petty cash book is a ledger account and forms part of the double entry. This obviates the need to keep a petty cash account in the ledger. It will be seen in the example in Figure 5.7 that an amount has been paid to the petty cashier and entered in his book equivalent to the amount he spent during the period which has just ended, so that the amount in the petty cash float has been made up to its original sum. This is known as the imprest system of maintaining cash. At any time the amount of cash, together with the vouchers for amounts paid out since the last reimbursement, should equal the amount authorized for that float. Such a system is beneficial to management, who can conduct a spot check easily at any time and who are also responsible for reviewing the petty cash spending for each period as they make the reimbursement; it is also helpful to the petty cashier, who knows constantly that the total of the paid out vouchers plus the cash remaining must equal a fixed figure.

The imprest system of keeping petty cash can be maintained whether the petty cash book is analysed or not and is highly recommended. The petty cash book should always be thoroughly checked when expenditure is reimbursed, ruled off, and initialled up to that point.

BANK RECONCILIATION

When the duties of the cashier/receptionist include maintaining both sides of the cash book, it is necessary from time to time, when a true cash position is required, to reconcile the balance as shown by the cash book with the balance recorded on the bank statements. Neither figure may represent the real position.

Differences between the two balances may arise from any of the following causes:

(*a*) Cheques paid out to creditors and credited in the cash book have not yet been presented by them for payment at the bank.

(*b*) Cheques received by the hotel and debited in the cash book have not yet been credited to the hotel by the bank.

(*c*) Payments made to or by the hotel by bankers' order or by trader's credits may not have been entered in the cash book, the entry on the pass sheets of the bank statement being the first intimation to the cashier of such a transaction.

(*d*) Similarly, the first intimation of the exact amount of bank charges and bank interest may be found on the pass sheet, and this figure is not included in the cash book entries at the time when they are recorded by the bank.

(*e*) Dishonoured cheques may not yet have been received back from the bank and thus not credited in the cash book prior to being re-presented, although they have already been debited by the bank.

The usual reconciliation procedure is first to agree all the items which can be agreed between the cash book and the bank statement, ticking the debit entries of one against the credit entries of the other and repeating the process for the opposite side. The writing up of the cash book is then completed by entering any items not previously recorded and ticking these off. Finally a reconciliation statement is prepared between the newly ascertained final cash book balance and the balance on the bank statement.

The items unticked on either side of the cash book represent those transactions which have not yet passed through the bank. There will be no unticked items on the bank statement as this has been used to write up and complete the cash book.

The items not credited by the bank, i.e. the unticked debit entries of the cash book, should be listed and totalled and, where the bank balance is not overdrawn, added to the balance at the bank. From this figure must be deducted the total of the cheques outstanding, represented by the unticked credit entries of the cash book, similarly listed for con-venience and information. The resultant balance must equal the final cash book balance.

If the bank balance is overdrawn, the total of the items not yet credited by the bank must be deducted (thus reducing the overdraft) and the total of the cheques outstanding, which the hotel creditors have not yet presented, added (their effect will be to increase the overdraft) to arrive at the true cash position.

Illustration

When the bank statement up to the end of June 1971 was checked with the cash book, it was found that bank charges of £16·50 had not been entered in the cash book. This was done. The final cash balance was now £818·00. Items paid into the bank on the last day of the previous month had not yet been credited in the hotel's bank account. These were: cheque Smith £28, cheque Jones £18, cash £110. Cheques drawn by the hotel in favour of Lock £10, Stock £24, and Barrel £38 had not yet been presented. The balance on the bank statement was £734 to the credit of the hotel.

The bank reconciliation statement would appear as follows:

Reconciliation of Bank Statement with Cash Book as at 30 June 1971

			£
Balance as per Bank Statement			734·00
Add Amounts not credited			
	Smith	28·00	
	Jones	18·00	
	Cash	110·00	
		———	156·00
			890·00
Less Cheques not presented			
	467 Lock	10·00	
	480 Stock	24·00	
	501 Barrel	38·00	
		———	72·00
Balance as per Cash Book			£818·00

If the facts were the same as in the previous illustration but the bank balance was an overdraft of £410 and the cash book showed a final balance of £326 (overdrawn), the reconciliation statement would be compiled thus:

Reconciliation of Bank Statement with Cash Book as at 30 June 1971

			£
Balance as per Bank Statement			410·00 (*overdrawn*)
Less Amounts not credited			
	Smith	28·00	
	Jones	18·00	
	Cash	110·00	
		———	156·00
			254·00

                                                            £

  Add Cheques not presented
                   467 Lock   10·00
                   480 Stock   24·00
                   501 Barrel   38·00
                                  ─────
                                                          72·00
                                                       ─────────
  Balance as per Cash Book   326·00   (*overdrawn*)
                                                       ═════════

In both cases the final cash book balance presents a figure £84 better
from the hotel's viewpoint than the current balance at the bank, and
the reason for this difference is explained.

With one or two exceptions, the banks do not nowadays print any
names in the body of their statements, merely placing the last three
digits of the cheque number next to the amount debited. It is, therefore,
advisable to enter on the payment side of the cash book not only the
name of the creditor and the amount paid to him but also the cheque
number. This makes agreement with the bank statement much simpler.

Where separate cash books are maintained for cash receipts and cash
payments respectively, each has to be checked against the appropriate
side of the bank statement and, if necessary, entries made in both. The
new totals would be posted to a general cash book or total cash account,
balanced off, and the reconciliation then made.

Paying In to the Bank

Often one of the duties of a receptionist is to prepare the money to be
banked. The notes are sorted and coin bagged up appropriately. The

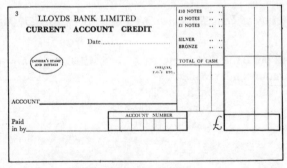

Fig. 5.8 Paying-in slip

amounts of each type of note and coin are entered on a paying-in slip (Figure 5.8) and sub-totalled. Any cheques being presented are listed separately on the slip and added to the cash total to give a total being banked. The person paying in the money signs the slip. When the bank cashier receives the money and cheques, he counts this, checks it against the paying-in slip, and stamps the slip.

Most hotels use a duplicate paying-in book so that a copy of the paying-in slip remains in the book. This is also stamped by the cashier. Where it is necessary to send a copy of the paying-in slip elsewhere (e.g. to a head office to give details of a banking) a triplicate paying-in book is used. It is more acceptable to the bankers and easier for record purposes if foreign currency is entered on a separate paying-in slip.

6. *Mechanized Hotel Billing*

THE introduction of machines into hotels for accounting purposes has the same basic objects as their use in any other field of industry or commerce. The main aims are to save time, to lessen the possibility of error, and to reduce the size of the labour force.

To be worthwhile, mechanization calls for a large number of transactions requiring similar entries. In this respect the visitors' ledger is an ideal object for mechanization. It was the first of the accounting processes, apart from the use of cash registers, to be mechanized in an hotel and, with the exception of the larger hotels, is the only one likely to prove economic and worthwhile. Even in this area the smaller hotels of less than, say, fifty rooms, may not have sufficient postings to the tabular ledger to warrant the installation of a special machine. However, it should be clearly understood that it is the number of postings to the ledger rather than the size of the hotel in terms of rooms that is the main factor to be considered. A large hotel with weekly 'en pension' terms or with a high incidence of cash sales is less likely to utilize a machine fully than a medium-sized hotel with a highly transient clientele and a large number of departmental charges to be posted. Other factors, which we shall consider later, play a part in determining whether a machine should be installed, but the number of entries remains the prime consideration.

OPERATIONS

The operation of the visitors' ledger can be broken down into five main processes:

(*a*) The recording of transactions – charges, allowances, transfers, payments.

(*b*) Analysing the debits and credits.

(*c*) Reproducing the guest's account shown in the tabular ledger, to provide the guest's bill.

(*d*) Adding and balancing.

(*e*) Posting the analysed charges to the summary book.

All these operations can be carried out by mechanical means. Indeed they lend themselves to this very well.

Recording of Transactions

Transactions have been recorded mechanically since the days of the first typewriter, and the uniformity and clarity of presentation thus provided are features of the hotel bill produced by mechanical means.

Analysis

Analysis can be simply achieved with a machine by installing a separate adding register and a corresponding key on the keyboard for each category required. When the figures are set on the machine and an analysis key is depressed, these figures are accumulated in the corresponding adding register, as well as being utilized in other non-analysis adding registers and printed out elsewhere. At any time a reading can be taken of the analysis registers to give a breakdown of the figures recorded since the registers were last cleared.

Reproduction

The reproduction of figures mechanically can be accomplished by two main methods. One is for the information to be printed out in several documents simultaneously. This may be achieved either by the use of carbon or other reproductive paper or, alternatively, by setting several registers with one setting of the keyboard, so that printing takes place at various points on the machine at the same time. The principle of the other method is to store the details of all the transactions, which the machine has recorded in a given period of time, and to reproduce all, or part, of this information as required. This may be done by using punched cards. The advent of electronic machines has produced several ways for storing information, punched cards having been augmented by punched paper tape and magnetic tape. Some hotel billing machines are designed to work in conjunction with punched cards and punched tape, which does enable a more detailed analysis of the various charges. However, the majority of hoteliers find the amount of analysis which can be achieved by purely mechanical means to be sufficient for their purposes at present.

Additions

Additions are done quickly and accurately by machine. It should be noted that where an hotel billing machine is not an economic proposition, assistance can still be given to receptionist/book-keepers in even the smallest hotels by installing a small adding or add-listing machine. They are so easy to operate that one can teach oneself in a few minutes and speed can be achieved with a little perseverance and practice. They are of particular assistance in cross-casting handwritten tabular ledgers, a process which is slower and leads to more mistakes than vertical additions.

Posting of Totals

The posting of totals of charges and credits to summary sheets is a simple matter, as the cumulative registers remain at any given figure until another figure is added, or until the registers are cleared and returned to zero.

BASIS OF MECHANIZED BILLING

The emphasis on analysis, with each charge and credit having its own separate register, means that a normal accounting machine is not really suitable for the purpose, and special hotel billing machines have been devised. Their development from the cash register can be seen in the design of several models by their shape, cash drawers, and by the inclusion of visible evidence of what has been registered.

The basis of the mechanized system is posting the guest's bill and the ledger copy of it, and also producing a running total of them in one operation, whilst at the same time storing in the analysis registers the details of the charges or credits which have just been recorded. At the end of each shift the ledger can be balanced with the aid of sub-total readings of the analysis registers. At the end of each working day, after the operator has balanced the ledger, the readings of analysis registers are posted on appropriate cards and cleared. They fulfil the same purpose as the cross-additions of the vertical tabular ledger and the ledger copies of the guests' bills replace its individual vertical columns. The total of balances on all the ledger copies of the bills at any one time represents what the guests in residence owe the hotel. The figure at the end of the day is the same as the total carried forward in the handwritten tabular ledger.

The two account cards (the guest's bill and the ledger copy of it) maintained for each guest in the hotel may be compared with the hotel copy of the bill as used with the duplicate handwritten bill system. However the cards differ from the conventional handwritten hotel bill in their layout. Charges and credits for each day are not posted at predetermined separate times, but subsequent to one another in the order of posting. An abbreviation or symbol is printed alongside each entry to indicate its nature. There is usually room for about thirty entries on each card. The exact number varies with the model and make of machine and the depth of the bill heading; with some models the only limit to the number of entries is the length of the bill which the hotelier wishes to present to the guest, whilst with others the size of the bill is predetermined by the machine.

When one pair of cards is completed, the balance is transferred to a new pair of cards, regardless of the length of stay. It is, therefore, possible that a current guest's account consists of two or more cards at the end of a week's stay, depending on the number of items posted. At the end of each posting run for each guest's bill the cumulative total of the bill is posted. The simpler machines post the debits, credits, and running balances in successive lines of the same column on the bill, but the more sophisticated models print these three sets of figures in separate columns as shown in the guest bill with its ledger card illustrated in Figure 6.1.

VISITOR'S ACCOUNT

1st Column – Remarks

Here are entered remarks when a further explanation of any item is required.

2nd Column – Item No.

Lines to which items are posted are numbered consecutively. On some models there is a depth-finding mechanism. The number of the next vacant line is pressed or set on it and the card inserted as far as it will go. The next 'print out' will be on that line. This ensures a neat, evenly spaced bill, with no waste of space or paper. When such mechanisms are employed, the depth of the bill heading is predetermined by the machine.

Where there is no depth-setting mechanism, these numbers are

Room No
345

Welcombe Hotel
Bournehampton, Wessex

Name   J. Blank, Esq.

ITEM NO	DATE	DETAILS		CHARGES	CREDITS	BALANCE DUE	ROOM NO.
1	-2·4-71	FLOOR	MEAL	★ 7·00			
2	-2·4-71	FLOOR	DRNK	★ 5·00			
3	-2·4-71	FLOOR	CIGR	★ 2·00		★ 14·00	
4	-2·4-71	— DISBT	TLGM	★ 0·50			
5	-2·4-71	PHONE	—	★ 0·05		★ 14·55	
6	-2·4-71	FLOOR	(-)DRNK	★ 5·00			

345   J. Blank, Esq.

REMARKS	ITEM NO	DATE	DETAILS		CHARGES	CREDITS	BALANCE DUE	ROOM NO.
	1	-2·4-71	FLOOR	MEAL	★ 7·00			# ·345
	2	-2·4-71	FLOOR	DRNK	★ 5·00			# ·345
	3	-2·4-71	FLOOR	CIGR	★ 2·00		★ 14·00	# ·345
	4	-2·4-71	— DISBT	TLGM	★ 0·50			# ·345
	5	-2·4-71	PHONE	—	★ 0·05		★ 14·55	# ·345
	6	-2·4-71	FLOOR	(-)DRNK		★ 5·00		# ·345
	7	-2·4-71	FLOOR	DRNK	★ 3·00		★ 12·55	# ·345
	8	-2·4-71	APART	—	★ 10·00			# ·345
	9	-2·4-71	MISC.		★ 0·50		★ 23·05	# ·345
	10	-3·4-71	FLOOR	MEAL	★ 0·40			# ·345
	11	-3·4-71	— NEWS —		★ 0·05			# ·345
	12	-3·4-71	REST	MEAL	★ 0·60		★ 24·10	# ·345
	13	-3·4-71	— TAILR —		★ 0·50		★ 24·60	# ·345
	14	-3·4-71	GRILL	MEAL	★ 4·95			# ·345
	15	-3·4-71	SURCH.	SERV	★ 0·50			# ·345
	16	-3·4-71	LNGE	DRNK	★ 0·40		★ 30·45	# ·345
	17	-3·4-71	— ADJST	CIGR		★ 0·45	★ 30·00	# ·345
	18	-3·4-71	MISC.	AUTO	★ 3·00			# ·345
	19	-3·4-71	— DISBT	THEA	★ 2·50		★ 35·50	# ·345
	20	-3·4-71	APART	—	★ 10·00			# ·345
	21	-3·4-71	MISC.	—	★ 0·48		★ 45·98	# ·345
	22	-4·4-71	FLOOR	MEAL	★ 0·55			# ·345
	23	-4·4-71	— NEWS —		★ 0·05			# ·345
	24	-4·4-71	REST	MEAL	★ 1·10		★ 47·68	# ·345
	25	-4·4-71	— LNDRY —		☆ 1·83			# ·345
	26	-4·4-71	SURCH.	—	★ 4·27		53·78	# ·345
	27	-4·4-71	— CASH —			★ 50·00	★ 3·78	# ·345
	28							
	29							
	30							
	31							

ACCOUNTS DEPT

Fig. 6.1 N.C.R. posting machine: specimen guest's bill (*above*) and ledger card (*below*)

still of use in lining up the cards manually, with the help of guide lines in the machine.

One manufacturer's depth-finding mechanism is based on holes punched in the card at each entry. Line numbers are then superfluous. On these machines (Sweda Model 76, *see* Plate 6.1), the bill and ledger card are entered into the machine so that the bill heading is nearest to the operator and pushed forward until a small wire engages the latest hole. The bill is then in the correct position for the next entry, which is made with the figures facing away from the operator, but in the correct way on the bill and ledger card.

3rd Column – Date

The date of each item is automatically printed here. A dating device is enclosed in each machine, but it is easily accessible and the date is changed from day to day quite simply by moving one or two dials. The date is of some importance to the control department as it can be easily seen when an item was posted, besides being of interest to the guest on his bill.

4th Column – Details

Here is printed the department, in which a charge originated, and also a further description of the charge or other item.

When abbreviations are used, a key to their meaning is often printed in a vacant space on the bill. The abbreviations of the bill illustrated are normally explained at its foot. They are reproduced below partly as a guide to reading the bill, but mainly as an indication of the type of breakdown into departments a large machine with many analysis registers can achieve:

ADJST	– Adjustment or allowance	NEWS	– Bookstall/news-stand
APART	– Room charge	NGHT	– Night waiter
AUTO	– Car hire or garage	PHONE	– Telephone
CHEM	– Chemist/drug store	REST	– Restaurant
CIGS	– Cigars or cigarettes	SERV	– Service charge
DISBT	– Paid out	SURCH	– Surcharge
DRNKS	– Drinks	TAILR	– Valet and dry cleaning
FRUT	– Fruit/flower shop	THEA	– Theatre tickets
LNDRY	– Laundry	TLGM	– Telegrams or cables
LNGE	– Lounge		

Most of the smaller machines limit the abbreviations to three letters or to printing the international hotel symbols on the bills and the ledger cards, and have considerably fewer analysis headings. One of the manufacturers (Anker) has a model with seven letters allowed for each explanation, which means that frequently no abbreviations are necessary, the source of the charge being entered in full (Plate 6.2).

5th Column – Charges

Only charges (debits) are posted here.

6th Column – Credits

Only credit items are posted here.

7th Column – Balance due

The balance of the account at any time is shown here. The maintenance of this running balance of each account, as a by-product of the posting of an item or series of items, is one of the noteworthy features of mechanized billing machines.

The simpler machines save space and cost, at some sacrifice to clarity, by combining the last three columns in one.

8th Column – Room Number

The room number, to which the charge has been posted, is printed on the ledger card only, together with the operator's symbol, mainly for control and audit purposes.

The ledger card is invariably the bottom or carbon copy, and the guest's bill is kept on top of it. The copies have been reversed in Figure 6.1 so that an extra column, which appears only on the ledger card (and then only with the more complex machines) can be seen clearly. When using the smaller machines the posting routine is altered. The room number either appears elsewhere on the ledger card and incidentally also on the guest's bill (usually before the amount of the charge); alternatively (in the case of the Sweda 76) the relevant number is posted straight on to the audit roll before the insertion of the bill and card and is, in consequence, omitted from them entirely.

AUDIT ROLL

The audit roll is a roll of paper which is usually kept locked within the machine. On it are printed the details of every entry which has been made by the machine, including the picking up of old balances and the printing out of totals and sub-totals. The used audit strip for each day is removed by the control clerk or night auditor when the trial balance has been completed, the summaries posted, and the registers cleared and returned to zero. He uses this strip to check the day's postings against the prime sources, mainly the vouchers and, where necessary, against the bills. To assist in this 'marrying-up' process and, indeed, to aid any query where a voucher must be produced to verify a charge, a tally roll number is printed specially for this purpose on the bill, the audit strip, and—by most machines—also on the individual voucher, which is placed on a separate special platform on the machine prior to activating the registers. The guide number increases by one every time the machine makes a total of a guest's bill.

It is possible to post the charge to the bill without inserting the voucher (some earlier models do not provide for this) and, conversely, it is possible for the machine to mark a voucher as posted without the bill having been printed on at the same time. The sense of the routine of the operation and some check devices in the more sophisticated machines make this latter error unlikely to occur accidentally. In both cases the amount is printed also on the audit strip, which cannot be by-passed. The advantages of the machine marking a voucher when it is posted are that the details of the posting can be seen and compared with the handwriting on the voucher itself – date, room number, type of charge, and amount – and, of equal importance, it can be seen at a glance that the voucher has been posted and the likelihood of double posting is lessened. Where it is routine practice to insert the vouchers into the machine when posting them to the guest's bill, and the operator has omitted to do this, the simplest procedure is to wind forward the audit roll until it is visible in a window of the machine and note by hand on the voucher the details of the entry, including the tally roll number, which appear on the audit roll.

Three billing machines made by the National Cash Register Co. Ltd. are shown in Plates 6.3 to 6.5. In addition, Figure 6.2 illustrates how posting is accomplished simultaneously on four records.

PROCEDURE

As soon as a guest arrives, a bill is opened with his name and room number (and frequently the room tariff and length of stay). The hotel duplicate copy is completed at the same time using carbon or specially prepared paper. If arrival notifications are interleaved between these two copies, they also can be compiled as part of this one operation. If the room rate is entered, it may be marked both at the top of the bill so

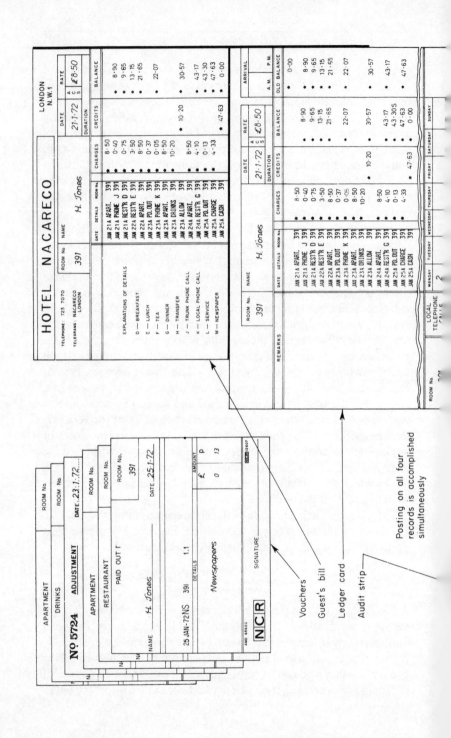

Vouchers

Guest's bill

Ledger card

Audit strip

Posting on all four records is accomplished simultaneously

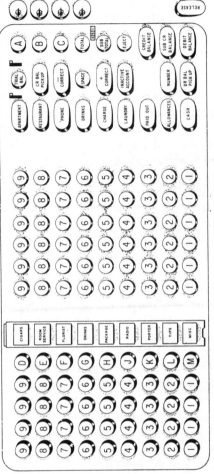

Fig. 6.2 N.C.R. Class 42 key board and related stationery

that it can be included in the arrival notification, and again in a space designed for it in the bottom left-hand corner of the bill. When using some machines this latter entry is visible and can be referred to when posting the accommodation charges.

The bill is then placed in a ledger tray conveniently situated beside the machine on the same side as the bill platform on the machine. The bills are kept upright in room number order, being either placed between guide cards bearing the room numbers or slipped into individual folders similarly marked. Where folders are used, they can be cut at the right-hand side with advantage so that the room number and a large part of the cumulative total column are visible. This saves a great deal of time by overcoming the necessity of taking each card out of its folder to ascertain its running balance when constructing the trial balance at the end of each day.

Where the volume of transactions is large and more than one machine is in operation, the work is usually divided between the machines by floors and separate ledger trays of account cards are used with each machine, say 200 rooms per machine.

Charges are usually entered two or three times a day in batches arranged in room number order; early morning, after lunch, and late evening are common times. The frequency depends on the busyness of the hotel and the other work of the machine operator, but too many posting runs entail extra work, both in handling the bills and in making more entries on the machine. However, where there is a substantial number of entries to be made, operators tend to make these as they arise. This often occurs, because in the larger hotels one person may have the operation of the machine as his main responsibility and wants to be continuously up-to-date. This does not alter the fact that proper organization can lessen the work-load. When vouchers are received from the various departments they may either be left in one pile until immediately before the posting run, when they are sorted by room numbers into ascending order, or they may be sorted by room numbers as soon as possible after arrival. If the latter procedure is adopted, the vouchers can either be placed in small numbered pigeon holes or, together with the bills, in the folders in the ledger tray. The advantage of this method is, that should a guest request his bill prior to leaving, it is only a matter of seconds to see if any vouchers have not yet been posted. There may otherwise be a long search through a pile of unposted vouchers. Time is saved in this way on a guest's departure at the cost of more time being spent in sorting during the day. Which method is adopted depends on the particular circumstances prevailing in each hotel.

POSTING CHARGES

The exact procedure to enter a charge varies with different machines. The following outline covers the essential actions, although the order of some entries differs with various models.

First, the bill together with the hotel copy, on which the charge is to be posted, is taken out of the tray. The relevant room number and the last figure on the bill, that is the cumulative total to date, are entered into the machine. This is done by setting the amount on the keyboard, then pressing the key marked 'old balance'. If the keys are not self-activated, the motor bar has to be pressed subsequent to this (and, indeed, every) entry before it is recorded by the machine. With most machines the bill may be placed on the bill platform and set at its correct depth (by using the depth-setting mechanism if available, or manually) either before or after this operation. If done beforehand, the amount of the old balance 'picked up' is 'printed out' on the bill. If the bill is inserted after this operation, the 'pick up' appears only on the audit roll. The advantage of printing the old balance is that it saves a great deal of time later, if there has been an error in picking up an old balance which has passed unnoticed, and which has to be found before the daily balance can be achieved. The 'pick up' and the previous total can be quickly compared visually, otherwise the additions of every bill have to be checked for all the day's postings until the error is discovered.

The disadvantages of this method are held to be:

(*a*) that it uses more paper and, therefore, if it makes the difference between using one bill and two, it adds to stationery costs;

(*b*) that the guests will not understand the entries; this may be valid, but in introducing innovations there is frequently a tendency to underestimate the intelligence of (most of) our guests.

(It depends on the type of hotel whether (*a*) is a material factor. Where guests stay only one or two nights a page of a bill is rarely completed in any case.)

Once the bill and ledger card have been placed in the machine and the old balance has been picked up, charges or credits may be entered. Charges are posted by depressing the appropriate room keys (except with the Sweda models), followed by departmental and descriptive keys and the amount. The order in which these are depressed varies with different makes of machine. An activating or motor bar also needs depressing on some makes. Where it is the practice to insert the voucher in the machine, this should be left as late as possible in the operation. Most of the information to be recorded can be read straight from the voucher; thus the details which the operator has to remember before operating the keys are reduced to a minimum. This practice reduces operator errors considerably. After one charge has been made, the voucher is removed from the machine, the next charge for that room set up on the machine and entered on the bill, and so on, until all charges then known for that room have been made.

The appropriate key is then pressed to print out on the bill and on the audit roll the new total, which the guest owes. The adding register, which has accumulated the old balance picked up and all the debits or credits which have been posted to the guest's bill, prints out the total with some symbol to indicate its significance and is cleared automatically to zero to await the compilation of the next bill total. If a bill is removed from the machine without being totalled, the amount of that bill is added to the next, as the register will not have been cleared. There may thus be errors on two bills and, particularly where the amount of the first bill is small, these can be difficult to trace. In order to prevent this, some models are so designed that it is not possible to remove a bill from the machine without first totalling the guest's account.

The posting process is repeated until all the vouchers have been entered. It can, however, be interrupted at any time to attend to another guest's account, provided the last bill on the machine is totalled before dealing with the new matter, say the payment of a bill by a guest.

The procedure for entering a payment is the same as when entering a charge, except that cash or transfer-to-ledger keys must be depressed instead of the charge keys. These registers also accumulate all entries made in them throughout the day and their totals assist in the balancing of the ledger at the end of a turn of duty.

Where a service charge is added to guests' accounts, the following procedure may be followed when the guest asks for his bill.

First it must be ascertained if any further charges are to be entered. If this is so, the room number and the old balance are entered in the machine in the normal way, followed by any unrecorded charges.

The sub-total key, which most machines have, is utilized to arrive at the balance, which can be seen. (This is particularly easy to do if the machine is of the cash register type.)

The appropriate percentage of this sub-total is calculated at this stage

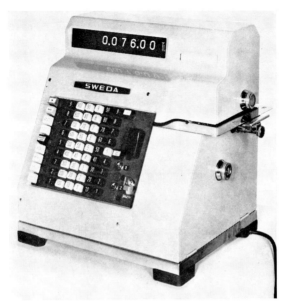

Plate 6.1. Sweda hotel billing machine

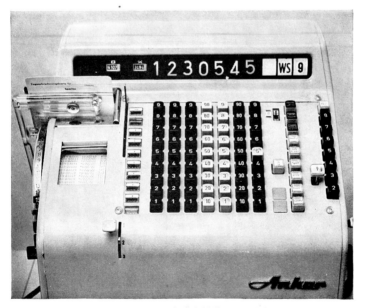

Plate 6.2. Anker hotel billing machine

Plate 6.3. N.C.R. Class 42 posting machine

Plate 6.4. N.C.R. Class 3A billing machine
for smaller hotels

and added to the bill by inserting the amount in the machine and depressing the 'service' key.

The bill is totalled and presented to the guest for him to check. If he agrees, he hands the bill back to the receptionist who then obtains the guest's signature on both copies if he is not settling the bill immediately.

The operator enters the room number and the old balance in the machine and inserts both copies of the bill. The amount of cash or the amount to be transferred to ledger is posted and the bill is closed, i.e. balanced at zero.

If the machine line finder is a visual one, the placing of the bill in the machine may with advantage be so arranged that the last ('settling') entries appear at the bottom of the bill, after a gap between them and the rest of the entries. This provides subsequently a clear and quick indication that the bill should no longer be in the 'live' section of the ledger tray.

If the guest has settled his account by an immediate payment, the top copy of the bill is returned to him together with his change. The bottom copy (the ledger card) of the guest's account is placed in a separate section at the back of the ledger tray marked appropriately (e.g. 'cash payments'). However, if the guest has arranged to have his bill settled at some future date, both copies of the bill are retained and placed in another separate section of the ledger tray marked 'transfers to ledger'. It is prudent to keep both these types of closed bill to hand as they may be needed should the trial balance fail to balance at the end of the day and the day's postings have to be checked on all bills posted that day.

SALES LEDGER

Some hotels keep a separate ledger tray for all unsettled accounts. Accounts are placed in it in alphabetical order of name of debtor, and fresh accounts are added at the end of each day. At the end of each month, or at some other established period, the top copies of the bills for each debtor are assembled, a statement is prepared, and the bills and the accompanying statement are dispatched to the debtor, that is the person or company responsible for paying the bill. The bottom copies, i.e. the ledger cards, remain in the sales ledger tray until payment is received, when they are marked 'paid' and removed. The sales ledger tray thus contains all the debtors of the hotel and control over them is facilitated as only live accounts are contained there. A coloured-tag system can be also incorporated (attaching a different coloured tag each month to the top of the ledger cards remaining) so that the long outstanding accounts can be seen at a glance.

CASH TRADING

Separate columns or lines are sometimes maintained in the handwritten tabular ledger for the various bars and for chance trade, so that the cash received, its source, and the nature of the sales may be recorded and included in the business done; this may also be provided for with mechanical billing machines. The simplest method is to maintain separate bill and ledger accounts with fictitious room numbers for chance restaurant, lounge waiter, bar, and other sales. The account card is entered in the machine and the amount paid in is simply recorded as so much drink, food, and so on, in their appropriate registers. At the end of a week or month the cards can be added to ascertain the business done in that department. The cash received is entered on a separate card. As the debits and credits must be equal, the inclusion of these cash transactions does not affect the daily trial balance of the ledger, but ensures that these sales are included in the total business done.

ADJUSTMENTS

If an error in posting is made and discovered, rectifying entries have to be made. Some examples of the action to be taken are shown below; they are intended merely to indicate the approach to adjustments and are by no means exhaustive.

(a) THE TOTAL OMISSION OF AN OLD BALANCE. The room number, the last total printed on the bill, and the last balance which had been omitted, are entered in the machine and the total key is depressed. The new correct balance now appears on the bill. The bill is removed from the machine and the incorrect figure is neatly crossed out.

(b) AN UNDERSTATEMENT OR OVERSTATEMENT OF AN OLD BALANCE. This may be dealt with similarly by entering only the difference between the wrong and correct amount. However, the calculation of the difference may lead to a further error, and it is for this reason considered safer to deduct from the last printed total the whole amount of the old balance incorrectly posted by using the adjustment key and to enter the correct amount additionally. If this is done, a note should be kept of the details on an adjustment sheet, in order to explain and analyse the amount appearing in the 'adjustments' total. Sometimes a separate voucher is used for each adjustment, which is made through the adjustment register; the total of their credits must equal the total of the adjustment register.

(c) CHARGES UNDERPC TED TO THE CORRECT ACCOUNT. These may be dealt with similarly to the first method outlined above. Once again, because of the possibility of error being made in calculating the difference, the second method may be adopted.

(d) CHARGES OVERPOSTED TO THE CORRECT ACCOUNT. These require the use of the adjustment key outlined under (b) above.

(e) CHARGES POSTED TO THE WRONG ACCOUNT. This type of error also calls for the use of the adjustment key and its attendant procedure. In this case the balance of the account, which has been incorrectly charged, has to be entered in the machine together with its room number. The bill is inserted in the machine and the adjustment voucher (if one is in use) is placed on the voucher platform. The amount of the incorrect charge is deducted from the bill by entering the amount in the machine and pressing the adjustment key; a new correct balance is obtained. The bill is removed from the machine.

Next the bill which should have been charged is inserted in the machine, after the room number and the last balance have first been registered. The charge is entered in the machine and the appropriate charge key is pressed. The adjustment voucher is removed and a new balance is printed.

It will be seen that in order to enter the charge in the correct account, it has been necessary to pass the same amount through the same register for the second time (the first time this happened when the wrong account was debited). Consequently, at the end of the day the machine total for the particular type of charge will be in excess of the true business done by the amount of the double posting. In order to arrive at the true figure, a manual adjustment is necessary in the trial balance card, as is the case with any double posting.

Miscellaneous Key

Some machines provide only a limited analysis of charges; a composite key is used for a variety of miscellaneous sales and further analysis may be required subsequently. In this case it is common to use an appropriately ruled form, on which the operator enters manually various charges in the appropriate columns at the same time as they are entered on the bill by the machine. The individual columns are totalled at the end of a turn of duty and the sum total is agreed with the reading of the miscellaneous key. This approach may also be adopted for the analysis of other registers including credits; it may be continuous or periodical.

'X' and 'Z' Readings

Furthermore, when sub-totals of the analysis registers are printed out, the symbol 'X' is printed alongside the figures to indicate that it is a sub-total and that the register has not been cleared. When the register is being totalled and cleared, the symbol 'Z' alongside the amount advises the reader of what has taken place. It is not possible to take out these sub-totals and totals unless the keys (marked 'X' and 'Z' respectively) have been utilized to unlock certain sections of the machine. Normally sub-totals may be freely obtained by all operators, who can thus balance the ledger, but to guard against fraud, the 'Z' key is usually kept by the control clerk or night auditor and it is he who finally clears the registers at the end of the day's business.

New Audit Roll

In some hotels, in order to ensure that no entries have been unrecorded on an audit roll, the following procedure is adopted. When the old audit roll is nearly completed, as indicated by a red band appearing on the roll and visible through the audit roll window, an 'X' reading, or sub-total, is taken of all the debit and credit analyses. This prints on the audit roll. A new audit roll is then inserted and the 'X' readings are taken again. Subsequently the control clerk sees that these two sets of entries agree so that he can be sure that the two audit strips are virtually continuous.

Individual Operator Keys

Some machines require the insertion of an operator's key before they will function at all. Other models possess a refinement of this whereby each operator's key is different and fits into a separate lock. By this means it is possible to identify which operator made each entry, as his identifying mark is printed everywhere in addition to all the other details.

DAILY TRIAL BALANCE

The balance referred to in this context is equivalent to balancing the tabular ledger at the end of the day. The purpose is the same, to prove the accuracy of the balances on the guests' bills being carried forward to the next day; and to check, subject to errors of omission, misreading the charge vouchers, and compensating errors, that the postings which have been made, are correct.

The 'balance' may be expressed as an equation.

Total of the current guests' bills at the beginning of the day (or balance brought forward)
+ the total of charges entered into the machine
− the total of credits entered in the machine
= total of the guests' bills at the end of the day (or balance carried forward).

The total of the current guests' bills at the beginning of the day would have been entered on the daily trial balance card the previous night after that day's balance had been agreed.

To obtain the total of charges for the day, the trial balance card is placed in the machine and, after using the 'X' reading key (or appropriate sub-total key), each of the charge keys is depressed in turn so that a reading of each key is imprinted on the card. As the register readings started at zero at the beginning of the day, this represents the totals posted through each register during the day. Some machines automatically add these amounts and print out a total of the debits. In the simpler models this addition must be done manually.

The daily trial balance card is then moved further into the machine, lining it up with the relevant narration and the readings of the credit registers for the day are extracted similarly.

The difference between the total debits and total credits must then be added (if the former exceed the latter), or subtracted (if there is a greater amount of credits than debits) from the balance brought forward. This will be the calculation of the total amount of current guests' bills which are now in the ledger tray. The last total of all these guests' bills must then be added – alternatively this may be done before any 'X' readings are taken. Most machines are so designed that this can be done on the machine. When all the bill totals have been entered, the daily trial balance card can be inserted and lined up with the narration 'machine trial balance', and the grand total of all the final balances on the guests' bills printed out. To balance, this figure must agree with the calculated total. If it does not, an error has occurred and must be sought out as detailed below but, if the two figures agree, the arithmetical accuracy of the figures has been proved.

Net Figures

If there have been no adjustments, the machine readings will reflect the business done. It is possible, however, that some of the charges have been overstated. For example, where an account is wrongly charged, say 30p for drinks, and this has been discovered, the adjustment register will have been utilized to deduct the 30p from the wrong bill and ledger account, and the drinks register used again when posting the drink charge to the correct account. If no other entry had been made for drinks, at the end of the day the machine readings for drinks would be 60p and, *inter alia*, the adjustment register would read 30p. The net difference of 30p is correct and the trial balance can be achieved, but the drinks figure is an overstatement and must be corrected to arrive at the record of business done.

The adjustment book or slips are referred to for details of adjust-ments made and all reductions of charges noted opposite the relevant charge heading in the designated column of the trial balance card. The total of these adjustments is deducted from the machine reading of the adjustment figure and the net amount of each adjusted charge is entered in the first column of the trial balance card together with any unadjusted machine readings. This column shows the actual business done.

The final trial balance may be done by the operator, but frequently the control clerk or night auditor completes this. Many cards contain memoranda of other checks and actions which are to be carried out at this time.

Shift Balancing

One of the advantages of using an hotel billing machine is that it is possible to balance the ledger at any time. It is usually done at the completion of the duties of each shift. The operator has to find his own mistakes and to hand over a balanced ledger. The procedure is the same as for the daily balance. When doing the second or subsequent balance during a day, it should be noted that the brought-forward figure to be used is always that for the whole day when all the debit and credit registers were at zero, and not the total at which the last shift balanced.

Summary Cards

When a final trial balance has been achieved at the end of a day, the machine totals for debits and credits are posted on to individual summary cards. One card is kept for each type of charge or credit and is headed appropriately. The card usually has a line for each day of the month and is divided into three columns. In one of these is printed the machine total for that charge for the day. As this is the last time the readings of the registers are required, the 'Z' or totals key can be used so that the registers are cleared at the same time and are reduced to zero for the next day. Adjustments, as recorded on the daily trial balance cards, are entered in the second column, and the business done for the day calculated and entered in the third column.

The business done, recorded on these summary cards, is totalled at the end of each month and posted to the monthly summary. As with the handwritten tabular ledger, the sales figures are posted from the monthly summary to the credit of the sales accounts in the main ledger. The guests' bills have provided the debit. When these bills were paid, they were credited and the debits entered via the daily summaries into the cash book, itself part of the ledger. Thus in total (and taking into account unpaid bills) the debits will equal the credits in the ledger.

COMMON ERRORS
AND METHODS OF DETECTION

When the outstanding totals on the current bills are listed and added and the total is not that required to balance the trial balance, the difference may be due to one or more causes:

(*a*) A simple amount over or short (e.g. a difference of 10p or £1). This can easily be caused by pressing the wrong key during the add-listing.

(*b*) An amount over or short below £1, which is divisible by 9. This is likely to be caused by a transposition of figures (e.g. 37p being listed as 73p).

(*c*) A fairly large uneven figure, by which the list total is short of the required balance. This could easily be due to the complete omission of a balance: the bill could have been mislaid, taken out of the ledger tray, misfiled so that two bills are in one folder and only the balance of the top bill has been read, or merely overlooked.

In each of these instances the first action to take is to check all the balances on the bills against the figures which have been listed. It is advantageous, if possible, to have an independent person calling out the bill totals.

If the error is of type (c), it can also be helpful to check the room numbers of the 'live' bills against the up-to-date alphabetical index of guests (or preferably the index of guests in room number order if one is kept). This will not locate the missing bill but will indicate if a bill is missing, or if the difference is due to some other error.

When the error is not discovered by these means, it is necessary to check each bill for the period since the last balance was taken, as the error may well be one of the following:

(d) A mistake in picking up the old balance when posting to the bill, or

(e) a complete omission of the old balance.

Such errors may appear on the bills in the following manner:

(d)	Jan 16	4761	£19·80	T
		Food	0·75	
		Drink	0·35	
			20·90	T

Here the old balance has been picked up as £19·50, and an error of 30p has been recorded in the new balance, which will make the total of the balances 30p short.

(e)	Jan 16		£19·80	T
		Food	0·75	
		Drink	0·35	
			1·10	T

Here no old balance has been picked up at all. The total of the balances will, therefore, be £19·80 short.

To detect such errors it is necessary to examine all the postings since the last balance and quickly re-check the additions, in each case seeing that the old total plus the succeeding entries equals the new total recorded on the bill. This can be a long, tedious task. It must include not only all those bills which are still active, but also entries on those bills which have been transferred to the sales ledger account and on those which have been paid. For this reason, if no other, it is prudent to keep such bills in the back of the 'live' bills ledger tray until the trial balance is achieved.

Where this type of error occurs frequently, or where there are new operators likely to make errors, the procedure of entering a bill may be slightly altered on some machines so that the bill is inserted into the machine after the old balance has been entered, but before the motor bar is pressed to activate the registers. The balance picked up will then be printed out on the bill immediately below the old balance thus:

$$\text{Jan 16} \qquad \text{£19·80} \qquad \text{T}$$
$$\text{£19·80}$$
$$\text{etc.}$$

To check for any errors in the 'pick up' in these circumstances it is only necessary to agree each total since the last 'X' reading with the figure immediately succeeding it. This can be very time-saving. The arrangements for and against such a procedure have been outlined earlier in this chapter.

ADVANTAGES OF A MECHANIZED SYSTEM

Mechanized systems have the following advantages:

(*a*) The guest is presented with a clear printed bill as compared with a handwritten one containing possibly several different kinds of handwriting.

(*b*) The machine ensures greater accuracy of visitors' accounts by eliminating errors which often result from careless handwriting and faulty arithmetic.

(*c*) The machine eliminates much of the drudgery of additions and other arithmetic.

(*d*) The machine permits quick balancing.

(*e*) The machine permits extraction of revenue analysed by department and also the extraction of a trial balance at any time of the day; the ledger can thus be balanced at the end of each shift and the person responsible for an error has to find it before balancing.

(*f*) Cash reports can be prepared quickly.

(*g*) The machine helps to keep each bill up-to-date and ready for presentation at any time.

(*h*) The machine enforces strict control and a simple check on visitors' accounts.

(*i*) The hotel retains an exact copy of the bill presented to the guest. In larger hotels the use of machines results in labour saving both in the operating staff and in the night audit staff.

Night Audit

The night audit of visitors' accounts is greatly facilitated by the use of a posting machine:

(*a*) If the machine total for a department is the same as the total of residents' charges shown in the sales records of that department, a proof is established that all charges of that department relating to residents have been entered.

(*b*) A comparison of the class of charge as written by the department with the name of the department printed on the voucher by the machine also reveals whether the voucher was registered for the correct department.

(*c*) To establish that all items have been posted to the correct accounts, advantage is taken of the room number printed on the ledger card and on the voucher. Usually when room charges are posted at night, the operator can observe at a glance whether the correct room number is printed after each item on each ledger card.

(*d*) If no error is found on the ledger card, it is only necessary to examine the vouchers and to compare the room number written on each by the department with the room number printed by the machine. If these two numbers are the same on every voucher, all items may be assumed to have been posted to the correct rooms.

FACTORS INFLUENCING THE INSTALLATION OF HOTEL BILLING MACHINES

When considering whether to install hotel billing machines or not the hotelier will be influenced primarily by three factors: his needs, the price of the machine, and its ability to do the work and analysis he requires. He will try to equate these.

His needs may be manifold and may prove the overriding factor in his decision. Staffing problems may be the key. He may hope to save staff, and thus money, by the introduction of a machine, or may seek to assist the present staff to cope with their work more effectively or to release them for other duties.

The billing machines remove a lot of the drudgery from the recording of charges and, in making the work more attractive, may assist in reducing the turnover in reception staff. In some areas, as more and more receptionists become competent in the operation of billing machines, it is becoming increasingly difficult to engage receptionists/book-keepers to operate a handwritten tabular ledger well, for once people become efficient in using a machine, they are loath to return to the drudgery of handwritten records. The machines may thus attract the staff required.

The actual number of entries on the visitors' accounts will be the major determining factor. Where these are few, staff is not unduly concerned and the cost is hardly justified. As the number of entries increase so the other factors play a proportionately greater part in the decision to mechanize. A desire to appear modern, to have neatly presented bills, and all the other advantages of mechanized accounting may affect the decision to a greater or lesser degree according to the circumstances.

The next step is to equate the amount of money, which the hotelier is prepared to pay, with the amount of analysis he requires. As a general rule the more sophisticated the machine and the more registers it has, the more it will cost. This often means that the hotelier streamlines his analysis to fit in with the machine he can afford. On inspection, this streamlining is not always to the detriment of his management control as frequently dissections in the tabular ledgers are unified in a ledger account and the separate analysis totals are not used.

The choice of machine will depend on cost and the ability to do what is required. Other considerations may well be training of operators, after-sales service (and its cost), the speed of dealing with a breakdown, stationery costs, the ability to obtain trained operators, the reliability of the machine and the space it will occupy, the delivery date of the machine, and any additional features it may possess, particularly safeguards against inaccuracies.

7. *Sundry Guest Services*

THE reception department in the smaller hotel provides several services to guests, which are performed in the larger establishments either by the uniformed staff or by separate units. Among these services are the handling of mail, the safe custody of guests' valuables, the provision of information to guests, and dealing with callers on behalf of residents. It should be appreciated that the work of the independent units of the larger hotel in these matters differs mainly in volume from the situation where the receptionist performs these duties. The problems and basic routines are the same but the receptionist may find that some of the aids or details of procedure are unnecessary as there is a smaller volume to deal with, and that it is practicable to approach this work in a simpler manner, without the use of some of the *aides-mémoire*. Maintaining a large number of books and registers is pointless where a good service can be given to the guests without these aids, and where information which the guest may require is readily available. The general approach outlined below should therefore be followed and utilized (or developed) as necessary.

UNIFORMED STAFF

The uniformed staff of an hotel is usually under the control of a head hall porter. His is an important post in the hotel hierarchy and one which is frequently underestimated by outsiders and newcomers to the industry. He often engages and dismisses his staff, organizes their duties, arranges for the distribution of their tronc, and is responsible for the running and well-being of his departments. He is one of the key members of hotel staff on closest terms with the guests. He may be the first person to greet arriving guests and is the one who will attend to their departure. He has long been personalized by his first name so that he is 'Charles' or 'John' to the guests. It is usually to him that they will turn, should they require help or information of an unusual kind, besides making use of his knowledge and the facilities of his department in the more routine everyday matters.

Arrangements ranging from a dinner on the Continent to a funeral in

Africa are made as a matter of course by the head hall porters. For their services they are not ungenerously rewarded by the guests. The scope of a head hall porter varies according to the size of the hotel and the limitations imposed on his department by the management of the hotel. In the larger hotels his reponsibilities tend to be greater. The information and enquiry bureaux may be within his aegis. His department may distribute mail and look after car-hire, the sale of newspapers, theatre tickets, and travel agency bookings, where these services are not provided on a concession basis.

The uniformed staff in an hotel may include the porters (including night porters and the luggage porters), the liftmen, the commissionaires at the doors, the linkmen who greet guests and attend to the cars, male cloakroom attendants, valets, and page boys (*see* Figure 7.1). They

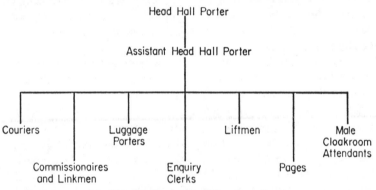

Fig. 7.1. Uniformed staff in a large hotel

provide front-of-house personal service for guests, which may include opening doors, delivering messages, paging guests, attending to luggage, and supplying information. In a large hotel the head hall porter may control as many as fifty members of staff. In the smaller hotels, while these duties may still be performed there may not be persons appointed with the various titles, but a generic term 'porter' may be applied instead.

As the centre for these staff is mainly the front hall where the hall porter's desk is located, there is obviously a great deal of interdependence between the work of the reception unit and that of the uniformed staff. There are also areas of responsibility which are sometimes allocated to the reception unit and in other cases to the uniformed staff. Guests' mail may be dealt with by reception in the smaller hotels, and

by either a separate mail unit or by the uniformed staff in other establishments. Similarly, enquiries may be dealt with and information
supplied in some hotels by one department and in some by the other. It
is customary in some hotels for the receptionist to show the guests to
their rooms. Where there are women employed as receptionists, the
management may deem it preferable for male guests to be escorted to
their rooms by the uniformed staff who take the guests' luggage. However, many hotels rely entirely on the porters taking guests and their
luggage to their rooms.

Guests' Luggage

Although the uniformed staff have many other duties, which may
include the letting and setting up of stock rooms and the setting up of
furniture for functions, the handling of guests' luggage is a duty connected with the reception unit which is invariably undertaken by the
head porter's staff.

Where the receptionist does not show the guest to his room, the
porter should be summoned, given the key to the room, and told 'please
show Mr X to room 49'. This enables the porter to check that he has the
right key and also to learn the guest's name; he is, of course, expected to
take the guest's luggage as well. Where the receptionist is showing the
guest to his room, he will ask the porter to bring the guest's luggage to
his room. In hotels with separate luggage lifts this may take a separate
route to the guest's room. Should no porter be available, the receptionist
advises the guest that his luggage will be sent up. Some indication of the
room number should be placed on each article whenever it is not being
placed straight into the hands of a porter to be taken up to the guest's
room. Tags, sticky labels, or simply a chalk mark are all methods used
to identify the luggage.

Where large parties are arriving, or where there are a large number of
departures at the same time, considerable strain can be placed on the
head porter's department to deliver or collect luggage as quickly as
possible. The organization of this is not the receptionist's responsibility.
He can, however, assist considerably by advising the head porter of all
anticipated movements, which is done in an arrivals and departures list
(*see* Chapter 8), noting any particularly heavy luggage commitments
which are known (for example, visitors arriving from abroad for a long
stay) so that the uniformed staff duties can be arranged accordingly.
The reception can also help by explaining the reason to the guests,

should there be any delay. Many hotels have luggage rooms adjacent to the street so that the luggage of departing guests, especially heavy luggage, can be brought down in good time and kept there prior to their departure. A common practice is for the luggage porter to note in a small book a guest's name, the number of pieces of luggage he left with, and the number of the taxi where one was used.

The Night Porter

The task of the night porter is to maintain such services as the management deem necessary during the night. He often has a stock of liquor and sandwiches for the convenience of residents when the bar is closed. He may perform the duties of a night telephonist where a separate person is not employed, and also often undertakes some cleaning duties in the public rooms during the night. However, his prime concern is security. He makes periodic patrols within the hotel and admits late guests. Where there is no night receptionist, he is also responsible for registering new guests and showing them to their rooms. The last receptionist to go off duty provides the night porter with details of any guests still expected to arrive, together with the numbers of the rooms allocated to them. The porter is also given a list of rooms to be used if there are any chance late arrivals. He may also be responsible for calls during the night and for organizing the morning call sheets.

An understanding of the problems and viewpoint of the uniformed staff makes for a better relationship between the two departments to the ultimate benefit of the guest and of the hotel.

GUEST MAIL

In a small hotel incoming mail presents little difficulty: the volume is relatively small and most guests are personally known to staff. But in a larger hotel an efficient system for handling mail is essential so that incoming mail is speedily distributed and no letters (for which the hotel may be liable) are mislaid. In any case the Post Office should be informed who is authorized to receive mail on behalf of the hotel; otherwise, an employee may be assumed to be a sufficiently responsible person to whom a postman is justified in handing letters. This is particularly important when handling registered mail.

All incoming mail is first divided into three main categories:

(*a*) HOTEL MAIL. This is usually given to the manager for his attention and sent by his office to the relevant department to be dealt with. In some instances certain things, e.g. bookings or accounts, are sent directly to the appropriate department.

(*b*) STAFF MAIL. This may be distributed through the staff office, a staff housekeeper, or some other person appointed for the purpose.

(*c*) GUESTS' MAIL. Here there are three possibilities which will affect the manner in which the mail is handled: the guest may be in residence, the guest may have left, or the guest may not have arrived.

As a protection against charges of negligence, both to the hotel and to the person dealing with the mail, many establishments insist that all incoming mail is date- and time-stamped on arrival. While this does provide evidence of the time interval between the stamping of a letter and its receipt by the guest, it is not unassailable evidence of the time at which it was received – it is only evidence of the time when it was stamped. For any credence to be placed on this system it must be an absolute routine to stamp all letters immediately on arrival, before any of them can be mislaid.

Mail Sorting

The most common procedure for sorting guests' mail is to go through it and, with the aid of an alphabetical strip index, to ascertain whether the guest is resident and, if so, to insert his room number in pencil on the mail. The individual pieces are then placed in the key and mail rack. The mail which is not disposed of in this way should, therefore, be that of a past or future guest.

Whether or not mail is delivered to the guests' bedrooms largely depends on the class of hotel but, apart from the risk of unwelcome disturbance to the guests, the cost of the labour used for this purpose rarely justifies it as normal practice. It is becoming more and more customary for guests to call for their mail at the desk. Where there is no key and mail rack, the mail may be sorted and placed in compartments arranged in alphabetical order of name; a suitable letter desk is shown in Figure 7.2.

A simple letter rack, placed where guests may help themselves to their mail, is a common method of distributing mail for guests in the very small hotel (*see* Figure 7.3). Whilst this may save a certain amount of time, the practice has the disadvantage that there is a lack of privacy and security for the guests' mail. The separate letter rack may be placed behind the reception desk to overcome this but the letter rack and separate key board probably take up more wall space than a combined key and mail rack and have no particular advantage over it.

In any case a complication arises with larger mail and parcels. Apart

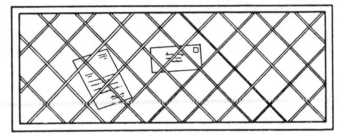

A — D	I — L	R — U
E — H	M — Q	V — Z
Packets	Packets	Registered Mail
A — M	N — Z	Future Guests

Fig. 7.2 Layout of a letter desk

Fig. 7.3 Letter rack

from not being suitable for a letter rack, they are also too large to be placed in a key and mail rack or in a letter drawer. Where larger mail is received it has to be stored separately; a form on the lines of the one illustrated in Figure 7.4 is made out and placed for the guest in the appropriate pigeon hole in the key and mail rack. When the guest collects his mail he can read, or be advised by the receptionist, that a piece of large mail (or a parcel) is being held for him.

Mail for Past Guests

Small hotels normally forward all mail received for guests who have departed, as this does not amount to many letters each day and does not involve much time on the part of the reception staff. Large hotels, on the other hand, find that the time involved in redirecting mail can be considerable and they try, therefore, to limit their responsibilities.

Guests requiring mail to be forwarded to them are asked to fill in a special card before departing. This includes all or most of the details shown in Figure 7.5, although reimbursement is frequently not requested.

The period during which mail should be forwarded is shown so that the hotel staff know exactly when the obligation is at an end.

The advantages of using mail forwarding cards are that it restricts the obligations of the hotel, firstly, to those guests who have completed

Fig. 7.4 Mail advice note

Fig. 7.5 Mail forwarding card

the cards and, secondly, to a definite period of time. Furthermore, should the hotel require reimbursing, it is easier to claim where a guest has already signed a form agreeing to it.

The mail forwarding cards are kept in a separate alphabetical index by name of guest. At each delivery, after the present guests' mail has been sorted out, the residue is checked against this index and, where appropriate, re-addressed. The mail-forwarding card index should be cleared regularly every few days and the expired cards should be removed. Some hotels have found it advisable to list all redirected letters and keep a record of them for six or twelve months in case there is any enquiry regarding forwarded mail. The list can be recorded on the back of the mail forwarding card (Figure 7.5).

It is sometimes not practicable to have a mail forwarding card; where individual registration cards are kept and not used subsequently for any other purpose part of these cards may be ruled to show a forwarding address. The guest completes this when registering, or subsequently, so that his forwarding address is known. On his departure the registration form is filed in 'recently departed guests' and the forwarding address is then available until it is refiled under 'departed guests'.

Future Guests' Mail

Once present guests' mail has been distributed, and past guests' mail re-addressed where possible, attention must be turned to the future guests' lists. This is a very good test of the efficiency of the reception unit. If advanced bookings are filed alphabetically, they can be checked through fairly quickly. If this is not done, it may be necessary to look through the advance bookings diary – a time-consuming process. This in itself is in many cases a good reason for alphabetical filing of advance bookings.

A note of the mail awaiting arrival must be made in the bookings diary against the name of the addressee. It should be the practice either to consult the diary or the arrivals list (on which the note would have been copied) as each guest arrives. The mail must be stored separately from that for the current guests, possibly in a convenient drawer, and arranged in alphabetical order.

Any ordinary guest mail which now remains is either for guests who have left and whose forwarding card has expired, or is mail mistakenly addressed to the hotel. In both cases the most expedient course is to mark it 'address unknown', and to return it to the postal authorities. Practice varies on this point: frequently mail is kept for a short period before being returned to the postal authorities in case a chance guest arrives who has given the address of the hotel in advance to his correspondents.

Registered Mail

Mail is registered by senders for security. In receiving registered mail for guests the hotel assumes a greater responsibility for it than for ordinary mail. One cannot expect guests to be present personally to sign the postman's receipt for registered mail. It is, therefore, signed for by hotel employees appointed to receive registered mail (usually the head porter, the letter desk clerk, or the head receptionist).

The registered mail must be kept in a secure place – a safe or a locked drawer. The guest may be informed, or the receptionist reminded, that registered mail is awaiting collection by means of a note placed in the key and mail rack. Alternatively, a message may be sent to the guest's room asking to call at the letter desk where registered mail awaits him.

Date Recd.	Regn. No.	Addressee	Room No.	Date Collected	Guest's Signature	Clerk's Initials

Fig. 7.6 Registered mail book

When registered mail is received by the hotel, the particulars must be entered in a registered mail book (Figure 7.6). The guest signs this book when receiving his mail from the letter desk.

Recorded Delivery

On payment of a small fee, which is in addition to the postal charge, the sender receives a special certificate of posting. (He may, on payment of a further small fee and completion of another form, also arrange to receive a certificate of delivery.) This service is used mainly when the sender is more interested in obtaining a record of posting than receiving compensation for loss. The value of the contents is restricted to less than £2 and all money, jewellery, and negotiable instruments are expressly forbidden. The service is mainly used for documents. The mail receives no special security in transit. However, as with registered mail, the Post Office requires a signature when delivering this type of mail. The same procedure should be followed in an hotel as with registered mail; it may be found advisable to keep a record of this mail separately from registered mail.

Telegrams, Cables, Telex Messages, Express Letters, and Communications by Personal Messenger

In large hotels the receipt of these communications is sometimes recorded in an appropriate book ruled in a similar way to the registered mail book, with the exception of the second and fifth columns. The time of delivery is inserted in column two instead of the receipt number unless all such communications are time-stamped. The date of collection may be omitted, but the type of message, 'cable', 'express letter', etc., should be noted.

Before accepting the delivery of any urgent message, the mail clerk must first ensure that the guest is resident in the hotel or see from the arrival list that he is due to arrive later in the day. The purpose of these messages is speed; their acceptance in respect of guests who are no longer resident usually delays them and the responsibility for that delay is then often placed on the hotel. Where telegrams or cables have been

```
            Welcome Hotel

Please call at the Reception Office

(Letter Desk) where

    REGISTERED MAIL/MESSAGE/TELEGRAM

awaits you.

Mr/Mrs/Miss ........................ Room ...........

Kindly hand this card to the mail clerk
```

Fig. 7.7 Mail advice note

taken in for guests no longer resident, strenuous efforts should be made to contact them by telephone, advising them of the receipt.

The guest should be contacted as quickly as possible. If the guest is resident, the clerk telephones his room advising him of the delivery and enquires whether he wishes it to be sent to his room or whether he will collect it from the desk. Where there is no room telephone, a note is sent up to the guest's room advising him of the delivery. If the guest is out of the hotel and his key is in the key and mail rack, the message or letter should be placed in the rack so that he receives it as soon as he collects his key. However, where the letter desk is separate from the key rack, an appropriate note should be attached to the guest's room key (Figure 7.7).

Special keys are available with slots in the room number tag to facilitate the passing of messages in this fashion (Figure 7.8).

In the case of a guest who is due to arrive that day, a note should be made in the diary or on the arrivals list (whichever is always checked on the arrival of a guest), and the communication placed in the appropriate space or drawer. The expected date of arrival of the guest is marked on it.

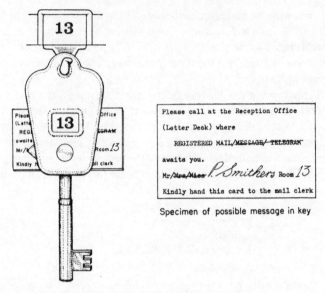

Specimen of possible message in key

Fig. 7.8 Key with slot for messages

Mail Checks

At fixed times towards the end of the evening duty and again before the first mail delivery, the key and letter racks or the current drawers of the letter desk should be checked to ascertain what is uncollected. The purpose of this is to prevent mail staying at the desk longer than necessary. There should normally be no mail there at these times. If there is mail, a ticket or note should be sent to the guest advising him that there is mail awaiting collection at the desk.

SAFE CUSTODY OF GUESTS' VALUABLES

An hotel which is an inn in law (as defined in the Hotel Proprietors' Act, 1956) differs from a private hotel (where visitors are received by permission of the management and do not have a right to accommodation) by being liable for the loss or damage of a guest's property unless the guest has been negligent. The private hotelier is not liable for the loss of a guest's property unless he can be proved to have been negligent. Where the innkeeper exhibits the notice as laid down in the Hotel Proprietors' Act, 1956, this provides for some limit to his liability (*see*

Appendix B). However, even when such a notice is exhibited, there is no limit to his liability in certain circumstances. These include the case of loss or damage where

'property (has been) deposited by or on behalf of the guest expressly for safe custody with the proprietor or some servant of his authorized or appearing to be authorized, for the purpose, and if so required by the proprietor or the servant, in a container fastened or sealed by the depositor.'

Unlimited liability also applies as regards the property of a resident guest which had been offered for deposit in the proper manner, and which the hotelier or his servant had refused to accept; and property which the guest wished to offer for deposit but was unable so to do, due to the default of the proprietor or his servant.

In the case of the private hotelier, he may be held to have been negligent should he not provide a place of safe custody; he may also be responsible should there have been a loss of goods in safe custody if the guest can prove the proprietor has been negligent. However, here the onus of proof lies on the guest.

It is important that each hotel should have a clear procedure for the handling of property left for safe custody and that this should only be undertaken by responsible and authorized persons. Where the manager or assistant manager undertakes the control of property for safe custody, and the receptionist is approached by a guest with goods for deposit, the receptionist should contact the relevant person at once and acquaint him with the guest's request. Where there is a cashiers' office, it is usually there that property is deposited for safe custody. Sometimes, however, the responsibility is undertaken within the reception unit. Details of procedure to be followed vary, but a fairly common system is the following.

The guest, having indicated that he wishes to deposit some property for safekeeping, is handed a specially designed strong envelope, into which he places his property. The guest seals and signs the envelope, which clearly bears his name. The envelope is placed into the safe, and the guest is handed a receipt immediately. The receipt book is used solely for this purpose and has one copy for the guest and a carbon copy which remains in the book. The serially numbered receipt states the date, the depositor's name, details of the deposit (normally 'one envelope said to contain...' or 'one envelope'). It is signed by the hotel employee receiving the property. Additionally, a deposit register may be kept in which the details of the receipts are posted. If a triplicate receipt book is used, the third copy of the receipt is attached to the envelope.

When the depositor wishes to collect his property, or even a part of it, he must present his receipt, which will be cancelled and married to the relevant page of the receipt book. He also signs for the returned property in the deposit register. If the guest wishes to take out part of his property, he does this and then the procedure starts afresh with a new receipt and a fresh envelope.

From time to time the envelopes in the safe should be checked against the deposit register or the receipt book to ensure that there is an envelope, properly signed and sealed, for each entry that has not been completed (as evidenced by the lack of a signature in the deposit register). The deposit receipt book is checked against the deposit register to ensure that all deposits have been entered in the register, and that cancelled receipts have been properly returned to the deposit receipt book.

INFORMATION AND ENQUIRIES

This work may be undertaken by reception, the hall porter, or a separate department. There are two distinct aspects to the work and they are sometimes dealt with by different persons, or even persons in different departments. One service is to answer enquiries regarding guests resident in the hotel. The other is to furnish guests with miscellaneous information which they may require. In general, the smaller the hotel, the more likely it is that these duties will be undertaken by the reception unit.

Enquiries Regarding Guests

It is essential that the person handling this type of enquiry knows who is in the hotel, and this is usually achieved in the larger hotels by maintaining an alphabetical index of every guest who is staying in the hotel. This must be maintained as up-to-date as possible, names of new arrivals and their room numbers being entered in the index as soon as they have checked in at the reception desk. A large proportion of enquiries for guests tend to be on the day of their arrival, and it is important to ascertain immediately and as a matter of routine whether or not they have booked in.

Telephone enquiries regarding guests are dealt with by the telephonists who maintain, or have easy access to, an up-to-date alphabetical index of resident guests with their room numbers; guests having telephones in their rooms can receive the call. Where this is not the case, the telephonist passes on the call to the person dealing with enquiries who establishes whether the guest is in the hotel and, if so, tries to contact him. Should the guest be out or not available, the enquiry clerk takes a message, if required, and places it in the letter rack. Sometimes the details of the call are also recorded in a book. A typical layout of such a book is illustrated in Figure 7.9.

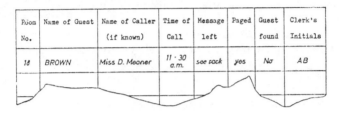

Room No.	Name of Guest	Name of Caller (if known)	Time of Call	Message left	Paged	Guest found	Clerk's Initials
18	BROWN	Miss D. Meaner	11·30 a.m.	see rack	yes	No	AB

Fig. 7.9 Guest telephone calls book

It is of assistance to telephone operators if all the extension numbers and the room numbers are the same. This not only speeds up incoming calls but also tends to lessen errors in the charging of outgoing calls; otherwise the extension number instead of the room number may easily be inserted in error on the charge voucher.

Personal Callers

If a personal caller enquires about a guest, the guest's room number is ascertained first; the second requirement is to establish whether he happens to be in the hotel. If there is a telephone in the guest's room, the clerk contacts the room and by using a phrase such as 'Mr Lake is calling on Mr Black' passes on the information that Mr Lake is at the enquiry desk but leaves the initiative with the hotel guest, Mr Black, to say whether or not he is available. Where there is no internal telephone, a message should be sent to the guest's room. If the guest is not contacted in his room and it appears that he is in the hotel he should then be paged. The page boys walking through the hotel calling for the guest have been superseded in many places by a public address system to all the public rooms. In the larger hotels this can result in considerable saving of time in contacting a guest as well as in saving labour. The paging may be done by name, but where there is the possibility of more than one person of the same name staying in the hotel at any one time, it is often done by using the guest's room number.

A 'callers' book' is sometimes kept to note details of all telephone and personal calls on guests. The layout of such a book would be similar to that of the 'telephone calls for guests' book illustrated in Figure 7.9.

Information

The amount and nature of information sought by guests in an hotel varies widely according to the type and location of the hotel. Most common enquiries are about local facilities, entertainments, how to travel to various destinations, accommodation outside the locality, and the times of public transport. It is advisable to acquire a number of reference books to deal with such inquiries. A good basic library would be:

FOR TRANSPORT FACILITIES	An *A.B.C. Railway Guide* A route map and time-table of local bus services In London, an Underground route map also
FOR LOCAL ADDRESSES	A local *Kelly's Street and Trade Directory* A street guide and street map of the area In country districts a local Ordnance Survey map The local telephone directory The local classified telephone directory
FOR ENTERTAINMENTS	The current entertainments page from the local press Any local publication of what is currently on A local guide book
ACCOMMODATION OUTSIDE THE LOCALITY	*A.A.* or *R.A.C. Handbook* B.H.R.A. or B.T.A. *Official Guide of Hotels and Restaurants in Britain*
FOR POSTAL INFORMATION	*Post Office Guide*

FOR GENERAL INFORMATION *Whitaker's Almanack*
FOR LOCAL INFORMATION Guide Books
Maps
List of local church services

Additional books should be available as required; for instance, where cable and telex enquiries can be sent from the enquiry desk, appropriate directories will be necessary. Many American visitors rely on the *Fodor Guide to Europe*. Where they are frequent guests, the information clerk should be at least as well equipped and should be able to anticipate the questions which arise therefrom, and be able to provide the answers.

Apart from directories, maps, guide books, and lists to provide immediate information, the clerk should familiarize himself with other sources, from which he may obtain quick answers to other enquiries. Local facilities, such as hairdressers, retail shops, restaurants, and bars, should be known and a list should be available for easy reference; where such facilities are available within the hotel, however, these should be recommended.

The information desk may also be asked to advise both residents and other guests about functions in the hotel. An information board is usually made up daily showing the functions and where they are taking place but, nevertheless, queries can arise which require personal attention.

The scope of information required depends on the class and location of the hotel, and the aids should be assembled to provide answers to the type of question expected. It should also be borne in mind that hotel staff are particularly transient and that frequently they are not local people. Therefore information which is common local knowledge must also be available, so that new staff may advise guests correctly.

Finally, these books and guides must be readily available and up to date; the staff should not only know where they are but be capable of using them and know where quickest to find the information required.

8. *Communications*

THE reception unit has been described as the nerve centre of the hotel. It is certainly the centre of communications concerning the guests. Much of the information regarding guests originates in, or passes through, this office. Once a guest has advised reception of his wishes or intentions, he feels that he has automatically advised every relevant department in the hotel. It is left to the receptionist to do this. The methods used range from word of mouth and printed forms to internal telegraphic and television circuits. Which method is used in a particular hotel largely depends on cost and necessity. It is, therefore, more common to find the more expensive and elaborate systems in the large hotels, where their use is not only justified, but frequently essential. Modern hotels have an advantage in this respect as regards cost, as it is usually cheaper to install a communication system in an hotel at the construction stage than to do so subsequently.

The most reliable method of communication within an hotel is by writing and this is often best done on forms specially printed or duplicated for the purpose. Such forms act as reminders to the originator of the communications of what information is required and also contribute to speed and clarity. Carbon copies enable information to be prepared for several departments simultaneously. One copy can be retained for use in the sender's office and as a confirmation of the information which has been sent.

The reception office's most urgent needs for inter-departmental information, especially in transient hotels, are to ensure that all guests have been fully charged before their departure and to know the current occupation of rooms and the availability of rooms for letting. Advising other departments of the anticipated arrivals and departures is another service which the reception unit often provides as a regular aid to the smooth running of the hotel. We shall consider this first and follow with an outline of several methods used in communicating other information about guests and rooms.

ARRIVALS AND DEPARTURES LISTS

Daily lists are used in many hotels to advise other departments of the expected arrival and departure of guests. They should not be confused with the arrivals and departures book, described in Chapter 2, nor with arrival and departure notifications, which are discussed later in this chapter. In some hotels, the copies of the lists retained in the reception office are suitably marked and adjusted and then used as an historical record of the arrivals and departures which did take place, no arrivals and departures book as such being kept. However, the primary purpose of the arrivals and departures lists is to advise departments of the anticipated movements of guests. The lists are usually prepared and distributed each evening before the day to which they refer. Helpful information, such as an excessive amount of baggage, or a guest's expected time of arrival or departure, is noted in the lists, if known. When a guest arrives or departs, the receptionist ticks his name on his copy of the appropriate list.

The arrivals list is compiled from the bookings diary or from the booking chart if no diary as such is kept; alternatively, the list may be compiled from the sets of bookings if these are filed by date of arrival. Whichever source is used for the original preparation of the arrival list, it is advisable to check it against another source. (*See also* Chapter 3 for methods of dealing with advance bookings.) The list cannot include chance guests who become known only on their arrival and are included in the arrivals and departures book. Where it is the practice to allocate room numbers before the arrival of guests, these are inserted. For ease of reference the arrivals list is usually arranged in alphabetical order. At the end of the day the names of any expected guests who have not yet arrived are given to the night porter or to the night receptionist, together with their room numbers.

The departures list may be compiled from information on the reception board (in larger hotels this may be replaced by the room record index), which will also indicate the expected departure date; the list may also be compiled from the room booking chart. It is usually set out in room number order, but it may be arranged alphabetically.

Examples of both types of list are given in Figures 8.1 and 8.2. It should be noted that these two lists may be separate or combined in one document.

The number of copies of these lists and their distribution varies according to the needs of the hotel. We have seen a medium-sized hotel

Name	Confirmed	Type of Accn.	Nights staying	Rate	Room	Remarks
ARRIVALS LIST FOR 1ST MARCH						
ALDER, L.	CF	T.B.	4	15.00		A/C to Elvis Ltd.
BRIAR, S.W.	DEF	S.B.	2	9.50		V.I.P. Call Manager on arrival
BRILLIAM, K.	CF	S.B.	5	8.00		SP. Rate
BROWN, N.G.	CF	S.B.	2	9.50		
COPSLEY, P.	CF	D.B.	4	15.00		Flowers in Room
DEMBO, K.	N/C	S.B.	2	9.50		To be confirmed by 10 a.m.
DERBY, L.P.	N/C	T.B.	3	15.00		
ENGDALE, J.	VCF	S.B.	2	9.50		Regular
GREGG, P.	N/C	T.B.	1	15.00		Stays before not confirmed
HARRIS, L.	CF	S.B.	1	9.50		Inside Rooms
HAWSER, P.	DEF	S.B.	2	9.50		Returns on 9.3.
JOHNS, A.	CF	S.B.	2	9.50		Late Arriv. Tour.

CF — Confirmed   DEF — Definite i.e. Not confirmed but certain   N/C — Not Confirmed   VCF — Confirmed Verbally

Fig. 8.1 Specimen arrivals list

DEPARTURES LIST FOR 1ST MARCH

Room No.	Name	Remarks
107/8	WALKER	
110	LEE	
115	FRANKS	
205	EVANS	
210	KING	Heavy luggage
306	ADAM	

Total Departures   6

Extra Departures

Fig. 8.2 Specimen departure list

preparing fourteen copies of each! However, most hotels use considerably fewer and the main persons to whom they may be distributed are indicated below.

(*a*) The *manager* may require a copy so that he may show 'the personal touch' to his guests. This reminder assists him where it is his practice to greet his guests on arrival or see them off on departure, and also enables him to take any other action when a particular name is brought to his attention.

(*b*) The *head porter* makes use of the information to allocate his staff with particular regard to transporting the guests' luggage.

(*c*) The *head housekeeper* wishes to know from which rooms guests are departing and to which rooms new guests are allocated, so that she may arrange the allocation of work to chambermaids.

(*d*) The *head waiter* often receives a copy, especially where it is the practice to allocate guests to permanent tables for the duration of their stay.

(*e*) The *chef* is usually only concerned with the number of guests, but the lists are sometimes used as the means of advising him of a change in the number staying, particularly in a seaside hotel with few or no chance arrivals. What may be of more concern to him in certain types of hotel is whether the guests are receiving full board, demi-pension, or taking breakfast only, and this information may be briefly indicated on the arrivals list.

(*f*) Where there is a separate *cashiers' office*, a departures list is usually sent to it daily.

(*g*) *Telephonists* may also be included in the distribution, so that they may inform callers of guests still to arrive.

(*h*) One copy of both lists is retained in the *reception unit* itself.

In hotels where a departure list is used, names of guests are ticked off the reception or cashiers' copy when the guests finally return their room keys and book out. By this means it can quickly be seen which guests are still expected to depart. Where it is customary for guests to vacate their rooms by noon, it may be the duty of the receptionist or the housekeeper to check the rooms of such guests as noon approaches.

If it is the housekeeper's duty to check such rooms, she must be informed by reception of the room numbers they wish her to check, and she will advise them of the result of her investigation. The receptionist will mark his departure list accordingly. If the guest is not in the room, but has not departed, the coded notes may be:

P = Guest has packed – luggage to be removed
NP = Guest has not packed – guest to be found
DND = A 'do not disturb' sign on the door – guest is then to be
contacted by internal telephone.

Normally, the larger the hotel, the more departments are found necessary to be advised. Conversely, the smaller the hotel, the less distribution is required to the extent that in hotels of less than about fifty rooms it is frequently found that there is little need for arrivals or departures lists at all.

ARRIVAL AND DEPARTURE NOTIFICATIONS

The arrival notifications are made out by the receptionist at the time of the guests' arrival. The departure notification is completed by whoever is acting as a cashier on the guests' departure. Notifications are sent out for all guests, including chance arrivals. They go to all departments interested in the fact that a guest is either now resident, or now no longer resident, in the hotel. These departments normally include the housekeeper, the bill office, enquiries desk, and the telephonists, with one copy retained for the reception unit itself; the distribution tends to coincide with that of the arrival and departure lists. The porters may also receive arrival notifications but their departure notification often takes the form of a luggage pass, which is referred to below. The notifications are commonly prepared in triplicate, quadruplicate, etc., according to how many departments are to be notified. The use of specially prepared paper which requires no interleaving carbon paper speeds the process. The names of the different departments are printed appropriately on each copy, and different colours may be used for different departments for additional clarity and ease in distribution (Figure 8.3). For the purpose of notifying an arrival to the bill office or to the bill clerk, the bill heading can be made out by the receptionist and the bill passed on for charging. Alternatively, in some hotels the notification slip to the bill office has an adhesive backing so that it may be affixed to a new bill and form its heading.

The arrival notifications contain the guest's name, initials, title, and room number. The bill office may also be advised of the room rate and most printed forms used for the purpose have additional space for notifying other details of the arrival, if necessary.

Large hotels sometimes use an internal teleprinter system to pass on this information to the various departments; the receiving departments

Plate 6.5. N.C.R. Class 5 posting control register

Plate 6.6. Sweda Series 1000 Dataregister

Plate 8.1. Room status indicator, Royal Garden Hotel, London

Plate 8.2. PBX switchboard

are equipped with ticker-tape machines (*see* Figure 8.4). The operator in the reception unit sends out this internal information; he also receives and issues other messages. Like the internal telephone system,

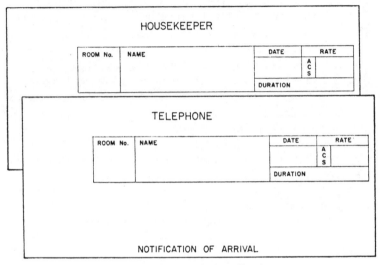

Fig. 8.3 Specimen arrival notifications

the internal teleprinter can also be used for conveying guests' requests. With one such system a guest requiring room service telephones the teleprinter operator and gives the order. The operator connects her machine both to the teleprinter in the kitchen, and to the machine at the

```
WED £21·50    SMITH MR MRS R A USA 435
```

The message received by the Bill Office reads as above, and is printed on gummed strip paper, which is stuck onto a bill, and becomes the authority to charge items to that account.

The message received by all other departments reads thus:

```
SMITH MR MRS R A USA 435
```

Fig. 8.4 Ticker-tape used for arrival notification

service point on the guest's floor and prints the room number, the order, its price, her own initials, and the time of receipt. The message is in this way transmitted to the kitchen and to the floor service. One copy of the message is retained by the teleprinter operator and one copy is sent by gravity tube to the bill office for immediate recording in the guest's account.

The departure notification is not sent out by the cashier until the bill has been settled by the guest. It does not necessarily mean that the guest has actually left the hotel but does indicate that his bill has been closed and thereafter any sales, such as drinks and telephone calls should be paid in cash; this is of particular importance in large hotels. The distribution of departure notifications should include all sales points where credit is normally given to guests.

It can be seen how important it is that such sales points are advised quickly of this change in a guest's credit position. Equally, the system of gathering vouchers for guests' charges into the bill office must be speedy enough to avoid recent purchases on credit not reaching the guest's bill until after his account has been settled.

The pneumatic or gravity tubes with special containers for the messages, of the type found in some department stores, form one rapid means of communication in some large hotels. The size of the hotel and the number of transactions make it not only economic but necessary. However, the initial installation cost is high.

Regular collection of vouchers from sales points forms a part of the routine of the hotel. When a guest is about to settle his account, the person responsible for making up the bill may check with these points by telephone to see if any vouchers for that room number have not yet been dispatched for charging. He must, of course, also ensure that no unposted vouchers are in the bill office.

MAIDS' REPORT SHEETS

In some hotels the maids' report sheets are filled in once (and in some hotels twice) per day. Their purpose is to ascertain the number of persons occupying each room. The chambermaid on duty on each floor enters in the form against each room number how many people are occupying that room. The sheets are given to the housekeeper or her assistant who takes them to the reception office.

In some hotels each maid reports only the number in her section and this information is entered in one big form known as the 'housekeeper's report' (Figure 8.5). The purpose and destination of this is similar to that of the maids' report sheets.

On receipt of these reports the receptionists can check the actual total number of sleepers against the total number according to their records. Where there is a difference, the numbers actually occupying each room are checked against the reception records of the number

HOUSEKEEPER'S REPORT

101		201	+ 1	301	
102		202		302	
103	X	203		303	
104		204		304	X
105		205		305	X
106	X	206	X	306	

131	X	231		331	X
132		232		332	
133					
134					

Housekeeper's Signature   *A.L. Risely*

Date   *5th June*

Rooms unoccupied last night   *7*

Extra sleepers last night   *1*

Fig. 8.5 Specimen housekeeper's report

who are supposed to be there and have been charged. When the difference is located, the room is re-checked to see whether the maid's count or the reception records are correct. If the error is in the reception unit, it is further investigated and appropriate adjustments are made. Alternatively the maid's sheet is corrected, if she had counted wrongly.

The sheets are also utilized to calculate each morning the number of vacant rooms and beds, to which are added the expected departures to give the total available rooms and beds for the night.

CHANGE OF ROOM

When a guest is to transfer from one room to another, the reception unit must advise not only the housekeeper, but also the telephonist, the enquiry office, the bill office and, where relevant, the restaurant and other sales departments. Persons responsible for maintaining alphabetical and visitors' room record indexes must alter them appropriately, and the reception board must be brought up-to-date.

The porter or floor valet, where there is one, receives a list of removals and moves the guests' luggage to the new rooms. These lists indicate simply the room numbers being vacated and, in each instance, the relevant new room number. Normally, where rooms are expected to be vacated by midday, any changes are also made at about that time too, if possible. Large hotels tend to have a higher number of room changes and frequently lay down strict procedures on how they are to be dealt with, ensuring that alterations have been made to all appropriate records.

Notifications of transfers may be sent out by serially numbered advice notes (Figure 8.6). One copy can then be passed from one individual to another, each noting on it that the necessary action for which he or she is responsible has been taken. Regard should be paid to the number of the transfer note, which serves both as a reference to the alteration and as an indication whether a note has gone stray.

Where arrival and departure notifications are in use, the reception office may simply notify the various departments of room changes by using the same form and sending it to the same departments as were originally notified of the arrival.

EXTENSION OF STAY

If a guest wishes to extend his stay beyond the period for which he reserved accommodation originally, or wishes to vacate the room after noon, the appropriate date or time should be noted on the departure list and the reception records checked immediately to see if the guest's request can be granted; the guest should then be advised accordingly.

A request by a guest to be allowed the use of a room after the normal

time for vacating it, which does not extend beyond the original departure date, does not call for an alteration of reception records, except
for a note to the effect that the room will not be available for letting to a
new guest until later in the day.

```
┌─────────────────────────────────────────────────────────────┐
│              ADVICE  OF  CHANGE  OF  ROOM                     │
│                                                              │
│                              Serial  Number  1234            │
│                                                              │
│  M _____ │
│                                                              │
│  Transferred                                                 │
│  from Room No.: _____  to Room No : _____   │
│                                                              │
│  Note on :      Reception  Board      _____       │
│                                                              │
│                 Alphabetical  Index   _____       │
│                                                              │
│                 Visitors'  Record     _____       │
│                                                              │
│  New  Terms_____ Date _____       │
└─────────────────────────────────────────────────────────────┘
```

Fig. 8.6 Specimen change-of-room advice note

But an extension of the guest's stay beyond the original departure
date, whether the request is made to the reception office or only during
the housekeeper's check, described above, necessitates an amendment
of the appropriate reception records. Moreover, these extensions of
stay have to be notified to all those who had been originally advised of
the departure date; this means that they would be included in arrival
and departure lists and notifications or in both.

RESIDENTS' LISTS

Some hotels produce a daily house list or residents' list for distribution
to all departments. This is usually compiled from the reception board
or room record index and checked against the booking chart; it simply
lists room numbers with guests' names opposite. Sometimes the residents' list replaces other lists and notifications. In other cases it is
produced in addition; whichever may be the case, it provides an
accurate list at the particular time of the day at which it was prepared,
but no more.

ROOM STATUS INDICATIONS

It is clear that none of the communications discussed so far indicate accurately whether a particular vacant room is ready for letting at any particular time. To this end a close liaison is necessary between the housekeeping and reception departments of the hotel. As rooms become available for re-letting, the housekeeping department advises reception. This may be done by a housekeeper periodically calling at the reception office and handing in a slip with the available rooms noted on it, but is more frequently done over the house telephone. Reception is usually informed of a batch of rooms becoming available when the housekeeper or her assistant return to their office, having completed an inspection of rooms.

–	– B	=	= B	+	+ B
104, 118, 120, 105, 113,	208, 108, 110,	209, 109, 117	115,		307,

Fig. 8.7 Rooms ready form

A useful aid for the reception office is a form similar to that illustrated in Figure 8.7. The room numbers available for re-letting are entered by reception as they are advised and crossed off as they are re-let.

Where a manual status indicator is maintained on the reception board, the room number should be noted and the status indicator brought up-to-date immediately.

The most modern method for indicating the exact status of each room is to use room status indicators. These indicators provide the receptionist, the cashier, and the housekeeper with up-to-the-minute information on the status of each room in the hotel. One of the indicators is situated in each of their offices. On it are three coloured lights and a switch against each room number (*see* Plate 8.1). When a guest is allocated a room, the receptionist presses his switch for that room number. All three indicators will now have, say, their red light shining for that room, showing it to be occupied. When the guest pays his bill, the cashier presses his switch, which changes the light from red to amber on all indicators. This advises the housekeeper that the room is 'on change'. When it has been prepared for letting, the housekeeper presses her switch. The amber light changes to green and the receptionist knows the room is available for re-letting.

This system is most useful where the hotel is of a highly transient nature with a high occupancy and where rooms are needed quickly. It does not interfere with other internal communications, it is speedy, and it does not require the presence of a person at the receiving end. One model of the indicator in the reception office has been developed so that the coloured lights and switch appear below each room on a normal reception board.

A further development to speed up communications even further is a deep-sunk switch located in each bedroom and wired to the boards in the various offices. By using a special key the housekeeper can alter the status boards as soon as she has checked a room; thus she does not have to return to her office on each occasion or wait until she has checked all the rooms ready for inspection before returning to her office and advising the receptionist that certain rooms are now available for re-letting.

LUGGAGE PASSES

In some larger hotels, when a guest pays his bill a slip known as the luggage pass is sent by the cashier to the luggage porter. This slip may take many forms. It is often a tear-off portion of the receipt or of the bill itself. Its purpose is simply to indicate to the head hall porter that the guest has settled his account and that the luggage can, therefore, be properly removed from the hotel. As mentioned earlier in this chapter, in these circumstances the luggage pass constitutes the departure notification and makes it unnecessary to distribute a copy of the general notification to the head hall porter.

Where a luggage pass is not used, the porter should check with the receptionist or cashier whether a guest has settled his account before the luggage is finally cleared.

A few hotels have a final departure notification giving a guest's name and room number and this is sent by the head hall porter's department to the telephonists and to reception to advise them that the guest is no longer in the hotel. Where this operates, the telephonists then do not alter the alphabetical guest index until they receive the hall porter's notification.

The cashiers' department notification will have been distributed normally only to sales departments extending credits to guests.

CALL SHEETS

Call sheets are often made out by the receptionists or the night porter and left for the persons responsible for giving the guests their morning

CALL SHEET

Date Monday, 3 Feb.

Room Number	Time	
11	7·15	T and Tel
12	8·00	Mirror
14	7·45	2T and Express
15		
16	8·00	---

Simple Call Sheet for Small Hotel

Room No	Paper	6·30	7·0	7·15	7·30	7·45	8·0	8·15	8·30
11	Tel.			1 x T					
12	Mirror						Call		
14	Expr.					2 x T			
15									
16							Call		
17	Mail					2 x C			

Analysed Call Sheet for Larger Hotel

Fig. 8.8 Call sheets

call and, if required, their tea or newspaper. This is usually done by the chambermaids. However, some hotels awaken their guests by telephone if they do not require any other service, and in such establishments this may be the responsibility of a telephonist or receptionist. The call sheets are simple in design and two illustrations are given in Figure 8.8. The second example has the great advantage of sorting out the calls according to their time; which rooms have to be dealt with next can be seen at a glance. The room number order may be varied to suit particular establishments, and separate sheets may be used for individual floors or parts of the hotel where, as is the case in larger hotels, duties in connection with morning calls may be divided between several members of staff.

One common problem faced by many hoteliers is that guests leave instructions regarding their morning call with various members of staff. It is as well to have one unit responsible for the centralization of this data and guests should be directed to it. Where another member of staff does accept instructions from the guest, he must see to it that the request is correctly recorded. Messages on scraps of paper are liable to be mislaid, misread or forgotten.

In many smaller hotels there are call boards with the room number and a space where the time of the call and any requests for tea or papers can be chalked. A more modern version of this replaces the blackboard with a pegboard, and one can indicate with pegs in appropriate columns when the guest would like to be called, his choice of newspaper, and his preference for tea or coffee. Boards are still sometimes fixed on the floors for guests to enter their requests. This is not good practice; apart from being unsightly it can lead to errors and practical jokes.

MESSAGES AND OTHER COMMUNICATIONS

Internal telephones are a great boon for communications within the hotel. They are direct and save time in delivering messages, but they do have certain drawbacks; the main one is that the caller wastes time waiting for the call to be answered. This may happen because there is no one to answer the call, a frequent occurrence with housekeepers, or because the person called is attending to a guest. This difficulty can be overcome by using a device to record the message at the receiving point; at the same time an indicator lights so that the person called can see that a message awaits him when he returns or becomes free and can receive the message by picking up the receiver and listening to the recording.

While this can save time and lessen exasperation, there are still reservations on its usefulness. Members of staff find some models difficult to use correctly, there is no guarantee that the message has reached the right person, and urgent messages may wait for some time before being received.

A simpler system, which is frequently employed, is to have a light on each internal telephone. This light is controlled by the operator of the internal exchange. If a caller fails to contact the person required when the number rings out, the operator activates the light and is also advised whom the caller wishes to contact. When next someone sees the indicator light glowing, he lifts the receiver and the operator either passes on a message or contacts the original caller and completes the connection.

Another device for transmitting messages to another part of the building, where they await collection, is the electro-writing machine. A message is written on the sender's machine and transcribed electrically on to the paper on the machine to which it is directed. The message can thus be read as soon as the called person returns. These machines are also used in some hotels to transmit charges to the bill office or orders from the floors to the kitchens.

Where there is a frequent and urgent need to contact staff who may be moving around the hotel, there is a growing tendency to employ radio location devices (Plate 8.2). Designated staff carry small receivers in their breast pockets. A particular person is contacted by a signal sent out from a central point, usually the hotel telephone exchange, which is picked up only on his receiver. On hearing distinctive 'bleeps' which give these machines their nickname, the carrier goes to the nearest telephone and contacts the central point, when he is given the message or placed in contact with the person who wants him.

These devices may also be lent to guests, on request, when they are expecting outside telephone calls. They form a quick and personal paging system.

Referring again to Plate 8.2, it will be noted that on the right of the operator are two Shannon boards, one listing the guests in alphabetical order and the other listing them in room-number order. Above the board (top left) is a master station for internal radio contact.

9. *Control*

AN internal checking system in an hotel has a threefold purpose. Firstly, it must ensure that all charges and allowances to guests and any moneys received from them have been properly recorded in the guests' accounts and in the hotel records. Secondly, its aim is to prevent fraudulent and negligent practices by hotel employees. Thirdly, it should aim to eliminate waste.

The control function may be performed by an individual clerk in a smaller or medium-sized hotel or by a separate department in a larger one. In either case the function remains the same, although the scope and amount of work may vary. The control department plays a large part in most systems of internal check in an hotel, but it often also fulfils a wider function in providing management with statistics and other information. Some of this work is of a routine nature but much information produced can be of real assistance to management in the running of the hotel, the relevant data being extracted from the many sets of figures which are available to the control department. In this latter respect, particularly, the department may fulfil the role of an internal auditor. However, it is the part which the control department plays in the systems of internal check, which brings it into closest contact with the reception unit and related hotel services, and which concerns us most here. In this chapter internal checking is explained with particular reference to hotel reception but an indication is also provided of its application to the restaurant and other hotel activities.

The principle of internal check is proving the accuracy of one person's work by another who is preferably working with data derived from independent sources. The object is the early detection of error. In an hotel with guests leaving every day this is of particular importance. Internal checking systems must, therefore, be organized as part of the day-to-day routine of the business. They do not automatically involve the control department and many internal checks exist independently of it. Thus, for example, the bill office clerk may check the total of accommodation charges for the day against the corresponding amount calculated independently by the receptionist in the arrivals and departures book. Errors in guest and financial records may result in a loss of revenue, lack of satisfaction on the part of the guests, and also make the records unreliable for future reference. Much the same is true of other hotel records.

However, in many hotels, such is the past record of complicity and such are the temptations, that procedures have to be laid down which involve not one but two checks, so that three persons would have to be involved to achieve a fraud, one of them a person in the control department. A system of internal check includes procedures for recording transactions, arrangements for regular collection and collating of data, allocation of responsibilities, the division of work between persons (including irregular changes of duties of persons checking a particular aspect), and the use, wherever possible, of grand totals independently compiled to check a mass of individual figures. The system should be flexible and it should be suited to the particular hotel.

CONTROLLING VISITORS' ACCOUNTS

The functions performed by a separate bill office, found in large hotels, may be carried out within the reception unit itself in smaller establishments. The main methods of control are basically the same, irrespective of size and irrespective of whether guest accounts are recorded in a tabular ledger or by means of a billing machine. It is necessary to ensure that all sales are charged at the correct price to the correct guest and that they are analysed under the correct headings.

The controller or his clerks build up the individual totals of the different types of charge into which sales are analysed, drawing on independent sources of data, sorting, checking, and – if necessary – pricing the sales. After adding up the amounts, they see if their totals agree with the totals produced by the bill office. Ideally this is done daily for each of the analysed headings of charges. In practice, which varies from one hotel to another, some charges receive less attention than others. Where the totals agree, this is regarded as prima facie evidence that the entries under that heading are correct. At least, in the absence of compensating errors, the amount which has been charged is correct, although this test does not guarantee that the right person has been charged. Should the totals not agree, a more detailed individual investigation has to be carried out to try and trace the mistake.

The first hope is that there has only been a single error to account for the difference, and all vouchers and entries for that amount are first checked individually with the ledger or audit roll entries. If the difference is under £1·00 and is divisible by 9, it is possible that it has been caused by a transposition of figures either in the original entry or in the control check (e.g. 17p entered as 71p, the difference being 54p and thus divisible by 9). In these circumstances particular attention should be paid to this aspect when re-checking. Where no inspired checking is possible, a complete scrutiny is necessary if the total is to be agreed. At this stage, despite the possibility of two large nearly compensating errors causing a small difference, many controllers do not regard a re-check as worthwhile if the error is small, bearing in mind the cost of the control clerk's time.

Large hotels tend to break the work down into areas of responsibility. One clerk may be responsible for checking room charges, another food and drink sales, another telephone and other sundry sales, and so on. The total figures of the various types of charge are checked as indicated below.

The controller compares the totals of the various debits and credits in the tabular ledger against totals at which the control clerks have arrived (or which, in the smaller hotels, he has reached himself). The detailed procedure varies from one hotel to another, but an illustration follows of the manner in which the overall control is accomplished.

Balances Brought Forward

The total of individual balances owing by guests and brought forward is checked against the total carried forward from the previous day. Each total should be reached by an independent addition of the outstanding balances.

Accommodation

The accommodation total is checked, where possible, against the total of accommodation sales calculated in the arrivals and departures book by the reception unit (*see* Chapter 2). Where the housekeeper submits a daily report to the control department, stating which rooms have been occupied the previous night, it can be checked in detail against the rooms charged. This may be shown on a special type of room list where the amount charged for accommodation is inserted against the number of each occupied room; a new sheet is prepared daily by the receptionist. A similar check may be made against the audit roll of a mechanized billing machine. Where handwritten tabular ledgers are compiled on a loose-leaf principle, the check may be made against the actual entries on these sheets.

Food

Charges for early morning teas are compared with the call sheets (if beverages are recorded in them) or with the chambermaids' lists. The breakfast total can also be checked by reference to the housekeeper's room report if only a single-priced breakfast is served and included in the room tariff; the breakfast price multiplied by the number of sleepers gives the requisite total. If breakfast is not part of an inclusive tariff and particularly where breakfast prices vary, the vouchers are sorted separately, priced if necessary, and a total compiled. Lunch and dinner totals are checked against the restaurant cashier's summary. Afternoon teas are checked against the lounge waiters' check pads, stillroom vouchers, and/or afternoon tea book, which contains details of after-noon teas served. Other food may include sandwiches, coffees, and sundry refreshments, which are usually recorded in the stillroom and by the lounge waiter.

Sometimes, particularly when some models of hotel billing machines are used, all the food items above are simply included under the one heading 'food', in which case the same process of checking is followed but built into one total.

Drink

The drink total is obtained by adding the drink sales recorded in the restaurant cashier's summary to those of the lounge waiter and night porter. Where credit is allowed in the bar, the signed vouchers must be seen and totalled.

Sundry Sales

The total tobacco sales are calculated in a similar way to drink sales if credit is allowed to residents.

Newspapers may be recorded in call sheets with early morning teas and checked against these or against the porter's list.

Telephone charges are controlled in two ways, depending on the type of call. Where there are many trunk calls, these are recorded separately in a duplicate check book. The room number of the guest, the number called, the duration, and the price charged are all noted in the book (the hotel telephonist may obtain the charge from the telephone exchange by requesting A.D.C. – Advise Duration and Charge). If the hotel is connected to the Subscriber Trunk Dialling system and a meter is installed, this is unnecessary, the meter being read by the operator before and after the call. The top copies of vouchers are passed to the bill office for charging, which is normal practice when posting all vouchers; the control department can check these charges against the duplicates in the books to ensure that all trunk calls have been debited to the guests. Local calls with guests' room numbers are all noted on a telephone sheet. These sheets are passed to the bill office several times a day. When the individual trunk calls have been agreed and totalled, the local calls are added and the sum of these two is agreed with the tabular ledger.

The growing practice, under the Subscriber Trunk Dialling system, of installing separate meters for each room enables a meter reading to be taken on the arrival and again on the departure of the guest and each unit charged to him at the appropriate rate. A direct comparison is then available between the calls which will be charged to the hotel and those which should have been charged to the guest.

Laundry charges can be controlled by using a numbered duplicate bill book and entering therein all the laundry bills of guests. The method of control is the same as for trunk calls, and the total is found by adding the entries in the duplicate book for the day.

Other charges, such as flowers, hire of rooms for meetings, and valet service, are checked in a similar way, either against duplicate books or against other confirmatory data; they are then compared with their respective totals as they appear in the tabular ledger or combined to agree with the total of 'miscellaneous' or 'sundry charges'.

Visitors' Disbursements

The total of 'visitors' paid out' is compared with the total cash disbursements recorded by the cashier in the visitors' paid out book(s) or in the appropriate column of the petty cash book. The cashier's entries are checked against the vouchers held and, where possible, against appropriate duplicate books. As always in checking against duplicate books, this is to ensure that not only correct entries are made and supported by documentary evidence, but also that no charges have been omitted. When charges have been transferred from one analysis heading to another or, with mechanical bill posting, there have been errors which have been discovered and rectified in the bill office, the charges must be checked with the separate transfer sheet on which they have been recorded. It is important to see that the totals of debits and credits on this sheet are checked and agreed.

Service Charges

If service charges are in operation and, as is usual, added to the guests' accounts on departure, it is relatively simple to check that each account closed on a particular day has been subjected to the service charge and that the correct amount has been added. The total of service charges for a particular day is easily ascertained from the tabular ledger or copies of the bills closed on a particular day.

Cash, Allowances, Ledger Transfers

The total of cash receipts recorded in visitors' accounts is agreed with the cash receipts book, when receipts are always given. Where it is the practice to bank the previous day's takings, they are compared with the total when possible, allowance being made for any other money received for banking. The total of visitors' accounts balances posted to 'ledger' is agreed with the entry in the sales ledger control account.

The total of the allowances made to guests is checked against the total of the allowances vouchers and against the duplicate book. Particular attention is paid to seeing that all allowances given have been properly authorized.

Balances Carried Forward

The total of visitors' accounts balances carried forward is usually checked within the bill office, this procedure being part of the system of internal check. Where the bills are handwritten, this is done by adding all balances on guests' bills to date and then comparing the total with the figure carried forward, which has been separately calculated. On bill posting machines the totals of all current bills are listed and this forms an integral part of the daily balance by the bill office.

Finally, the arithmetical accuracy of the totals column is checked and the total debits and credits agreed.

In this section an attempt has been made to indicate those aspects of control which affect visitors' accounts. However, control is normally undertaken of all charges of the same type together; for example, all food sales are controlled in one operation arriving at a composite total of sales to residents, banqueting, and other sales.

In practice, control is usually undertaken as the control of the whole tabular ledger, and in cases where transactions other than those appearing in the visitors' account have been passed through the tabular ledger, these also form part of the tabular ledger control.

Night Audit

Some large hotels employ a night auditor whose main task is to see that all guests have been properly charged, that there are no omissions, and that there are no cases of charging the wrong guest. It is not a satisfactory form of internal check to rely on the guest to advise the staff when there is an error in his bill. The night auditor also checks the totals charged against departmental sales. Where no night auditor is employed, the checking of each item to the correct account may be done as part of the work of the control department. The vouchers are first sorted into order. Where handwritten tabular ledgers are maintained, room-number order is most convenient, but where mechanical bill posting machines are used, the sequence of entries on the audit roll is indicated by consecutive numbers appearing both on the vouchers and on the audit roll and these should be taken as the guide to sorting. The amount, the source of the charge, and the room number can now be read off each voucher and it can be seen that it is correctly recorded in the tabular ledger or on the audit roll. The entries of charges are ticked as they are agreed and if a total check is being carried out, the reason is ascertained for any unticked entries for which there is no supporting voucher or other documentary evidence.

In the case of some hotel billing machines, the charge voucher is inserted in the machine when the charge is being posted to the guest's bill; the entry (including the room number) which appears on the bill, is simultaneously overprinted on the voucher. It is then possible to see at a glance whether a particular guest's bill has been debited with appropriate charges and whether a particular voucher has been posted with the correct details. An explanation of this method of audit is given in Chapter 6.

Sometimes only a test check is carried out. If this is to be acceptable, all errors or omissions found must be thoroughly investigated and, if the amount of these exceeds the limit of tolerance laid down (e.g. two errors in 100 entries) then the size of the test sample must be increased

until an acceptable percentage has been achieved or all entries have
been checked for that day.

RESTAURANT CONTROL

The main purpose of this checking is not only to control the bill office
and restaurant cashiers, but to ensure that all food used has been properly requisitioned and properly charged. The exact form the control
takes depends on the checking system in use and whether or not
mechanical means of voucher compilation are used. The basic approach
with handwritten vouchers is to marry up the various copies after the
transaction has taken place. Where waiters' vouchers are made out in
duplicate, one copy is passed on to the cashier to be priced and the
charge added to the guest's bill, and one copy is sent to the kitchen,
stillroom, or dispense bar to authorize the issue of the food or beverage
to the waiter. The second copies are best placed in locked boxes after
the goods have been requisitioned, so that they are not lost, and also so
that they cannot subsequently be altered or re-used.

Both sets of vouchers are collected by the control clerk on the completion of a meal and are checked as soon as possible. Delay in control
tends to lessen its impact. The effectiveness is also lessened where a
query arises some time after the particular meal to which it appertains.
People's memory becomes confused and it is increasingly difficult to
obtain satisfactory explanations as more time elapses. Where a triplicate system is used, the voucher books, in which the third copy is
retained, are also collected after the meal and form part of the control
process.

The restaurant cashier, as well as making out the individual bills in
duplicate, compiles a summary sheet during the meal, and completes
and balances it at the end of a meal. She pays the cash takings in to the
cashiers' office and obtains a receipt for them. Copies of bills for
posting to resident guests' accounts, signed by the guests, may be sent
to the bill office during the meal.

An example of a restaurant cashier's summary sheet is given in
Figure 9.1. The amount and nature of analysis varies. Analysis of particular items by count is not as common in hotel restaurants as in other
restaurants, but more use is being made of this method for control and
information. The items in these columns may be constant or may be
altered on a weekly or even daily basis.

The division between 'residents'' and 'ledger' accounts (which include credit card holders and other non-resident customers granted credit) may not be necessary in hotels if both are posted to the tabular ledger individually, as is a frequent practice where handwritten tabular ledgers are used in smaller hotels. However, in some hotels, particuarly

BILL No.	TABLE No.	No. of COVERS	ROOM No or 'CASH' or ACCOUNT	COUNT ANALYSIS OF ITEMS				VALUE OF SALES OF :				TOTAL	SETTLEMENT		
				a	b	c	d	FOOD £	DRINK £	TOBACCO £	SERVICE £		CASH £	RES. £	LEDGER £

Fig. 9.1 Restaurant cashier's summary sheet

where billing machines are used, one figure is posted to 'ledger' and the control or accounts department post the various ledger accounts direct from the signed top copies of these bills, which are passed directly to them, checking to see that the total posted agrees with the figure entered in the tabular ledger or its equivalent.

The duplicate copies of the bills have the appropriate vouchers attached to them by the restaurant cashier and these, together with the cash summary sheet, are passed to the control office. The control work commences with collecting the vouchers from the locked boxes and arranging them in table number order. They are then married up with the vouchers received by the restaurant cashier by reference to the consecutive numbers printed on them. A test is made to see that there are no differences between the two copies. Where a triplicate system is used and the waiters' voucher pads have also been collected, all three copies are compared.

The bills are then controlled. Where prices appear on the vouchers, they must be seen to be correct and to have been entered exactly on the bill. Where vouchers are unpriced, the items must have been entered on the bill and correctly priced by the restaurant cashier. The totals of the individual bills are checked and then the bill is checked on the cashier's summary sheet, under the analysed headings. Finally, when all bills have been controlled, all additions of the cashier's summary sheet are checked.

If errors are discovered, appropriate action has to be taken. Additions and subtractions must be made not only to the summary sheets, but the bill office and, if necessary, the sales ledger clerk must be advised and alterations made to guest accounts and to the totals of analysed charges. It is a matter of house policy whether or not a cashier is held responsible for undercharging cash customers and whether he has to make up such differences.

CONTROL STAFF DUTIES

Apart from the verification of the work of the bill office and the cashiers, part of which may be performed by a night auditor if one is employed, the control staff have to check the departmental sales in some detail. This work may be broken down into several main groups.

We have seen that one major task consists of the marrying up and comparison of all copies of particular vouchers to ensure that they are all correctly recorded, none having been altered or misappropriated, and that no mistakes in them have been left undiscovered. An example of the approach and of the work involved is shown in the section dealing with restaurant control. Also, at this stage, any quantitative analysis of sales that may be required can take place; for instance, analysis of the number of portions sold of particular dishes or of the number of bottles of wine sold in the restaurant. These statistics may be used for a sales promotion campaign or to check that the number of portions sold is related to the number of portions purchased. This work requires patience and attention to detail and is frequently the first training ground for those starting work in the control office. The more advanced aspect of control work consists of investigating errors and of completing the departmental sales figures. Where the staff is large enough this may be done by a more experienced control clerk.

Another duty frequently undertaken by the control department is stocktaking in the bars and other sales points, in the cellars and food stores and, at longer intervals, taking the inventory of various items of equipment.

A lot of control work is based on routine and the completion of laiddown schedules. These schedules are best grouped so as to allow the allocation of individuals' responsibilities and to constitute the end-product of their work. The nature of the schedules required will vary from one hotel to another according to the size and scope both of the hotel and of the control office. In any event, the purpose of these schedules should be examined from time to time to see if they are producing the required information in the best possible way and, indeed, to see if they are still needed at all.

Some hoteliers prefer to have the bar and cellar stocks taken by an outside firm of stocktakers, as they believe that this lessens the chance of collusion in a fraud. Although there is some reasoning behind this, the same result may be achieved by changing round the stocktaking duties of various control clerks from time to time. Also an outside firm is usually retained on a fixed fee and their time is, therefore, strictly limited if they are to make a profit from their service. When the hotel control staff deal with the day-to-day sales of liquor and possibly have knowledge of the purchases, stocktaking and the preparation of the bar trading results is the natural completion of their work. Having seen all the stages through which goods pass, they frequently develop a 'feel' for the trade and probe and investigate, because they may sense something wrong or because they have found a small clue. A good control department is so organized that there is time available to pursue these investigations and not, as some are, so that industrious and continuous ticking just produces a result at the end of each day. Other small but important tasks may include such aspects as the collection of cash from self-service machines and the reading of cash register till rolls.

The control clerks may also perform other duties which are not strictly a part of the control function. These extraneous responsibilities vary from one hotel to another. The control and issuing of bill pads, receipt books, and other numbered documents, recording when and to whom they were issued, is part of the system of internal control which is usually regarded as one of the duties of this department. One often finds that this practice is extended to include the issue of all stationery. Also the posting of ledgers, while strictly an accounting procedure, may be performed by control clerks in the absence of more suitably qualified persons on the staff. Similarly, in small hotels, where there is no wages clerk, or in company hotels where there is a central wages office, the control clerk often undertakes this work or assists where necessary.

The reception unit is concerned with all the clerical work related to receiving, accommodating, and charging the guests. By the very nature of its work, frequent interruptions make clerical work requiring continuous concentration unsuitable for this department. As in many hotels there is usually only one other office, the control office, in which persons used to clerical and confidential duties are to be found, it is to the control office that the manager turns for the completion of most other clerical work within the hotel.

10. *Reports and Statistics*

BASIC RECEPTION STATISTICS

THE statistics which are most commonly required from the reception unit by management are those relating to the sale and occupancy of sleeping accommodation. There are, it is true, hotels which do not compile these data. However, where even only very few figures are kept apart from the financial books of account, those relating to the actual numbers accommodated on a daily basis by the hotel are among the first to be recorded and used for comparisons and for other management purposes.

The main reason for compiling statistics in business is to enable management to be aware of facts and to draw inferences which would not be apparent solely from a consideration of the financial books of account. Aspects of the business can be recorded in other than money terms, although financial statistics may also be kept, and from these two sources the development of the business may be noted. The data, which have been recorded, have then to be marshalled in such a way as to be meaningful and useful to management.

Many businesses require to know how active they are in terms of numbers of customers or of their volume of transactions as well as their value of sales. Inflation and constantly changing prices have lent weight to this move away from purely monetary values as the best indication of the relative activity of a business. The number of customers may also be of interest to management in assessing such matters as staffing requirements (one customer spending £5 may not require as much attention as five customers spending £1 each). The pattern of customer spending is also pertinent. Much analysis may be carried out to provide the answers to the questions, 'when was money spent?' and 'on what was it spent?' The sources of income and their relative magnitudes are also a common and worthwhile study. We are concerned here solely with the reception unit and not with the wider analysis required to obtain a detailed account of the trading of the hotel. However, the data produced in the reception department are among the most important and, where only a few statistics are produced, most of them originate in this department.

Occupancy

The first and simplest statistics to be kept are those of the number of
guests staying at the hotel each night. These figures may be used as a
rough guide to the activity of the hotel; the past pattern may be
examined, comparisons made, and, most notably, future expectations
assessed. There may be more than one pattern of business; for instance,
a weekly pattern and a seasonal pattern may exist in the same hotel. It
may be seen that Mondays to Thursdays have had high occupancy
with a dropping off on Fridays and very few guests staying at weekends,
and that this pattern has repeated itself week in and week out. At the
same time it may be observed that during certain months of the year
weekly totals have been higher than in others.

The simplest comparison made is to take the number of guests staying in the hotel for a particular night and compare it with the corresponding night for the previous year. This is done to provide an answer
to the question, 'is the hotel more or less active than at this time last
year?' It is frequently found to be more useful to express this figure as a
percentage of the total bed capacity of the hotel. In this way comparisons can be made not only with the previous experience of one's own
hotel but also with other hotels for the same period under review. This
figure, known variously as the bed occupancy, sleeper occupancy or
guest occupancy, is calculated as follows:

$$\text{Bed occupancy percentage} = \frac{\text{Number of beds sold}}{\text{Total bed capacity}} \times 100$$

For this purpose twin beds or a double bed count as two beds as far as
availability is concerned and are also included as two beds in the
number of beds sold, if they are sold as twins or doubles. However, if
they are sold for the price of a single bed (no other singles being available), they are included only as a single sleeper place in the number of
sleeper places sold. In theory this percentage cannot exceed 100,
although in practice occasions arise when 100 per cent is exceeded (a
person may be accommodated in an extra bed or elsewhere, or a bed
may be sold and occupied more than once in twenty-four hours). Bed
occupancy is, therefore, an indication of the utilization of the sleeping
accommodation and often regarded as a figure by which may be judged
the efficiency of the reception unit in filling the hotel to capacity.

It is quite possible to let every bedroom in the hotel and yet not have
sold every bed. This is important to realize if, as is often the case, the

number of occupied bedrooms on a particular night, or over a period, is used as an indication of usage rather than the number of beds. This figure, expressed as a percentage of the total number of bedrooms available, is known as the room occupancy. It is calculated as follows:

$$\text{Room occupancy percentage} = \frac{\text{Number of bedrooms sold}}{\text{Total number of bedrooms}} \times 100$$

In many hotels both bed and room occupancy are calculated; the difference between the two on a particular night or over a particular period provides an indication of the extent to which twin- or double-bedded rooms have been sold for single occupancy.

Whether bed occupancy statistics are provided or not, it is desirable particularly in larger hotels, to calculate separate occupancy figures for each type of room as well as for the total. Over a sufficiently long period this approach provides some indication of the relative popularity of particular types of room with visitors.

For the purpose of arriving at weekly, monthly or annual bed or room occupancy the formulae given above also apply, but it must be remembered that for weekly occupancy, for example, the number of beds or bedrooms sold is the sum total of these for the seven days and that the total number of beds or bedrooms in the hotel must therefore be multiplied by seven.

Table 10.1 gives a monthly calculation of room and bed occupancy for three hotels for the month of April and also the cumulative figures for the year to the end of April. Interesting comparisons may be made of the relative room and bed occupancy percentages of the three hotels for the month as well as of the movement of cumulative figures (as opposed to the monthly ones).

TABLE 10.1

OCCUPANCY OF THREE HOTELS

	Hotel A 80 rooms (120 beds)		Hotel B 150 rooms (240 beds)		Hotel C 200 rooms (370 beds)	
	April	*Year-to-date*	*April*	*Year-to-date*	*April*	*Year-to-date*
Total room/nights	2,400	9,600	4,500	18,000	6,000	24,000
Actual room/nights	2,299	8,296	3,396	14,091	4,819	19,012
Room occupancy	96%	86%	75%	78%	80%	79%
Total bed/nights	3,600	14,400	7,200	28,800	11,100	44,400
Actual bed/nights	2,232	11,088	3,744	21,600	4,440	24,864
Bed occupancy	62%	77%	52%	75%	40%	56%

The definition of the total number of beds and bedrooms must be understood and the definition remain constant, whoever is compiling the figures. Complications may arise when rooms are taken off for any purpose (i.e. they are not available for letting) and when suites and other rooms are sometimes let as a bedroom and sometimes as a sitting room.

Any calculations may reflect not only the ability of the reception unit to sell rooms, but also a management decision to take rooms out of service. For example, if one floor representing, say, one-fifth of the rooms is closed, then the highest room occupancy figure which reception could achieve would be 80 per cent. Once that figure has been achieved, it ceases to be by itself an indication of the efficiency of the receptionist in selling rooms unless some other information is provided; this latter could be the total number of rooms not available or, more usefully, for comparison purposes, the percentage of rooms not available to the maximum number of bedrooms in the hotel.

When the purpose is to use the figures only as an indication of the ability of the reception department to sell rooms, it is more meaningful to omit any rooms which are not available for letting. However, where, as is more usual, the main purpose is to determine the percentage utilization of the sleeping accommodation of the hotel, the rooms taken out of service must be included in the total number of bedrooms. It is useful to record the reasons why rooms are not available for letting under general headings, e.g. repairs, re-decoration, temporary use by staff, etc., in order that management may be made more aware of the facts and judge which causes are controllable and have resulted in an unnecessary loss of revenue. Moreover, management should also know just how much revenue has been lost because the rooms were not available. This information is rarely recorded, mainly because it is often difficult to ascertain accurately. There are situations, apart from those outlined above, when it would be of use. For example, where cancellations are uncommon, some head receptionists will hold back two or three rooms in order to satisfy important or favoured guests who may require accommodation at the last minute. Normally such rooms are only released for letting late at night if they have not been taken up and if all the other rooms have been sold. Occasions arise when such rooms remain unsold although previous inquirers have been refused. While a case might be argued for satisfying regular clients, management should be aware of the cost of these individual actions by their receptionists. It should be realized by all concerned that such a loss is not only a reduction of revenue but, as hardly any additional costs are incurred by the letting of one room, an almost equivalent amount is lost to the net profit of the hotel.

Suites may also cause an inaccuracy in the room occupancy percentages if they are not dealt with in a consistent manner. It is best to divide suites into the number of saleable bedrooms. Then one out of two bedrooms of a suite sold is reflected in an occupancy of 50 per cent and, if both bedrooms are let, the contribution to room occupancy is 100 per cent. When other rooms are converted into temporary bedrooms, such rooms should not be considered part of the total bed and bedroom capacity of the hotel, but should be included in the number of occupied rooms for occupancy calculations. It is thus possible to achieve a percentage in excess of 100.

Any decisions on a programme of expansion are greatly facilitated by a knowledge of the amount and pattern of business which had been lost in the past, i.e. giving an indication of the potential market which a new building or alterations could hope to satisfy. Where the policy of the company justifies it the maintenance of such records can be very useful but attention must be paid to their accuracy. Thus a record of all requests for accommodation which have been refused for each night over a sufficiently long period provides a good indication of undercapacity, but the record must be accurately compiled and differentiate between definite requests for accommodation and mere inquiries.

Accommodation Income

The third piece of information which is frequently required is the total income from letting of rooms on a daily, weekly or monthly basis. Where the receptionists work independently from the bill office, the figure can also be of interest to the control department. The receptionist calculates and submits the figure, which ought to have been charged, by multiplying the number of each type of room let by the appropriate room rate and making any necessary adjustments for items such as cots or for special terms. The bill office clerk submits independently the amount which has actually been charged. The two figures are then compared and, if they do not agree, checked.

The daily turnover from rooms is often reported to management as another indication of the level of business. It has certain disadvantages for long-term comparative purposes as a change in room rates means that like is not compared with like. The current inflationary trend is leading generally to an increase in room rates over the years, so that in comparing one amount with the income of the corresponding period in a previous year it must be remembered that part of the current figure may be due to increased charges. Except where the increase has been of a similar proportion on each of the various room rates, it is not easy to calculate exactly how much of the change in income is due to the increased room rates and how much is due to a difference in the volume of business. The same problem arises when hotels with more than one rate during the year for any given type of room wish to use this method of comparison for the various periods. Some hotels overcome this difficulty by expressing the value of the actual room sales for a day or period as a percentage of the maximum possible income from room sales, i.e. assuming all were let during that time. The resultant percentages then provide a meaningful comparison.

For some purposes the actual room income may be of real assistance. Many managers like to know their daily revenue from the sale of rooms just as they require their restaurant and bar sales. Some utilize the figures to calculate on a daily, but more frequently on a weekly or monthly, basis the contribution that each department has made towards the running of the hotel, after deducting all costs directly attributable to each department for that period. In this way income and direct costs are related. Where, for instance, a rise in the pay of receptionists and chambermaids has led to an increase in room rates, the manager can see at a glance if the net result is a higher or lower contribution towards the running of the hotel (and towards its profits).

Average Price per Room

Another figure, which is collected by some hotels from the reception unit, is the average income or price per room of those sold. This is derived from the daily income from rooms. The former figure may be utilized further and expressed as a percentage of the average price per room when all rooms are sold. This figure, commonly but erroneously described as 'the maximum average price per room', is strictly 'the per-room average of maximum room sales'.

It should be understood that, where hotels have a range of room prices, there will normally be a tendency for the lower priced rooms to be more popular. Therefore, when the occupancy is low, it is likely that the average room rate will also be low as a higher proportion of the lower priced rooms is occupied. An increase in the occupancy will lead to more higher priced rooms being sold and a consequent increase in the average room rate. Also, if, at times of low occupancy, double rooms are let for single occupation, there will be a fall in the particular room rate and in the average room rate of rooms sold. This rate, therefore, can vary as a result of fluctuation in occupancy as well as for the more obvious reason – a change in the overall price structure.

Illustrations

Some of the statistics so far discussed are further illustrated in the example below. Assume that the rates are as in Table 10.2.

TABLE 10.2

ROOM RATES

Type of room	Number of rooms	Guest capacity	Price per night £	Maximum room sales £
Single (–)	8	8	6·25	50·00
Single with bath (–B)	12	12	7·50	90·00
Twin (=)	10	20	12·00	120·00
Twin with bath (=B)	20	40	13·50	270·00
Total	50	80		£530·00

Average room price if all rooms sold = one fiftieth of last column = £10·60.

If on one night five single rooms, eight single with bath, eight twin, and nine twin rooms with bath were let, the information could be set out as in Table 10.3.

TABLE 10.3

OCCUPANCY AND ROOM SALES

Type of room	Rooms let	Sleepers	Price per night £	Room sales £
Single	5	5	6·25	31·25
Single with bath	8	8	7·50	60·00
Twin	8	16	12·00	96·00
Twin with bath	9	18	13·50	121·50
Total	30	47		£308·75

The basic reception statistics for the night would appear as follows:

$$\text{Room occupancy percentage} = \frac{\text{Bedrooms let}}{\text{Bedrooms in hotel}} \times 100$$

$$= \frac{30}{50} \times 100 = 60\%$$

$$\text{Bed occupancy percentage} = \frac{\text{Actual sleepers}}{\text{Total bed spaces for guests}} \times 100$$

$$= \frac{47}{80} \times 100 = 59\% \, approx.$$

$$\text{Room sales} = £308 \cdot 75$$

$$\text{Average price paid per room} = \frac{\text{Room sales}}{\text{Number of rooms let}}$$

$$\frac{£308 \cdot 75}{30} = £10 \cdot 29$$

Comparison of average room price of actual sales with the per-room average price of maximum sales:

$$\frac{£10 \cdot 29}{£10 \cdot 60} \times 100 = 97 \cdot 007\%$$

$$= 97\% \, approx.$$

That room occupancy is higher than bed occupancy reflects the fact that, ignoring contingencies such as twin-bedded rooms being let as singles, the proportion of single rooms to twin rooms actually let is higher than the proportion of single rooms to twin rooms available; or, put another way, that a higher proportion of single rooms available have been let than is the case with twin rooms.

The comparison of the average room price achieved with what would occur when sales are at a maximum also shows that a higher proportion of people have taken the relatively cheaper rooms than the proportion provided of cheaper rooms to more expensive ones. If the reception had succeeded in selling all the rooms with baths before selling any other, the income would have been £320·75, the average price per room £10·69, and the percentage comparison with the per–room average of maximum sales (£10·69/£10·60) × 100 = 100·85 per cent.

Individual figures should therefore be examined carefully before any conclusions are drawn. A collection of statistics over a period can, however, indicate a trend and this may be of use in determining future price policy, budgeting for future staff needs, planning an expansion programme, or merely noting the sales ability of the reception staff. Certainly, it may indicate where questions should be raised which call for an answer (although the statistics themselves may not give it).

Overseas Visitors

An increasing number of hotels maintain statistics of overseas visitors who stay with them; these include their number, the room/nights, how long they stay, and their country of origin.

Their main purpose is to know how much the hotel depends on this source of business and how much it derives from them. For example, Americans account for over two-fifths of the occupancy of several London hotels. It is important in these cases for the management to appreciate the extent of this and thus forecast more accurately the effect on the hotel of, say, a general curtailment of American spending abroad. The figures should also determine the attention to be given to catering for the particular requirements of that group of visitors. The effect of an advertising campaign or of a visit abroad by a director to stimulate business may also be seen through these figures, which the reception unit can keep.

To know the relative importance of all aspects of the overseas visitors it will be appreciated that adequate records should be kept of domestic visitors. It is sometimes useful also to produce a breakdown of domestic visitors by place of origin.

Average Length of Stay

Knowing the average length of stay of visitors aids in judging the type of business in an hotel. This may result in the provision of particular facilities, and assist in such matters as evaluating laundry costs or work loads in the housekeeping and reception areas.

Average Spending of Each Guest

Some hotels also note the amount of each guest's bill so that they can see in the future which guests it would be most profitable to encourage to stay again. From these figures the average spending per guest (as debited to their accounts) may be calculated and is sometimes recorded. This may give an indication of the success of the staff in selling those hotel facilities which are not part of the inclusive terms. The increasing tendency to request guests to pay cash wherever possible, and thus to simplify the book-keeping, may make the collection of such figures in an hotel not always worthwhile. But it is worth remembering that these are very well-known and pertinent statistics in restaurants where the information is usually broken down under the main headings of food and drink.

In concluding this section it should be emphasized that, while keeping certain statistics may prove an interesting exercise in itself, it is largely a waste of time unless such figures are put to good use.

STATISTICAL TERMS

It is not the purpose of this chapter to provide a summary of simple statistical methods. There are many good textbooks on this subject which are easy to read and understand for those who wish, or need, to study them. However, there are a few common terms which may, when understood, open the eyes of the reader to some methods of presenting figures, which may be more pertinent than those he currently uses or which may show more clearly important points.

Averages

When asked for the average guest occupancy percentage for a week, the simplest way is to add daily guest occupancy percentages and to divide by seven. This gives the *simple arithmetic average* (or the *simple arithmetic mean* as it is sometimes known). It is commonly used, easy to understand, easy to calculate, and can be worked out with mathematical exactness. However, it may be affected by a few very high or very low figures. For example, if the room occupancy had been 100 per cent from Monday to Thursday, 55 per cent on Friday, and 35 per cent on the other two nights, the weekly figure would be 75 per cent. This is computed as follows:

$$\frac{100+100+100+100+55+35+35}{7} = \frac{525}{7} = 75$$

The figure of 75 per cent is accurate and of some use, but it does not reveal that for over a half of the week the hotel had been fully occupied and that the only way the performance could be improved would be to concentrate on the poor nights, Friday, Saturday, and Sunday.

Medians

Other methods can be used to overcome this weakness of the arithmetic average. One method is to arrange first all the figures in ascending order. This is known technically as an *array*. It is then possible to select the middle figure or item in this array (the formula for determining the position of the middle item is $\frac{1}{2}(n+1)$, where n represents the number of items in the array). This middle figure is called the *median*. It divides the array into two parts, one half of the values being greater than, and the other being less than, the median. To give more information about the distribution of the figures, the array can be divided in a similar way into quarters, the boundaries of the divisions being known as the upper and lower *quartiles*.

The array would appear as:

1	35	
2	35	
3	55	
4	100	*Median*
5	100	
6	100	
7	100	

Applying the formula $\frac{1}{2}(n+1)$: when the number of items in the array is seven then $\frac{1}{2}(7+1)$ or the fourth figure is the median. The median is thus 100. The second figure (35) is the lower quartile and the sixth figure (100) is the upper quartile. The formulae for determining the position of the lower and upper quartiles are $\frac{1}{4}(n+1)$ and $\frac{3}{4}(n+1)$ respectively (n still representing the number of items in the array). With such a small sample either one figure – the median – would be provided or, where more figures were required, it would probably be more meaningful and not cause a great deal of trouble to show them all.

However, in larger samples the quartiles may prove very helpful to indicate the range of the figures and, in particular, to show the distribution of the middle half of the figures falling between the lower and upper quartiles.

One great advantage of a median is that it can be used for other than numerical data. With it, qualities and attributes, which have no arithmetical value, can be measured. Extreme items do not affect its value but it should be realized that if there are only a few items in the array, as in our example, the median is not likely to be representative. The necessity of making the array at all may take a great deal of time and in the end the median, whilst being a good indicator, is not suitable for arithmetical calculations or for determining total value.

Modes

Another term which statisticians use to help explain the distribution of a series is the *mode*. It is the name given to the most frequent item in a series. The modal rate of daily occupancy is the occupancy figure which is most often recorded. As with medians, extreme items do not affect the modal figure, but it does entail grouping the items and cannot be used for arithmetical calculations. It is not of great assistance in dealing with reception statistics. However, concepts which have a considerable place in the modern reception office in establishing and recording its statistics are the *weighted arithmetic average, the moving average, the moving annual total* and, particularly, the graphic presentation of the latter with other data in the form of a *Z-Chart*.

Weighted Arithmetic Mean

Sometimes, before calculating an average of certain figures, it is important to lay more emphasis on some of the figures than others. This is called 'weighting' the figures. For example, if told that in a group of guests some had stayed two nights, some four nights, and some six nights, it could be misleading to report that the average length of stay was four nights. Of that group perhaps fourteen had stayed two nights, five had stayed four nights, and the remaining three six nights. By multiplying each length of stay by the number of guests staying that length of time, the stays will be appropriately weighted. The products are totalled and divided by the number in the group to obtain the weighted arithmetic mean:

Length of Stay		Number of Guests		Product
2 nights	×	14	=	28
4 nights	×	5	=	20
6 nights	×	3	=	18
		22		66

Weighted average = 66/22 = 3 nights

Moving Average

One of the most useful averages for presenting reception office statistics is the *moving average*. This is a particular application of the arithmetic average. It is a means of indicating the trend of the figures over a period of time. The particular feature which is of most interest to the hotel industry is that the average can be extended over a period long enough to eliminate the effect of seasonal and other fluctuations.

A low guest occupancy figure for February is not received badly when it is compared with that for the previous February and an

TABLE 10.4

MOVING AVERAGES

	Room Sales		Moving Average		
	1970	1971	£		
	£	£	3,725	December	1970
January	3,080	3,200	3,735	January	1971
February	3,020	3,080	3,740	February	1971
March	3,500	3,620	3,750	March	1971
April	3,740	3,680	3,745	April	1971
May	4,360				
June	4,500				
July	4,550				
August	4,030				
September	3,520				
October	4,070				
November	3,500				
December	2,830				

improvement is observed. This comparison with the corresponding figure of the previous year is very common in the hotel industry (although only possible where statistics are kept) and is of great help. It is of greater assistance if it can be seen at a glance whether this figure is following the same general pattern as that of preceding months. The significance of a comparatively small change in the monthly figures is highlighted and there is less chance of its going unnoticed.

The total sales figure (Table 10.4) for January–December 1970 is £44,700, which divided by 12 gives the average monthly figure £3,725. At the end of January 1971 the twelve-monthly total sales (i.e. February 1970–January 1971) are £44,820 and the average is now £3,735. The sales figures for the period 1 March 1970–28 February 1971 is £44,880 with a monthly average of £3,740. At the end of March the figures are £45,000 and £3,750, respectively. But during April there is a small fall in turnover compared with the previous year. The moving annual total drops to £44,940 and the monthly average to £3,745.

These averages are worked out as follows. At the end of each period, here a month, the latest (current month's) figure is added to the annual total; the earliest figure (i.e. the same month last year) is deducted and a fresh average is calculated. Similarly, to eliminate daily fluctuation from a weekly cycle, seven days' figures are totalled and divided by seven to arrive at a moving daily average. These averages indicate the trend, which is easily shown in graphical form. When annual figures are taken, the trend can also be indicated by the *moving annual total*. This is the name given to the total sales figures for the previous twelve months (produced and shown monthly in the example above).

Z-Chart

The moving annual total indicating the trend is often drawn on one chart together with a curve representing the figures for each month, or whatever other period is chosen; a third line indicates the cumulative amount. Sales figures, number of guests accommodated, rooms occupied, are examples of statistics originating in the reception office, which can be well illustrated by this method. The Z-chart derives its name from the picture it presents at the end of the year (*see* Figure 10.1). The cumulative figure coincides with the current figure at the end of the first period and is plotted upward until at the end of the year it is bound to meet the curve of the moving annual total.

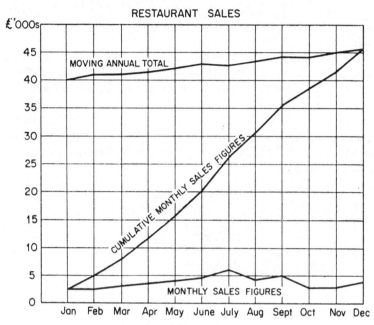

Fig. 10.1 Z-chart showing general trend in moving annual total

Each year a fresh chart is produced. If it is desired to place more emphasis on the current figure and to make it easier to read, two scales may be employed, a much larger one being used for the current figures.

Graphs

Graphs of reception statistics are sometimes kept on a daily basis. These not only save referring to detailed books when only a general picture is required, but can also be used as a stimulus to the general interest of the reception staff. They give a full and concise picture of the data which they portray and, most important, a picture that is quickly appreciated. When drawing a graph there are certain general rules which should be followed if it is to have maximum effect:

(*a*) The graph should have a clear and relevant title and descriptions; lettering should preferably be horizontal.

(*b*) As the purpose is to show figures over a period of time, the time scale in days, months or years follows the bottom horizontal axis and should be marked beneath it.

(c) The units (e.g. rooms) should be marked at the top of the left-hand vertical axis and the scale clearly indicated at intervals on its left side.

(d) The vertical scale should start at the bottom with zero if absolute changes are being shown. Otherwise changes can assume relatively more import than is warranted. Where all the figures fall within a narrow range and it is desired to show only this range, the scale should still begin with zero and the break in the scale should be marked with a break in the vertical axis before the first number of the scale is shown (*see* Figure 10.2). This warns readers of the graph against the danger of a false impression.

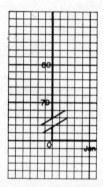

Fig. 10.2 To show break in vertical axis

(e) The scale should be chosen with care. It has been observed that information given to management in the form of a chart, the peaks of which are acute angles, often causes a state of anxiety. However, if the scales have been so designed that the same figures are presented with the peaks shown as obtuse angles, a much calmer atmosphere prevails!

(f) The plotted lines should be shown clearly. Where there is more than one curve on the graph, each should be distinguished. Colours are the simplest form of distinction but require a key, as do different types of line (dots, broken lines, etc.). Alternatively, the lines can simply be marked as illustrated on the Z-chart in Figure 10.1. There should not be too many lines in one chart.

Other methods of presenting information pictorially, such as bar charts, band curves charts, break-even charts, and even pie charts, may sometimes be of use when presenting reception statistics, although the graphs already described are most common.

REPORTS

Collection of information serves little purpose, unless it can be passed on to those who can use it. The presentation of facts can be as important as their accumulation. Where the report is of a routine nature, time should be taken in designing a form which highlights important features and changes, and this should be adhered to so that the reader knows where to expect the key information. Where comparisons are to be made, these should be included in the form and appropriately sited. Such comparisons might include figures for the corresponding period in the previous year or years, the figures for the previous period, or the budgeted figures for this period. This comparison of actual with anticipated achievement is, rightly, assuming more and more importance in operating an hotel successfully. The form also reduces to a minimum

The is a return for the period FROM ___ TO ___	MONTHLY REPORT ACTIVITY			FOR THE ATTENTION OF ___ COMPILED BY ___			
OCCUPANCY	Month	Year to date	Month	Year to date	OCCUPANCY %			
	No. of BED/BEDROOM NIGHTS 'SOLD'		Out of action Bed/Bedroom Nights Lost		Month		Year to date	
					this year	last year	this year	last year
BEDROOMS								
BEDS								
RESTAURANT	Number of covers sold				this year	last year	this year	last year
B'fast			Breakfast					
Lunch			Lunch					
Dinner			Dinner					
TOTAL			TOTAL					

Fig. 10.3 Monthly occupancy report

the time its compiler needs to spend on the report, concentrating on the changing facts and figures and not having to concern himself with details of layout. As with all reports, the form should be kept as brief and as simple as possible. Two routine reports are illustrated in Figures 10.3 and 10.4.

Routine reports of this nature should always be rendered promptly when due. To facilitate this, it is best to plan the timing of such reports so that their period coincides with the business cycle and their presentation follows as a natural outcome of the work cycle of the department or individual presenting them. For example, where returns are made weekly to end on a Saturday night, and Sunday is a quiet working day in the reception unit, the management can reasonably require that the weekly report from that unit be available each Monday morning.

PRIVATE AND CONFIDENTIAL

To ....

Compiled by ....

Week ending 19

WEEKLY REPORT

	W/E	19	W/E	19	Increase	Decrease
TOTAL						
Apartments						
Restaurant						
Cocktail Bar						
Lounge Bar						
Dispense Bar						
Night Bar						
Off Licence						
Snack Bar						
Cigarettes, Tob.,etc.						
Telephones						
Garages						
Sundries						
V. P.O.						
CASH BANKED						
Wages: Total						
Clerical						
Kitchen and Stills						
Restaurant						
Bars						
Domestic						
Porters						
Gardeners						
Snack Bar						
Casual						
CHEQUES DRAWN						

Fig. 10.4 Comparative weekly report

The frequency of routine reports should be carefully considered and they should not be rendered more often than is necessary. Each report will cost something in staff time, if nothing else, and in times of high labour cost this can represent a considerable monetary value. This cost must be measured against the possible benefits which may accrue, or losses which may be prevented, by the report. Its frequency may be flexible according to the nature of the report. Many hotels have monthly stocktaking reports of their liquor bar. When these are satisfactory, the stocktaking period may remain constant, but when a dubious report is received, weekly, or even daily, stock checks and reports are often required until the situation is corrected.

In the case of all reports, it is a waste of time collecting information only to present it too late for it to be of any use. The information may be of historic use for comparative purposes, but where management action has been deferred too long or the wrong action has been taken because the report was not available, the fault is obvious.

Some reports, such as the stocktaking and monthly bar results mentioned above, normally require a high degree of accuracy and detail; but in many cases a rounded-off approximation, which can be supplied more quickly, not only provides the information adequately but is, in fact, clearer, as the absence of minor figures makes the figures easier to assimilate.

Sometimes it is found most convenient to render reports in the form of the Z-charts or graphs dealt with above. Often this graphic presentation is the most striking and time-saving for the recipient.

From time to time written reports and reports of an individual nature may be asked for. As with the routine reports, the aim should be to keep the report simple, direct, and brief. It is sound practice to arrange the report according to a predetermined format. The simplest of these starts by stating the purpose of the report, is followed by the facts or figures required, and concludes (where asked for) with any observations and recommendations which the writer deems pertinent. More complex designs may be conceived as and when necessary.

There are a few basic details which should be common to all reports. Whilst their purpose is generally self-evident, they should not be overlooked. An appropriate title to the report is essential and this should include the period which the report covers and for whom it is intended. At the end of the report some indication should be given of when and by whom it was rendered. Furthermore, it is customary and good practice to include brief details of the distribution of the copies.

May we conclude by widening the theme applied to report-writing to the whole concept of reception work. In any situation there are a few basic principles which apply. The selection of particular methods, aids or procedures to provide the best or most practical system in given circumstances, depends on a variety of factors. We have endeavoured to set out the principles involved and to show what some of the better-known aids and routines can achieve and how they work. There is no ideal solution to all reception problems. Aids should be used where they are needed and useful but not otherwise. More complex (or simpler) designs may be conceived as and when necessary.

Appendix A

Hotels in Law

OUR guests stay in a wide range of accommodation – in hotels, motels, guest houses, boarding houses, holiday camps. But in law all establishments offering accommodation belong to one of two groups: they may be hotels in the legal sense or not. Those which are hotels in the legal sense have been defined in the Hotel Proprietors' Act, 1956; but the legal principles, which today apply to these hotels, have applied to inns for many centuries and it is convenient to refer to the hotels as defined in the 1956 Act as 'inns'. All other establishments, which are not inns, are referred to as 'private hotels'.

The distinction is of importance in three main ways: in determining the duty to receive travellers, the responsibility for guests' property,

	Inns	*Private Hotels*
(*a*) Duty to receive	Must receive all respectable travellers, if accommodation available, and their luggage.	Have a right to choose their guests and complete freedom to refuse them and/or their luggage.
(*b*) Responsibility for guests' property	Loss of or damage to guests' property is, with certain exceptions, the liability of the innkeeper.	Are not liable for guests' property unless they can be proved negligent.
(*c*) Unpaid bills	Have the right to detain a guest's property as security for an unpaid bill and a right of sale subject to certain conditions.	Have no right to detain a guest's property as security for an unpaid bill.

and the rights in respect of unpaid bills. The relative position of the two types of establishment is summarized above. It should be remembered that the name given to the establishment does not provide a reliable guide whether it is an inn or a private hotel. It is up to the proprietor to decide whether he wishes to conduct his establishment as an inn and to accept the duties and obligations arising out of it, or whether he wishes to be regarded as a private hotelier in the eyes of the law. He is absolutely free to describe his establishment as he chooses.

The main provisions of the Hotel Proprietors' Act, 1956, are given in Appendix B.

The innkeeper's right to detain a guest's property, and his right of sale, are explained in Appendix C.

Appendix B

Main Provisions of the Hotel Proprietors' Act, 1956

DEFINITION OF AN HOTEL

T HE Act defines an hotel as 'an establishment held out by the proprietor as offering food, drink and, if so required, sleeping accommodation, without special contract, to any traveller presenting himself who appears able and willing to pay a reasonable sum for the services and facilities provided and who is in a fit state to be received'.

HOTELIER'S RESPONSIBILITY FOR GUESTS' PROPERTY

The proprietor of any hotel has a duty to take reasonable care of the property of his guests brought to the hotel, whether resident or not. If it is lost or damaged through the negligence of the hotel, the proprietor may be liable. In addition to this duty, which an innkeeper has in common with others who are not innkeepers (private hoteliers), an innkeeper has, in certain circumstances, strict liability for the property of his resident guests.

The proprietor can avoid his liability only if he can prove that the loss or damage was caused by the guest's own negligence, or by an Act of God, or by an Act of the Queen's enemies.

Innkeeper's Strict Liability

This liability, which applies only to innkeepers, whether they have been negligent or not, extends to the loss or damage of guests' property only if

(a) at the time of the loss or damage sleeping accommodation had been reserved for the traveller; *and*

(b) the loss or damage occurred between the midnight immediately preceding and the midnight immediately following his stay at the hotel.

The strict liability does not apply to vehicles or property left in them, horses or other live animals or their harness or other equipment, although the innkeeper still has a duty of reasonable care for them. As strict liability no longer applies to these items, the innkeeper no longer has a right to detain them as security for unpaid bills.

Limitation of Strict Liability

The innkeeper's strict liability is limited to £50 for any one article and to £100 in respect of any one guest, if he exhibits a copy of the statutory notice, given in the Act, and in the way prescribed by the Act. If a copy of the statutory notice is not displayed, or not displayed as laid down by the Act at the time when the property was brought to the hotel, the innkeeper loses the protection of limited liability and becomes fully liable for the whole amount of the loss or damage.

Innkeeper's Full Liability

In addition to full liability arising when the innkeeper does not display a copy of the statutory notice as laid down by the Act, the innkeeper loses the protection of limited liability and becomes fully liable for the whole amount of the loss or damage if the property

(*a*) was stolen, lost or damaged through the default, neglect or wilful act of the proprietor or his staff; *or*

(*b*) was lost or damaged whilst expressly deposited for safe custody; *or*

(*c*) was refused for safe custody, or through some other default on the part of the innkeeper or his staff, it was not possible to deposit it for safe custody.

Notices of Disclaimer

An innkeeper cannot contract out of his liability to guests who have engaged sleeping accommodation by exhibiting notices disclaiming responsibility, or by informing a guest that the proprietors will not be liable unless goods are deposited for safe custody.

Such notices may have the value of serving as a warning to guests to take care of their property and thus tend to reduce the risk of loss. They may also be material when the issue of negligence is to be decided: the innkeeper may find it easier to prove negligent a guest who ignores any warning notices and thus reduce his liability or even avoid it completely.

But in an inn notices of disclaimer are not legally effective to relieve the innkeeper of his responsibility.

Application of Act

The Hotel Proprietors' Act, 1956, applies to Great Britain but not to Northern Ireland.

Appendix C

Innkeeper's Lien and Right of Sale

INNKEEPER'S LIEN

LIEN is a peculiar right of English law, which allows a man in certain circumstances to retain property even though it does not belong to him; for example, a craftsman who repairs has a lien over goods on which repairs have been executed.

An innkeeper has a lien for the whole amount of his bill on the goods of his guest. In the first instance the innkeeper is entitled to payment from the guest before receiving him (deposit may be requested) and has the right to demand payment of the bill before the guest leaves (the guest is not entitled to credit). If no payment is received, the innkeeper can exercise his lien, i.e. he may detain the guest's luggage until the bill is paid.

The lien applies to all goods brought to the hotel by the guest except vehicles and property left in them, horses or other live animals or their harness or other equipment. It makes no difference whether the goods are the property of the guest or not, provided that the innkeeper is not aware that the goods are not the guest's property.

The right of lien arises from the innkeeper's duty to receive all respectable travellers. It is a Common Law right, which was not created, but given statutory authority, by the Innkeepers' Act, 1878. The Hotel Proprietors' Act, 1956, affected lien only in that it excluded certain items; thus, for example, the innkeeper cannot detain the guest's car.

INNKEEPER'S RIGHT OF SALE

In addition to confirming the innkeeper's right of lien, the Innkeepers' Act, 1878, gave the innkeeper the right to sell the goods held on lien under the following conditions:

(a) The sale must be in respect of goods held by the innkeeper on lien. The innkeeper cannot, for example, exercise his right of sale in respect of property left behind by the guest and not claimed, if no amount is owing to him by the guest.

(*b*) No sale must take place until the goods have been held on lien for at least six weeks without the debt having been paid.

(*c*) The sale must be by public auction.

(*d*) At least one month before the sale the innkeeper must insert an advertisement in one London newspaper and in one other paper circulating in the district where the goods have been left, containing notice of the intended sale, with a description of the goods to be sold and the name of the owner or person depositing them where known.

(*e*) The innkeeper must pay to the guest concerned on demand the surplus, if any, arising from the sale of his goods, after allowing for the settlement of the debt and the costs of the sale.

Appendix D

Rules of Law relating to Hotel Registration

THE rules of law relating to registration of guests at hotels are contained in the Aliens Orders, 1953 and 1957, and can be summarized as follows:

(*a*) Every person of sixteen years of age and over who stays for one night or more at any premises where accommodation is provided for reward shall on arrival at the premises inform the keeper of the premises or another person acting on his behalf (that is proprietor, manager, receptionist, etc.) of his full name and nationality.

(*b*) Every such person who is an alien should give in addition:

(i) on arrival the number and place of issue of his registration certificate, passport, or other document establishing his identity and nationality, *and*

(ii) on or before departure his next destination and, if known, his full address there.

(*c*) The keeper of the premises must see that guests comply with these rules and must keep a record of all the above particulars in writing for a minimum period of twelve months; this record must also contain the date of arrival and be at all times open to inspection by any constable or by any person authorized by the Secretary of State.

(*d*) Any person acting in contravention of the Orders is liable on a summary conviction to a fine not exceeding £100 or to imprisonment for a term not exceeding six months; in England and Wales any proceedings for the above offences require the consent of the Director of Public Prosecutions.

One of the main objects of the rules introduced in the 1957 Order is to facilitate registration of parties by permitting a list containing the necessary details to be handed to the receptionist, instead of each guest making an entry in the register himself. But from the hotelier's point of view the register serves two main purposes, namely, to satisfy the law and to provide a useful record of his guests' particulars. In most instances it is impracticable to secure these two objectives otherwise than by asking arriving guests to enter the details themselves, i.e. 'to sign the register', as has been the practice for a very long time, and to state also the other particulars, such as their nationality and address for future communication. This procedure normally applies to all arrivals, except to members of organized parties, in which case the guide or another person may provide the details for all members of the party in order to speed up the reception procedure.

NOTES

(*a*) It is no longer legally necessary for a guest to enter the required information in the register himself: all that is required is that he should supply the details, either verbally or in writing. Moreover, the guest need not do so himself; anyone may do so on his behalf, for example a friend or the receptionist himself.

(*b*) 'Full name' means all Christian or fore-names and surname. It is not sufficient to enter in the register for example 'Mr and Mrs Jones' or even 'J. and E. Jones'; the entries in this case should be 'John Edward Jones' and 'Elizabeth Mary Jones'.

(*c*) The following categories are not regarded as aliens for the purposes of hotel registration and need not, therefore, supply the additional details required of aliens only:

citizens of the United Kingdom and Colonies; citizens of the Irish Republic (Eire); any Commonwealth citizens, including citizens of India; members of the armed forces of the NATO countries on active service in this country; foreign envoys or members of their households or their official staff; aliens subject to the service law as members of the armed forces of the U.K. or India.

(*d*) The hotel register need be produced on demand only to the two categories of persons stated above. In addition, hotels are sometimes required to supply evidence by providing witnesses to testify to the presence of certain persons in the hotel at certain times.

Appendix E

International Hotel Telegraph Code

NUMBER OF ROOMS, BEDS

1 room with 1 bed	Alba	3 rooms with 2+2+1 = 5 beds	Calde
1 room with 1 large bed	Aldua	3 rooms with 2 beds each	Caduf
1 room with 2 beds	Arab		
1 room with 3 beds	Abec		
		4 rooms with 1 bed each	Danid
2 rooms with 1 bed each	Belab	4 rooms with 2 beds each	Diroh
2 rooms with 2+1 = 3 beds	Birac		
2 rooms with 2 beds each	Bonad	5 rooms with 1 bed each	Emble
		5 rooms with 2 beds each	Ercaj
3 rooms with 1 bed each	Ciroc	6 rooms with 1 bed each	Felaf
3 rooms with 2 + 1 + 1 = 4 beds	Carid	6 rooms with 2 beds each	Feral

ADDITIONAL AMENITIES

Child's bed	Kind	Quality of rooms: very good	Best
Sitting room	Sal	Quality of rooms: good	Bon
Private bathroom	Bat	Quality of rooms: simple	Plain
Servant's room	Serv		
Room with good view	Belvu	Air conditioned room	Acond
Room facing courtyard	Inter	Box for 1 motor-car	Box
Room very quiet	Tranq	Ordinary garage for 1 motor-car	Garag
Room without running water	Ordin		

LENGTH OF STAY

Length of stay:		Length of stay:	
1 night	Pass	several days	Stop

ARRIVAL PROCEDURE

Meet at station	Train	Meet at bus terminus	
Meet at landing	Quai	from airport	Aeroz
Meet at airport	Aero		

TIME OF ARRIVAL

	Morning	*Afternoon*	*Evening*	*Night*
Sunday	Pobab	Polyp	Rabal	Ranuv
Monday	Pocun	Pomel	Racex	Rapin
Tuesday	Podyl	Ponow	Radok	Raqaf
Wednesday	Pogok	Popuf	Rafyg	Ratyz
Thursday	Pohix	Porik	Ragub	Ravup
Friday	Pojaw	Posev	Rahiv	Rawow
Saturday	Pokuz	Povah	Rajod	Raxab

This morning	This afternoon	This evening	This night
Powys	Pozum	Ramyk	Razem

Cancel rooms Anul

Appendix F

Addresses and Salutations

NAMES IN ADDRESSES

(*See* subsequent pages for Royalty, Peers and Baronets, the Church, the Law, and Civic and County Authorities.)

General Addresses

Mr. Norman Russell *or* Norman Russell, Esq. (more courteous).

H. R. Armstrong, Esq., O.B.E., M.A. (civil and military honours before academic degrees).

Sir John Blank, C.B.E., D.S.O., D.SC., F.R.S.
(The full order of letters after names is always: honour, decoration, degree, distinction.)

Frank Roberts, Jr., Esq. (a son bearing the same first name as his father).

D. Thompson, Esq., M.D.

Professor A. Bentley.

Miss Edith Churcher.

The Misses Brown (if two unmarried ladies).

Mrs. L. Brown.

Mr. and Mrs. Freeman.

Messrs. Thomas Brown & Co. Ltd.

Messrs Cameron and Somerville Ltd.

The Imperial Chemical Co. Ltd.

Military Addresses

Admiral of the Fleet Lord John Davis.

Colonel The Right Hon. The Earl of Blyth.

Wing Commander Lord David Courtenay.
(Service titles always precede hereditary titles.)

Commodore Bentley, D.S.O., R.N. (always write R.N. after the name of a naval officer except in the case of an Admiral, whose service is obvious from his rank).

Major Sir John James, V.C., M.O., Welsh Guards (in the Army indicate the name of the Officer's regiment).

Squadron Leader The Hon. James Black, D.F.C. (in the Royal Air Force the service is not indicated as it is obvious from the rank).

Members of Parliament

John Smith, Esq., M.P.

Sir John Black, K.C.M.G., M.P.

Dame Margaret Fincham, D.B.E., M.P.

(If an M.P. is a Knight or a Dame of an Order, the letters of that Order precede M.P.)

Privy Councillors

The Right Hon. John Blank.

The Right Hon. Lord Middleton, P.C. (if a peer who is Right Hon. in his own right becomes a Privy Councillor).

The Right Hon. John Meason, M.P. (a member of Parliament who is a Privy Councillor).

ROYALTY

	In speech	*On the envelope*	*A formal letter beginning*	*ending*
The Queen	*In the first instance:* Your Majesty; *subsequently:* Ma'am	To Her Majesty The Queen	May it please Your Majesty, *or* Madam,	I have the honour to remain, Madam, Your Majesty's most humble and obedient subject,
The Duke of Edinburgh	*In the first instance:* Your Royal Highness; *subsequently:* Sir	To His Royal Highness the Prince Philip, Duke of Edinburgh	Sir,	I have the honour to be, Sir, Your Royal Highness's most humble and obedient servant,
The Queen Mother	as for the Queen	To Her Majesty Queen Elizabeth The Queen Mother	as for the Queen	as for the Queen

	In speech	*On the envelope*	*A formal letter beginning*	*ending*
Princes, Princesses, Dukes, and Duchesses of the blood royal	*In the first instance:* Your Royal Highness; *subsequently:* Sir *or* Ma'am	To His (or Her) Royal Highness the Prince (*or* Princess) *or* Duke (or Duchess) of . . .	Sir, (*or* Madam,)	I have the honour to be, Sir (*or* Madam), Your Royal Highness's most humble and obedient servant,

Note: Letters to the Queen, the Queen Mother, and other members of the Royal Family should be sent to the Private Secretary or to a Lady- or Gentleman-in-Waiting in order to be transmitted. The letter must be a very real and urgent one to justify a direct approach.

THE PEERAGE AND BARONETS

Duke	Your Grace	His Grace The Duke of . . .	My Lord Duke,	I remain, Your Grace's most obedient servant,
Marquess	My Lord	The Most Hon. The Marquess of . . .	My Lord,	I have the honour to be, Your obedient servant,
Earl		The Right Hon. The Earl of		
Viscount		The Right Hon. The Viscount (name)		
Baron		The Right Hon. The Lord (name)		
Younger sons and all daughters of Dukes and of Marquesses, daughters of Earls	Lord (Christian name) *or* Lady (Christian name)	Lord (full name) *or* The Lady (full name)	Sir, (*or* Madam,)	as above

	In speech	On the envelope	A formal letter beginning	ending
Younger sons of Earls, sons and daughters of Viscounts and of Barons	Sir (*or* Madam)	The Hon. (full name)	Sir, (*or* Madam),	as above

Notes: There are five grades in the peerage: Duke, Marquess, Earl, Viscount, and Baron.

The wives of peers take their husbands' ranks and titles: Duchess, Marchioness, Countess, Viscountess, Baroness.

| Baronet | Sir (and Christian name) | Sir (full name), Bt. [In Scotland the territorial family title before the Bt.] | Sir, | I have the honour to remain, Your obedient servant, |

THE CHURCH (OF ENGLAND)

Arch-bishop (except Armagh)	Your Grace	The Most Reverend ...	My Lord Archbishop, *or* Your Grace,	I have the honour to remain, my Lord Archbishop, Your Grace's devoted and obedient servant,
Archbishop of Armagh	as above	The Most Revd. His Grace the Lord Primate	as above	as above
Bishop (except Meath and the Primus)	My Lord	The Right Revd.	My Lord, *or* My Lord Bishop,	I have the honour to remain, Your Lordship's obedient servant,

	In speech	On the envelope	A formal letter beginning	ending
Bishop of Meath	as above	The Most Revd.	as above	as above
Dean	Mr. Dean	The Very Revd.	Very Revd. Sir,	I have the honour to remain, Very Revd. Sir, Your obedient servant,
Provost	Mr. Provost	The Very Revd.	as above	as above
Archdeacon	Mr. Archdeacon	The Venerable	Venerable Sir,	as above but Venerable Sir
Canon	Canon (surname)	The Revd. Canon (full name)	Reverend Sir,	as above but Reverend Sir
Beneficed Clergyman	Vicar *or* Rector *or* Mr. (surname)	The Revd. (full name)	Reverend Sir, *or* Sir,	I beg to remain, Reverend Sir (*or* Sir), Your obedient servant,

Note: A temporal title is always preceded in writing by the spiritual one for example: The Revd. Sir John Brown, Bt.

THE LAW

The Lord Chancellor	According to his rank in the peerage	The Right Hon. The Lord Chancellor	My Lord,	I have the honour to be, my Lord, Your Lordship's obedient servant,
The Lord Chief Justice	If a peer, according to peerage, *otherwise* My Lord *or* Your Lordship	The Right Hon. The Lord Chief Justice of England	as above	as above

	In speech	*On the envelope*	*A formal letter beginning*	*ending*
The Master of the Rolls	as above	The Right Hon. The Master of the Rolls *or* The Right Hon. (according to rank)	as above	as above
A Lord of Appeal-in-Ordinary	My Lord	The Right Hon. Lord (name)	as above	as above
Judge of High Court	*In Court:* My Lord; *otherwise* Sir	The Hon. Mr. Justice (name)	My Lord, *or* Sir,	I have the honour to be, My Lord (or Sir), Your obedient servant,
Judge of County Court	*On the Bench* Your Honour; *otherwise* Sir	His Honour Judge (surname)	Sir,	Yours faithfully,

CIVIC AND COUNTY AUTHORITIES

Lord Mayor	My Lord *or* Mr. Mayor Your Worship *on public occasions*	The Right Hon. The Lord Mayor of [Bristol, Cardiff, Dublin, London, York, Belfast, and six Australian cities: Adelaide, Brisbane, Hobart, Melbourne, Sydney, Perth].	Sir, *or* Dear Mr. Mayor,	Yours faithfully, Yours sincerely,

	In speech	On the envelope	A formal letter beginning	ending
		The Right Worshipful The Lord Mayor of [all other cities]		
Wife of Lord Mayor (or acting lady)	My Lady	The Lady Mayoress of . . .	Madam,	Yours faithfully,
Lord Provost	My Lord *or* Sir	The Lord Provost of . . .	Dear Lord Provost,	Yours faithfully, Yours sincerely,

Notes: Equivalent rank in Scotland to Lord Mayor; wives do not share title. In writing, the Lord Provost of Edinburgh is addressed 'The Right Hon. (name)'; the Lord Provost of Glasgow is addressed 'The Right Hon. The Lord Provost of Glasgow'.

	In speech	On the envelope	A formal letter beginning	ending
Alderman	Mr. Alderman *or* Mrs. Alderman; Your Worship *on the Bench*	Alderman (full name) Alderman Mrs. (full name)	Dear Sir or Madam, or Dear Mr. (Mrs.) Alderman (surname)	Yours faithfully, Yours sincerely,
Bailie	Bailie (surname); Your Worship *on the Bench*	Bailie (full name)	Dear Sir (or Madam) or Dear Mr. (Mrs.) Bailie (surname)	as above

Note: If in doubt about civic authorities consult the Town Clerk

	In speech	On the envelope	A formal letter beginning	ending
Lord Lieutenant	According to rank	According to rank and add H.M. Lieutenant of (county)	According to rank	As appropriate for rank
Other county authorities	as above	as above and add position	as above	as above

Note: If in doubt about county authorities, consult the Lord Lieutenant's secretary

Appendix G

Postage Rates

POSTAL rates and regulations are quite complicated and it is essential for the reception staff to have access to the latest edition of the *Post Office Guide*. This is a large book which is published by H.M. Stationery Office every July, and is available from there or from larger post offices. By filling in a postcard the user of the *Guide* receives free all the amendments issued by the G.P.O. while the edition is still current, so that it may be kept perpetually up-to-date.

The receptionist or other staff handling guests' mail and endeavouring to answer enquiries is advised to extract from the *Post Office Guide* enough information to be able to give quick replies without the necessity of searching through the whole book.

A chart should be drawn up which will give the common rates of postage in the following categories:

Letters
Postcards
Printed papers – ordinary and reduced rates
Parcels – local and ordinary

Account should be taken of the differing rates applicable to Great Britain, Republic of Ireland, British Forces overseas, the Commonwealth, and foreign countries.

If many guests of foreign nationality use the hotel it is as well to make notes on airmail facilities, which are nowadays very extensive. Full particulars are given in the *Post Office Guide*, together with other useful information on rates and regulations for sending telegrams abroad and for telephoning foreign countries. The more attractive British postage stamps issued in recent years may give rise to enquiries from overseas visitors who are stamp collectors. It should be noted that the G.P.O. now operates a special Philatelic Bureau, whose address is 2–4 Waterloo Place, Edinburgh 1, Scotland.

A great deal of mental arithmetic may be avoided and the chances of error reduced if the quick-reference table is drawn up intelligently.

Below is an example of a simple table showing postage rates for mail as applicable in 1972:

POSTAGE RATES
INLAND AND IRISH REPUBLIC
LETTERS AND CARDS

Not over	First Class	Second Class
2 oz	3p	2½p
4 oz	4p	3½p
6 oz	6p	5½p
8 oz	8p	6½p
10 oz	10p	7½p
12 oz	13p	8½p
14 oz	15p	9½p
1 lb 0 oz	17p	11½p
1 lb 8 oz	24p	13½p
2 lb 0 oz	34p	maximum
each additional lb	17p	

Appendix H

Reference Tables for Rates of Exchange

HOTEL cashiers and receptionists need to draw up a reference table for converting the principal currencies likely to be offered by overseas visitors to Britain. Such a chart can take the following form; if several copies are needed, or if it is to undergo periodic amendment, the 'blank' chart as it appears here can be reproduced by stencil duplicator. The prevailing bank or 'hotel' equivalents in sterling currency can then be filled in the squares, as appropriate. (*See* Figure H.1. *overleaf.*)

	U. S. Dollars		AUSTRALIAN Dollars		BELGIAN Francs		CANADIAN Dollars		DANISH Kroner	
	£	p	£	p	£	p	£	p	£	p
1										
5										
10										
20										
30										
40										
50										
75										
100										
250										
500										
1,000										

Fig. H.1 Specimen reference table

FRENCH Francs		GERMAN Marks		NETH'DS Guilders		SWISS Francs			ITALIAN Lire	
£	p	£	p	£	p	£	p		£	p
								10		
								50		
								100		
								200		
								300		
								400		
								500		
								750		
								1,000		
								2,500		
								5,000		
								10,000		

for conversion of foreign currencies

Appendix J

Switchboard Operation

INTERNAL CALL SIGNAL

The disc flaps down, revealing the room number which is calling. To communicate with this caller:

(*a*) Plug jack *A* into the relevant socket *G* (yellow disc *E* will always show that the extension receiver is off its hook).

(*b*) Push switch *D* forward and speak to caller.

To connect caller with another internal extension:

(*a*) Plug jack *B* into relevant extension.

(*b*) Call this number by pulling switch *D* (when call is answered the yellow disc *F* will show).

When call terminates, the yellow discs *E* and *F* will disappear as the receivers are replaced. Then disconnect the jacks.

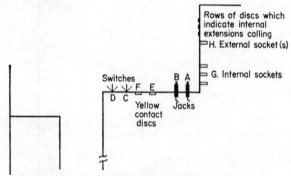

Fig. J.1 Side view of manually operated switchboard

To connect caller with an external number:

(*a*) Plug jack *A* into relevant internal socket *G* and then note number required.

(*b*) Insert jack *B* into any available external socket *H*.

(*c*) Push forward switch *D* to hear dialling tone.

(*d*) Push forward switch *C* and dial number. Bring back switch *C* into the upright neutral position.

A ringing tone should be heard after a few seconds. If engaged, return switch *D* to neutral to cut off the board from the call. Only by listening into the call for a second can the operator know whether the number has replied. To do this, simply push switch *D* forward.

When call terminates (shown by yellow disc disappearing) remove both plugs from the sockets immediately, otherwise the next external caller will ring directly to the internal extension.

EXTERNAL CALL SIGNAL

(*a*) External flap drops, revealing hotel's external number (e.g. 622 9191) and a ringing tone is heard as through an ordinary receiver.

(*b*) Connect jack *B* to relevant socket *H*.

(*c*) Push switch *D* forward and answer caller with the name of your hotel.

The caller will probably require an internal extension. Refer to the alphabetical index of guests if necessary.

(*d*) Connect jack *A* to the relevant internal socket *G*.

(*e*) Ring extension by pulling switch *C*.

(*f*) When caller answers, return both switches *E* and *D* to neutral.

Again when call terminates (shown by yellow disc disappearing) remove both plugs *A* and *B* at once.

Appendix K

List of Words for Use when Spelling Over the Telephone

A *for*	Andrew		N *for*	Norman
B	Bertha		O	Olive
C	Charlie		P	Peter
D	David		Q	Queenie
E	Edward		R	Robert
F	Father		S	Sugar
G	George		T	Tommy
H	Harry		U	Uncle
I	Isaac		V	Victor
J	Jack		W	Walter
K	Kitty		X	Xmas
L	London		Y	Yellow
M	Mother		Z	Zebra

Appendix L

Abbreviations

THE county name should be shown in full unless a shortened form for it appears in the following list of postally acceptable abbreviations (twenty-three in all):

Beds. *for*	Bedfordshire	Lincs. *for*	Lincolnshire
Berks.	Berkshire	Middx.	Middlesex
Bucks.	Buckinghamshire	Mon.	Monmouthshire
Cambs.	Cambridgeshire	Northants.	Northamptonshire
Carms.	Carmarthenshire	Notts.	Nottinghamshire
Co. Derry	Co. Londonderry	Oxon.	Oxfordshire
Glam.	Glamorgan	Pembs.	Pembrokeshire
Glos.	Gloucestershire	Salop.	Shropshire
Hants.	Hampshire	Staffs.	Staffordshire
Herts.	Hertfordshire	Wilts.	Wiltshire
Lancs.	Lancashire	Worcs.	Worcestershire
Leics.	Leicestershire		

ABBREVIATIONS OF MONTHS

January	Jan.	July	—
February	Feb.	August	Aug.
March	Mar.	September	Sep.
April	Apr.	October	Oct.
May	—	November	Nov.
June	—	December	Dec.

Appendix M

Specimen Extracts from Instructions to Reception Staff

THIS extract from instructions to reception staff and the one which follows on the use of telephone, have been included in this book as illustrations of the type of operating instructions which assist in the training of reception staff as well as in providing a constant source of reference for the correct approach and procedure to be used.

ROOM NOT READY

If a guest cannot immediately be shown to his room, act in this way:

(*a*) Apologize for the inconvenience he has been caused.

(*b*) Find out from the housekeeper when the room will be ready.

(*c*) Give the guest a time fifteen minutes later than you have been promised the room.

(*d*) Ask the guest to take a seat in the lounge.

(*e*) If the room is not available at the time you promised, contact the guest immediately and give him a new time.

(With acknowledgments to Grand Metropolitan Hotels Ltd.)

USE OF TELEPHONE BY RECEPTION STAFF

(*a*) This telephone is to be used only for reception business.

If you want to make a private call, use the call box in the hall.

If someone telephones you personally (not on business), keep your conversation as brief as possible and offer to telephone back from the call box when you are free. Unless you do this, you may keep waiting a potential guest who wants to make a booking.

(*b*) When the telephone rings answer it immediately.

If you are attending to a guest at the time, tell the caller 'Grand Hotel Reception. I won't keep you a moment'.

Do not let the telephone ring without answering it. Although it may at times be aggravating, the telephone call must always come before the tabular ledger.

(*c*) If you are attending to a guest when the telephone rings, excuse yourself.

But the telephone call should not take precedence over the guest at the counter with whom you were dealing before the telephone rang.

(*d*) Do not leave the caller waiting too long before attending to him.

A caller on the telephone should never be left longer than forty-five seconds without somebody picking up the telephone and saying again 'I'm sorry to keep you waiting'.

(*e*) Answer the telephone by saying 'Grand Hotel Reception; Good morning (Good afternoon, Good evening). May I help you?'.

Do not answer 'Hello'.

(*f*) Speak clearly.

Pronounce your words carefully – the caller may find it more difficult to understand you on the telephone than if you speak to him at the counter.

(*g*) Be brief and to the point, but not abrupt.

Remember that telephone time costs money and that the switchboard operator may be holding another call for you.

(*h*) Be polite, friendly, helpful.

On the telephone only your voice can indicate the welcome we want every potential guest to receive.

Do not interrupt the caller whilst he is talking.

You must never sound short, sharp, irritated or impatient.

(*i*) Be accurate in what you say.

The guest wants to have confidence in you. Do not 'think' or 'suppose'. If you do not know the answer, find out.

(*j*) Be courteous in explaining the hotel rules.

Do not use the phrase 'You have to'.

'I suggest' or 'Would you mind' is preferable.

Never argue with a guest; the guest is always right.

If there is a problem you cannot settle, let the head receptionist know so that he can deal with it.

(*k*) If you have to telephone the caller back, ask for his name and number.

Names of large commercial companies, like I.C.I. or Shell, are useless by themselves. The name of the caller and his telephone number (and extension) are essential.

(*l*) Finally, always remember that you represent the hotel.
Whilst you are dealing with a caller on the telephone, he does not
see you or the hotel – your voice is the hotel to him at the time. It is
up to you to ensure that the caller becomes and remains a satisfied
customer.

Appendix N

Reception Duties

THE following is an example of the reception routine as shown in a family hotel of 120 bedrooms in London where guests stay on average four or five nights. Not all the routine work would be suitable to other hotels but it has been found practicable in this particular instance. It has been included so as to give a picture of the main points of many a receptionist's day.

8 a.m.   Put through late arrivals; close old tab; complete summary.

Enter telephones, early tea checks, paid outs, papers, and late drinks from the lounge on new tab and on bills.

Write up bills of departing guests first; complete these and deal with departures and any other queries from guests as they arise.

9 a.m.   Letters for the following day's arrivals taken out, checked against diary, and placed in alphabetical order in file for next day.

10 a.m.   Arrival lists sent out to all departments (numbers having been checked with chart previously). Any changes of rooms also sent out about this time.

Letters are dealt with during the morning, charted, entered in the diary and then given to the typist for replies.

Menus typed and duplicated.

11 a.m.   Close cash and balance cash book. Prepare cash for bank. Order any change required.

11.30 a.m.   Necessary steps taken to check on rooms not cleared by guests expected to depart.

1 p.m.   Tab written up from chart for next day.

Departure list taken from chart and typed.

Papers for following day entered (as many of our

guests are here for long stays, and this saves time the following morning).

2.15 p.m.   Paid outs and papers on a petty cash voucher paid to the hall porter.

2.30 p.m.   Lunch drinks, lounge coffees, lounge drinks, luncheons, floor service entered.

All extras entered on bills.

Before 3 p.m. Tab completed as far as possible (except afternoon teas, drinks, dinners, floor service, and telephones).

3.30 p.m.   Change of brigades. Floats checked.

During afternoon and evening deal with arrivals as they arise, register guests, escorting them to their rooms when possible, notifying all necessary departments of the arrival, including marking reception arrival list and starting bill.

5 p.m.   Telephone vouchers entered and closed.

6 p.m.   Afternoon teas and floor service entered.

9 p.m.   Dinner books and lounge books entered.

Dispense money taken.

9.30 p.m.   Tab is now closed and everything else is entered on new tab, except new arrivals.

Tab and bills are brought down and balanced together. Tab balanced as far as possible. Bills are entered on new tab and agreed carried-forward figures from old tab.

10.30 p.m.   Lounge and bar cash taken.

All safes and cupboards locked. Float checked.

Rooms available for letting, late arrivals' names and rooms notified to night porter.

Appendix P

Reception Procedure for Arriving and Departing Guests

PROCEDURE FOR AN ARRIVAL

Greet the guest and establish whether or not he has a booking.

For a guest who is a chance customer

(*a*) Establish requirements; see whether accommodation is available.

(*b*) If no accommodation is available guest should be told and possibly alternative accommodation suggested in another hotel.

(*c*) If accommodation is available and the guest is not known, discreet observation or enquiries should be made to establish whether the guest has sufficient luggage or has stayed before. If this information is acceptable, no deposit should be asked.

(*d*) Tact should be employed when asking a guest for a deposit, which should amply cover the cost of one night's stay, including food.

(*e*) Proceed as for expected guest. (The booking should subsequently be written on the reservation chart.)

For a guest who has a booking

(*a*) Offer pen and invite guest to sign register.

(*b*) If an alien, give guest that form as well to fill in.

(*c*) Whilst guest is signing in, make a note that guest has arrived on the arrival list.

(*d*) Check that the room allocated is ready for letting. (If it is not, either exchange rooms – remember to alter chart – or ask guest to wait until room is ready: suggest he leave his baggage, have a coffee, etc.)

(*e*) Check length of stay and accommodation reserved by guest with him; if different, letter may easily be found in the file.

(*f*) Complete a rooming card with a guest's name, room number, and the terms. (Other information is often printed in these 'cards', which frequently take the form of a booklet, such as restaurant and other hotel facilities; also requests such as payment of bills, time period needed for acceptance of cheques, and vacation of rooms by a certain time on day of departure. This obviates many unsightly notices in the bedrooms. It also provides the guest with a future reminder of his room number.)

(*g*) Check for mail; obtain key; arrange for luggage to be taken up; escort guest to room or arrange for porter to do this.

(*h*) If escorting guest to room, *show* the room on arrival and demonstrate where the various switches are and how they work.

Thereafter complete the following bookwork

(*i*) Make out an arrival notification, including name and address of guest, room number, rate for room, number of persons, length of stay, and any special requirements or instructions; dispatch to the relevant departments, e.g. telephonists, porters, housekeeper, restaurant, bill office. When the receptionist is also responsible for making out the bill, the latter is obviously not required but the guest's bill must be headed up and opened.

(*j*) The reception copy of the arrival notification should be utilized in completing the rest of the records (hence the importance of its correct completion).

(*k*) From the arrival notification fill out a reception board card incorporating the following information in the appropriate places on the card: name, title and initials of the guest, arrival date, departure date, number of persons, price per night, and the room number.

(*l*) From the arrival notification fill in the arrivals section of the arrivals and departures book, putting the room number, name, title and initials of guest, number of persons, and terms.

(*m*) The arrival notification can be used to see whether there is a card in the file of past guests' record cards. If the appropriate card can be found it should be filled in with the date of arrival, room number, terms, and special remarks. If there is no card, then a new one should be typed to include the full name, address, and particulars (i.e. nationality, passport number, etc.) and details of the stay.

(*n*) The guest card is then filed in the current file.

(*o*) The arrival notification can be filed and destroyed after a day.

DEPARTURES

(*a*) When a guest requests bill on departure, check that guest is due to leave by consulting departure list.

(*b*) See if there are any further charges for guest.

(*c*) Compare bill with tab to see that they agree.

(*d*) Add up and present account.

(*e*) If there is an alien form to be completed, invite the guest to complete it. After the guest has completed the form it should be filed in reception.

then

If cash is to be paid

(*f*) Take cash and give change if necessary.

(*g*) Write out a receipt.

(*h*) Stick this receipt to the top copy of the guest's bill and hand it back to him.

(*i*) Pleasantly take leave of the guest. Summon a porter to deal with the guest's luggage.

(*j*) Remove the guest's card from the reception board. (Subsequently complete the details of the departure in the arrivals and departures book; also remove guest's card from the current file, date stamp it, and file in the *past* guests' file.)

(*k*) Send out departure notification (with time of departure, if not immediately).

(*l*) From the receipt book write up the cash book (debit).

(*m*) Close account on tab by entering amount paid in cash column and totalling it; also draw a line through the whole account to help prevent further entries being made.

If a cheque is paid:

Same procedure as for cash with the exceptions:

Check that the cheque is correctly completed.

Enter the amount against the cheque column in the tab.

If credit is to be allowed:

(*a*) Check that arrangements have been made. (These should be marked on the actual bill already.)

(*b*) If not, check with the manager.

(*c*) Credit being allowed, the bill having been prepared and presented to the guest, he will then be asked to sign the account. *Do not let the guest keep the bill at this stage.*

(*d*) Same procedure as (*i*), (*j*), and (*k*), above.

(*e*) Enter credit into the tab and close the account. This will subsequently be posted to the sales ledger.

Appendix Q

The Whitney Reception System

M ANY of the principles outlined in this book have been incorporated in various patent systems for the reception office. It is not our intention to advance the pros and cons of different systems. However, we describe one here, the Whitney system, to give an indication of how these principles can be incorporated in a system for a modern reception office.

The information for requests for future reservations, whether by telephone, telegram, personal or mail, is entered on a 'room reservation request' sheet. This becomes the master for all future action and the fact that this action has been taken is noted in the appropriate blocks on the request sheet.

The booking is pegged on a pegboard, the 'advanced bookings board'. One peg for every day the room has been booked is placed in the relevant section of the board.

The key information is typed on to a slip of paper, size $4 \times 1\frac{1}{2}$ in., showing on the top line the date of arrival, the guest's name, room rate, and expected date of departure. Below this is typed the date of the booking, how it was received, by whom, who dealt with it, and any other relevant information regarding the guest (e.g. V.I.P. or Director of XYZ Ltd.), or, if the booking was by an agency, the name of the agency. Block bookings show the name of the company or person responsible on the top line followed by the number of rooms of each type required.

A colour code enables quick visual distinction between private bookings, travel agents' bookings, company bookings, block bookings, and bookings requiring special attention.

The typed slip of paper is slipped into a metal slide and this in turn is placed in alphabetical order in the 'advanced reservations' rack so that the top line showing the essential information is visible. There is a separate rack for each day for the next month and these are less frequent allocations, usually one per month, thereafter. The supported typed slip is placed in the rack on the day when it is anticipated that the stay will begin. The advanced reservation rack replaces a bookings diary.

If there is time, a written acknowledgment of the booking is dispatched. A copy of this letter is attached to the reservation request form, to the front of which a copy of the typed Whitney slip has been clipped. Where there is an originating telegram or letter this is also attached to the rear. The initials of the receptionist making the booking, acknowledging it, pegging it, and racking it are all shown on the form. This batch of correspondence is filed in date order in a correspondence file.

On the day prior to the guests' arrival the correspondence is brought out and sorted into alphabetical order, then checked against the advanced reservation rack. Any adjustments for unconfirmed bookings are then made. For each reservation the name and initials, number of people expected, date of arrival, and price quoted are typed in a space printed out at the side of the guest's registration card. The card, which bears a serial number, is attached to the relevant correspondence. In the evening the next day's correspondence file goes to the front desk, as does the advanced reservation rack for the next day. The latter is the front desk's arrivals list for the next day, and it remains at the side of the reception board on the front desk. The reception board is usually attached to the back of the reception desk at an angle of 45° so that it can be seen at a glance by the receptionist whilst facing the guests. Alongside each room number is a slot which will take a Whitney slip, which indicates the occupant. Sometimes, when not let, a coloured room card is left in these slots to indicate the type of room and its details. Alternatively this may be done by putting a transparent colour guide over the room number.

When a guest arrives, the receptionist checks from the day's arrival rack that the guest has a reservation. If this is so, the receptionist finds the correspondence in the file which is on the counter with the registration card attached. When the guest has completed the registration card the receptionist checks the registration card and then completes by hand the portion at the bottom of the card. There are several slips which, by the use of N.C.R. paper, are simultaneously made out and serve as temporary arrival notification to such departments as the telephone operator, the hall porter and enquiries, and to the luggage porter for entry in the arrival book. These departments receive these temporary arrival notifications at once. The top slip is immediately put in the reception rack and thus denotes at once that the appropriate room is occupied. The slips state merely the room number, the rate, and the name.

The registration card is fully and correctly completed, re-attached to the correspondence, placed in a tray and, as soon as practicable, a bill is headed. The name and initials are taken from the registration card. The other information is taken from the Whitney slip. If there are no account instructions, 'A/C Guest' is marked on the bill followed by the guest's home address. Where it is an agency booking and covered by voucher, an 'Extras' bill must be started to cover all charges not specified in the voucher. In all events, deposits which have been received before the guest's arrival must be clearly marked in the top right-hand corner of the bill.

As the bill heading is typed, permanent arrival notification slips are simultaneously typed for notifying the same departments as previously, again by using N.C.R. paper: this is a single operation. On their arrival the temporary slips are destroyed and the type-written information entered in the alphabetical guest index racks in the telephone and enquiry departments, and in the reception rack.

The bill and registration card are sent to the cashier together with any vouchers from travel agents.

If there are guests with two different names in the same room, two notification slips must be completed.

When the guest has paid his bill before departure, the registration card is returned to reception by the cashier with the departure date completed. The notification slip is folded in the reception rack and marked with an 'H' when the housekeeper has been informed of the departure. The slip is taken out when reception is notified that the room has been prepared for the new guest. (Alternatively, with a slide system the sliders are adjusted to show the room first 'on change' and then ready for re-letting.) The departed guest's registration card is time-stamped and passed first to the enquiries desk and then to the telephonists to notify them of the departure so that they may adjust their alphabetical guest indexes.

The registration card is returned to the back office of reception where next day it is filed in exact alphabetical order.

If a guest stays more than twice (or a prescribed number of times) in the hotel a guest history card is made out. This is of the normal type except that an additional column is included so that the registration card number can be entered on the history card. When this card is being used the registration cards are filed separately in numerical order.

A periodic change of colour of the registration cards allows cards no longer required to be cleared from the filing cabinets with comparative ease.

Daily occupancy records and daily summaries of reception activity are kept in the normal way.

Appendix R

100 Examination Questions

This Appendix contains a wide range of questions designed to enable students to test their knowledge of the subject-matter included in the book.

Most questions have been selected from papers set for the former Examination in Hotel Book-keeping and Reception of the Hotel and Catering Institute in London. Some appeared for the first time in the Second Year Sessional Examination papers for the Associateship Diploma in Hotel and Catering Management of Battersea College of Technology, London. A few have been formulated by the authors of this book to test the students' knowledge of the subject as questions of the required type were not available from past examination papers.

Where necessary the original questions have been amended so as to express all amounts of money in decimal currency which replaced the existing currency in the United Kingdom on 15 February 1971, but at a level of prices generally appropriate when the questions were originally set.

Having studied each chapter, students are advised to work their way through the questions relating to that chapter. A further selection of questions is provided for revision purposes at the end of this section. This approach not only helps in consolidating previous work but also enables students to acquire speed and confidence in dealing with examination conditions.

INTRODUCTION AND CHAPTER 1 – GENERAL

1. Describe fully the duties of a receptionist in a small hotel where there is no cashier.
2. List the essential information about an hotel, which is required in

order to determine the most appropriate reception system, and indicate briefly in what way each characteristic of the hotel influences the records and procedures of hotel reception. (Visitors' accounts are not to be considered as part of hotel reception for this purpose.)

3. State, with reasons, what qualities an hotel receptionist should have.

4. What are the principal tariff structures to be found in hotels? Give the terminology and a brief description of each type of tariff.

5. Outline concisely what you consider the best reception office system for the following modern hotel and state the staff required to operate it:

Situation	large provincial town
Capacity	120 bedrooms, 160 guests
Guests	businessmen and tourists
Annual room occupancy	80 per cent
Length of stay	70 per cent one night; 25 per cent two nights; 5 per cent longer
Ratio of booked to chance	60 per cent to 40 per cent.

Notes: Visitors' accounts are dealt with in a separate bill office, the hall porter attends to most enquiries, and you should not concern yourself with either. All correspondence with guests regarding accommodation originates and terminates in the reception office.

You are advised to formulate your answer round the records, which should be briefly described, and to set it out in such order as to make their inter-relationship clear.

CHAPTER 2 – BASIC AIDS AND RECORDS

1. State the rules of law relating to the registration of guests in an hotel.

2. What forms of hotel register do you know? Describe each briefly. Choose one of them and state what you consider its three principal merits and three principal drawbacks.

3. What are the main advantages of the individual registration form over other methods of registration of guests in a large hotel?

4. Describe concisely the three basic reception aids given below and

explain their complementary nature in the work of a receptionist:
(*a*) reception board; (*b*) alphabetical guest index; (*c*) key and mail rack.

5. Give a specimen ruling of a room record card and explain the functions and use of a room record index in a large hotel.

6. State the purpose of a visitors' record index and how it is used.

7. What information should a visitor's record card give, and what is its purpose?

8. Compare and contrast the visitors' record index and the room record index.

9. What methods are used in hotels to provide a suitable record of 'black-listed' guests?

10. What are the functions of the arrivals and departures book? State the sources from which it may be written up and with which you can check its accuracy.

CHAPTER 3 – ADVANCE BOOKINGS

1. Give a specimen ruling of a reservation form and describe fully its function and use.

2. Give a specimen ruling of a bookings diary and describe fully its function and use.

3. Describe the various forms of booking chart with which you are familiar and how they are used.

4. (*a*) What information is required about each advance booking before a reservation can be made? (*b*) Outline a filing system suitable for advance bookings of an hotel of 100 bedrooms with a short average length of stay, in which most guests reserve their accommodation in advance by post.

5. Give a specimen ruling of a page from a bedroom book and describe its use as a record of advance bookings.

6. Explain the use of a reception board as a record of advance bookings.

7. By telephone, you, as receptionist, are asked to make a reservation for a certain night the following week. How would you determine the answer to be given, and what records of the outcome of the conversation would you make?

8. At the Beach Hotel the following bookings were made during April:

Name	Type and number of rooms	Length of stay	Remarks
Mr Hillman	Single	11–13 July	Garage
Mr and Mrs Oxford	1 twin and bath	1–14 July	Deposit £5
Miss Morris	Single	13 July (1 night)	Arriving 10 p.m.
The Misses Minny	2 singles (connecting)	4 days from 11 July	Quiet rooms
Mr and Mrs Austin	Twin	2–13 July	Meet at station
Miss Austin	Single	2–18 July	at 8 p.m.
Mr Ford	Single and bath	28 June–4 August	Deposit £10
Mr and Mrs Rover and small infant	Double and sitting room	10 nights from 6 July	Cot in room
Mr and Mrs Wolseley	Double bed	12 July for an indefinite period	Weekly account

(*a*) Draw up a room lettings chart for the period 1–15 July (inclusive) covering the above rooms.

(*b*) Post the bookings to the chart.

(*c*) Draw up three pages of an advance lettings *diary* and date them for 11, 12, and 13 July.

(*d*) Show the bookings as they would appear in this diary for these three days.

9. Describe in detail, in a system with which you are familiar, the channels and hands through which a visitor's letter requesting a reservation would pass, from the time it is delivered by the postman until it is finally filed.

10. What is the legal position when a guest cancels hotel accommodation which he previously reserved?

CHAPTER 4 – VISITORS' ACCOUNTS

1. Describe the main objects in keeping accounts in an hotel.

2. What are the principal types of charges to resident guests' accounts in an hotel? Describe each briefly and show how they reach the guests' accounts.

3. What is book-keeping? How are the principles of double entry book-keeping applied in the case of the tabular system of keeping guests' accounts?

4. Explain how the tabular ledger forms a part of the double entry book-keeping system of an hotel.

5. What is entailed in balancing the handwritten tabular ledger? Why is it necessary? Which types of error may not be revealed by this procedure?

6. What are compensating errors and how do they differ from other types of error? Illustrate your answers by reference to the tabular ledger.

7. What is a daily summary sheet and what are its functions?

8. Give specimen ruling of a tabular ledger and show on it the points stated below. Supply any figures necessary for your illustration.

(a) Mr Adam, who has been resident for two days, changes from room 7 to room 12.

(b) Mr Big (room 3) is given a loan of £10 by the hotel.

(c) Mr Charles's account amounts to £24·40. A service charge of 10 per cent is added to this, he pays the whole bill by cheque, and leaves. It is then discovered that on the day of his departure he has been erroneously charged with £1·10 for wine, which should have been debited to Mr Drake (room 17, still resident). Make the necessary corrections.

(d) It is found that Mrs Eve, who is a permanent resident (room 6), has been charged for a *Times* newspaper, price 3p, instead of a *Daily Telegraph*, price 2p, for the last three days.

(e) Cash received from restaurant for lunches £18·35, from American Bar, £8·35, and from Froth and Blow Bar, £10·80.

You are not required to balance the tabular ledger.

9. Mr John Field, a customer, stays at the hotel and incurs an account for £18·75 for which a credit account is opened when he departs on 4 March. He subsequently incurs the following bills:

		£
6 March	Dinners in Restaurant	2·50
18	Coffees in Lounge	0·30
20	Luncheons in Restaurant	3·25
25	Dinners in Grill Room	1·50
3 April	Garage Account	4·80
8	Dinners in Restaurant	5·70
14	Hotel Account	23·25
23	Luncheons in Restaurant	4·70
29	Coffees and Cigarettes in Lounge	0·35

On 25 March he paid a cheque for the amount of his account to 20 March, and this cheque was returned on 29 March marked 'R/D please re-present'. The cheque was re-presented on 1 April and duly met. Mr Field paid another cheque for £12·00 on 10 April. You are required to write up the customer's sales ledger account for March and April balancing the account at the end of each month.

10. On 22 February Mr Hancock sends a cheque for £15·00 to the hotel as a deposit against an advance reservation for the period 22–29 May, inclusive. An account is accordingly opened in the sales ledger.

His account amounted to £23·00, and on 30 May he paid the balance of his account in cash. He subsequently incurred the following bills:

		£
31 May	Dinners in Restaurant	6·05
3 June	Lunches in Restaurant	3·90
6	Dinners in Grill Room	4·85
17	Afternoon Teas	0·85
21	Lunches in Restaurant	1·00
21	Cigars	0·85
27	Dinners in Grill Room	3·00

On 4 June he paid his account by cheque up to and including 3 June· On 7 June Control discovered that dinners amounting to £4·85 charged to Mr Hancock should have been charged to the sales ledger account of Mr James, and this item was accordingly transferred. On 24 June a cheque for £2·70 was received from Mr Hancock. You are required to write up Mr Hancock's sales ledger account for May and June, balancing the account at the end of each month.

11. The following shows yesterday's business in the hotel. You are required to write up and balance the tabular ledger for the day. Suitably ruled paper is provided upon which you can draw up a form of tabular sheet with which you are familiar. *Lack of neatness may result in loss of marks.*

THE GREYFRIAR HOTEL

Visitors already resident

Room No.	Name	No. of persons	Amount b/f. from previous day £
103 (single)	Mrs S. Watson	1	11·85
117 (double)	Mr and Mrs J. Henson	2	29·60
204 (double)	Mr and Mrs H. Masters	2	14·75
221 (single)	Major B. Swain	1	7·20
313 (double)	Mr and Mrs D. Constant	2	34·40
324 (double)	Mr and Mrs P. Blair	2	4·85
407 (single)	Miss E. Thurston	1	19·15

Room Charges.
Single Room £2·50 per day.
Double Room £3·50 per day.

8 a.m.   *Early Morning Tea.*
Room No. 103, 10p   Room No. 313, 20p
Room No. 117, 20p   Room No. 324, 20p
Room No. 221, 10p   Room No. 407, 10p
Newspapers and Periodicals.
Room No. 103, 2p   Room No. 313, 9p
Room No. 117, 4p   Room No. 324, 3p
Room No. 204, 5p   Room No. 407, 2p
Room No. 221, 2p

9 a.m.   *Breakfasts.*
Room No. 103, 30p   Room No. 313, 50p
Room No. 117, 35p   Room No. 324, 60p
Room No. 204, 60p   Room No. 407, 30p
Room No. 221, 20p

Laundry.
Room No. 117, 60p   Room No. 313, 70p
Telephone Charges.
Room No. 204, 5p   Room No. 324, 8p

10.30 a.m. *Arrival*
Mr S. Watson arrived to join Mrs Watson who was moved
from 103 to 113 (double).

11 a.m. *Morning Coffees.*

Room No. 113, 20p	Room No. 324, 20p
Room No. 117, 20p	Room No. 407, 10p
Room No. 204, 20p	Chance 90p
Whisky.	
Room No. 221, 25p	

11.30 a.m. *Disbursements.*
Cash advance Room No. 204, £5·00
Theatre tickets, Room No. 113, £1·75

12 noon Room No. 117, Mr J. Henson paid account, £29·60
Arrival
Room No. 103, Lady Watkins (single).

1 p.m. *Luncheons.*
Room No. 103, Lunch, 50p; coffee, 10p.
Room No. 113, Lunch, £1·30; beer, 10p; coffee, 20p.
Room No. 117, Lunch, £1·00; whisky, 25p; minerals, 5p;
coffee, 20p.
Room No. 313, Lunch, £1·00; coffee, 20p.
Room No. 324, Lunch, £1·10; wines, 65p; liqueurs, 40p;
coffee, 20p.
Chance: £7·90; wines, £1·15; spirits, £1·75; liqueurs,
£1·20; beers, 50p; minerals, 35p; cigarettes, 75p; coffees,
90p.

2 p.m. *Disbursement.*
Room No. 313, cash advance £5·00

3 p.m. *Arrival.*
Mr and Mrs C. Carlton, Room No. 304 (double).
Major Swain, Room No. 221, paid £5·00 on account.

4.30 p.m.   *Afternoon Tea.*
               Room No. 113, 45p   Room No. 304, 45p
               Room No. 117, 45p   Room No. 407, 45p
               Room No. 204, 45p   Chance, £7·20
               Room No. 221, 25p

5 p.m.   *Departure.*

5 p.m.   *Departure.*
               Mr and Mrs D. Constant. Account suspended to Ledger.

7.30 p.m.   *Dinners.*
               Room No. 103, Dinner, 75p; coffee, 10p.
               Room No. 113, Dinner £1·50; wines, 75p; coffee, 10p.
               Room No. 117, Dinner £1·40; spirits 25p; coffee 20p.
               Room No. 204, Dinner, £1·50; liqueurs, 40p; coffee, 20p.
               Room No. 221, Dinner, 90p; beer, 10p; coffee, 10p.
               Room No. 324, Dinner, £1·50; wines, 90p; coffee, 20p.
               Chance, £8·65; wines, £3·60; spirits, £1·20; beers, 60p;
               cigars, £1·30.

10 p.m.   *Refreshments.*
               Sandwiches, 60p; biscuits, 10p; coffees, £1·50; minerals,
               35p.

               Copy of Cashier's Receipt book.

	£
Chance morning coffee	0·90
J. Henson, Room 117	29·60
Chance luncheons	14·50
Major Swain, Room No. 221	5·00
Chance teas	7·20
Chance dinners	15·35
Chance refreshments	2·55
American bar	24·75

12. The following shows yesterday's business in the hotel. You are required to write up and balance the tabular ledger for the day. Suitably ruled paper is provided upon which you can draw up a form of tabular sheet with which you are familiar. *Lack of neatness may result in loss of marks.*

THE GREYFRIAR HOTEL

Room Charges.
Single Room, £2·75 per day.
Double Room, £4·00 per day.
Suite, £4·50 per day.

Visitors already resident

Room No.	Name	No. of persons	Amount b/f. from previous day £
23 (single)	Mr H. Stansfield	1	4·95
32 (double)	Mr and Mrs L. Marsden	2	12·70
41 (suite)	Mr and Mrs Holden	2	29·35
43 (single)	Mrs P. Black	1	6·35
56 (double)	Major and Mrs Spencer-Jones	2	21·20
65 (double)	Mr and Mrs D. Caldwell	2	9·75
78 (double)	Mr and Mrs W. Tate	2	17·90
83 (single)	Miss C. Grant	1	7·15

8 a.m.   *Early Morning Tea.*

Room No. 23, 5p	Room No. 56, 10p
Room No. 32, 5p	Room No. 65, 10p
Room No. 41, 10p	Room No. 78, 10p
Room No. 43, 5p	Room No. 83, 5p

Newspapers and Periodicals.

Room No. 23, 3p	Room No. 56, 4p
Room No. 32, 4p	Room No. 65, 3p
Room No. 41, 7p	Room No. 78, 8p
Room No. 43, 2p	Room No. 83, 2p

8.30 a.m. *Arrival*
Mr V. Drew, Room No. 33 (single).

9 a.m. *Breakfasts.*

Room No. 23, 30p	Room No. 56, 60p
Room No. 32, 60p	Room No. 65, 65p
Room No. 33, 30p	Room No. 78, 60p
Room No. 41, 75p	Room No. 83, 35p
Room No. 43, 35p	

Telephone Charges.

Room No. 32, 3p	Room No. 83, 2p
Room No. 41, 5p	

Garage.
Room No. 33, Petrol 93p

11 a.m. *Morning Coffee.*

Room No. 23, 10p	Room No. 65, 20p
Room No. 41, 20p	Room No. 83, 10p

Chance: £1·50
Disbursement.
Rail ticket for Mrs Black, 80p

12 noon *Departure.*
Room No. 43, Mrs Black. Transfer account to sales ledger.

12.30 p.m.
Mr Holden paid account, £29·35
Mr Tate paid £15·00 on account.
Mrs Black returned having missed her train, and was given the room she occupied on departure.
Garage
Room No. 56, £1·70

1 p.m. *Luncheons.*
Room No. 23, Lunch, 55p; coffee, 10p.
Room No. 32, Lunch £1·10; whisky, 25p; coffee, 20p.

Room No. 41, Lunch, £1·25; wine, 85p; coffee, 10p;
cigarettes, 25p.
Room No. 65, Lunch, £1·10; beer, 10p; minerals, 5p;
coffee, 10p.
Room No. 78, Lunch, £1·20; whisky, 25p; minerals, 5p;
coffee, 20p.
Chance: Lunch, £8·75; wines, £1·70; spirits, £1·55; beers
60p; minerals, 20p; cigarettes, £1·20; coffees, £1·10.

2 p.m.   *Disbursement.*
              Flowers for Mrs Holden, £1·75

2.30 p.m.   *Arrival.*
              Mr and Mrs J. Seymour arrived and were shown up to
              Room No. 68 (double).
              Telephone Charges.
              Room No. 43, 8p   Room No. 78, 3p
              Room No. 56, 3p   Room No. 83, 3p

2.45 p.m.   Mr and Mrs Seymour returned to reception and asked for a
              different room. They were given room No. 46 (double).

3.30 p.m.   *Arrival.*
              Capt and Mrs R. Cornwall, Room No. 68 (double).

4.30 p.m.   *Afternoon Teas.*
              Room No. 32, 50p   Room No. 43, 25p
              Room No. 33, 25p   Room No. 65, 50p
              Room No. 41, 50p   Room No. 83, 25p
              Chance: £2·50
              Control disclosed the omission of 10p early morning
              teas for Room No. 32 and an overcharge of 25p on a dinner
              bill for Room No. 56 for the previous day.

7.30 p.m.   *Dinners.*
              Room No 23, Dinner, 65p; coffee, 10p.
              Room No. 32, Dinner, £1·40; wines, £1·10; coffee, 20p.

Room No. 41, Dinner, £1·50; spirits, 45p; minerals, 5p; coffee, 20p; cigarettes, 25p.

Room No. 43, Dinner, 70p; coffee, 10p.

Room No. 46, Dinner, £1·45; spirits, 25p; minerals, 5p; coffee, 20p.

Room No. 56, Dinner, £1·25; coffee, 20p.

Room No. 65, Dinner, £1·40; wines, 90p; coffee, 20p.

Room No. 68, Dinner, £1·35; beers, 10p; minerals, 5p; coffee, 20p; cigarettes, 20p.

Room No. 78, Dinner, £1·50; wines, 65p; coffee, 20p.

Room No. 83, Dinner, 65p; coffee, 10p.

Chance: £6·20; coffee, 65p; wines, £3·80; spirits £1·20; beers, 90p; minerals, 40p; cigarettes, £1·05.

8.30 p.m.   *Departure.*
Major and Mrs Spencer-Jones and transfer account to sales ledger.

American Bar Takings.
Spirits, £25·70; cigarettes, £4·90.

13. You are required to write up the tabular ledger during 5 May and balance it for the day. Suitably ruled paper is provided on which you should draw up a form of tabular sheet with which you are familiar. *Lack of neatness will cause loss of marks.*

THE MARINE HOTEL

Room and breakfast charge £1·25 per person, per night (allocated 95p to apartments and 30p to breakfast).

Inclusive terms £1·80 or £1·95 per person, per day (allocated 50p or 65p respectively to apartments and £1·30 to board). Inclusive terms include afternoon tea but not coffee after meals nor early morning tea.

The following visitors are already resident:

Room No.	Name	No. of persons	Terms	Amount b/f. from 4 May £
1	Mr and Mrs Young	2	Inclusive £1·80	37·45
2	Miss Purves	1	Inclusive £1·95	8·00
4	Col and Mrs Webber	2	R & B	2·50
6 and 9	Mr, Mrs, and Miss Elliston	3	R & B	31·40
7	Mr Lush	1	Inclusive 36s. 0d.	5·10
8	Mlle Maillard	1	R & B	1·25
11	Mr and Mrs Mackenzie	2	R & B	19·60

5 May.

8 a.m.   *Early Morning Tea.*
         Room 1, 10p   Room 6, 10p
         Room 2, 5p   Room 7, 5p
         Room 4, 10p   Room 9, 5p

8.10 a.m.   *Newspapers.*
         Room 1, 2p   Room 6, 2p
         Room 4, 3p   Room 11, 2p

8.20 a.m.   *Breakfasts.*
         Room 2, one.   Room 7, one.
         Room 6 and 9, three.

8.40 a.m.   *Departure.*
         Room 7, Mr Lush – account paid by cash.

9 a.m.   *Departure.*
         Room 2, Miss Purves – account transferred to sales ledger folio 152.

9.30 a.m.   *Breakfasts.*
         Room 1, two.   Room 8, one.
         Room 4, two.   Room 11, two.

9.45 a.m. *Disbursement.*
Flowers, £1·05, for Mlle Maillard.

10 a.m. Mr Elliston paid £24·20 on account.

10.15 a.m. Mlle Maillard transferred to Room 7.

10.30 a.m. *Telephone Charges.*
Room 4, 5p   Room 7, 35p
Room 6, 2p

11.15 a.m. *Morning Coffee.*
Room 1, 10p   Room 7, 5p
Chance: 45p

11.30 a.m. *Arrival.*
Mr Castell given room 2 to be charged room and breakfast terms.

2 p.m. *Luncheons*
Room 1, two luncheons; coffee, 10p; beers, 10p.
Room 2, luncheon, 45p; coffee, 5p.
Room 4, luncheons, 85p; whisky, 25p; minerals, 5p.
Room 6, luncheons, £1·25; coffee, 15p.
Room 7, luncheons, £2·75; wine, £1·15; liqueurs, 60p; coffee, 20p.
Chance: luncheons, £6·45; coffees, 30p; wines, £2·55; spirits, 75p; beers, 30p; cigarettes, 25p.
Ballroom: 33 luncheons, £13·20; 31 coffees, £1·55; to be charged to the Seabridge Rotary Club, sales ledger folio 17.

2.30 p.m. *Arrival.*
Mr and Mrs Woodward given room 3 to be charged inclusive terms £1·95 per day).

3 p.m. *Disbursements.*
Mlle Maillard, theatre tickets, £2·25.

4 p.m.   Control disclosed an overcharge of 30p on previous day for Room 4; also 25p for whisky charged in error to Room 9 instead of Room 4; also omission of coffee 5p for Room 11.

4.30 p.m.   *Departure.*
Room 4, Col and Mrs Webber account paid in cash – no charge for apartments today.

5 p.m.   *Afternoon Teas.*

Room 1, two.	Room 3, two.
Room 2, 30p	Room 6, 45p
Chance: 75p	

5.30 p.m.   *Telephone.*
Room 7, 4p

6 p.m.   *Arrival.*
Mr Blackwell given Room 10, inclusive terms (£1·95), to be charged to the account of Booksellers' Association; all extras to be paid cash by Mr Blackwell on departure.

8 p.m.   *Dinners.*
Room 1, two dinners.
Room 2, dinners, 50p; coffee, 5p; wines, 75p.
Room 3, two dinners; coffee, 10p.
Room 9, dinners, £1·50; coffee, 15p; beers, 15p.
Room 10, dinners, one; coffee, 5p; wines, £1·25.
Room 11, dinner, 50p.
Chance: dinners, £7·50; coffee, 65p; wines, £4·35; liqueurs, 70p; cigars and cigarettes, 65p.
Banquet Room: 15 dinners, £11·25; coffee, 75p; wines, £3·80; to be charged to the account of Mrs Parker, sales ledger folio 91.

8.30 p.m.   *Garage Charges.*
Mr Young, 10p; Mr Castell, 10p; Mr Elliston, 15p.

8.45 p.m.   *Telephone.*

Room, 2, 45p.	Room 3, 2p.

10.30 p.m. Room 7, sandwiches, 85p; wine, 75p.

11 p.m.   Hotel bar: liquors and minerals, £30·05; cigarettes, £4·15; sandwiches, 60p.

14. You are required to write up the tabular ledger during 5 May and balance it for the day. Suitably ruled paper is provided on which you should draw up a form of tabular sheet with which you are familiar. *Lack of neatness will cause loss of marks.*

THE IMPERIAL HOTEL

Tariff:
Room and Breakfast £2·75 per person, per night, allocated £2·10 apartments and £0·65 breakfast.
   Inclusive terms £4·20 per person per day, allocated £1·40 apartments and £2·80 food. Sitting room (No. 10) £4·00 per day.

The following visitors are already resident:

Room No.	Name	No. of persons	Terms	Amount b/f. from 4 May £
1	Mr Abel	1	R & B	11·00
3	Mr and Mrs Smith	2	Inclusive	8·40
4	Lady Fairweather	1	Inclusive	38·80
5 and 7	Messrs Todd, Linklater and Finlay	3	R & B	16·40
6	Mr James	1	Inclusive	34·80
9	Monsieur Petitjean	1	R & B	2·75
10 and 11	Mr and Mrs Palmer	2	R & B	70·40

5 May.

8 a.m.   *Early Morning Tea.*
             Room 1, 5p   Room 6,   5p
             Room 3, 10p   Room 11, 10p
             Room 4, 5p

8.15 a.m. *Newspapers.*

Room 1, 4p   Room 4, 4p
Room 3, 7p   Room 11, 9p

8.30 a.m. *Breakfasts.*

Room 1, one.   Room 5, two.
Room 4, one.   Room 7, one.

8.35 a.m. *Departures.*

Room 1, account paid by cash.
Rooms 5 and 7, account transferred to sales ledger folio 71.

9.30 a.m. *Breakfasts.*

Room 3, two.   Room 10, two.
Room 6, one.

9.45 a.m. *Disbursement.*

Monsieur Petitjean, railway tickets, £3·55

10.30 a.m. *Arrival.*

Mr Hunt, given Room 1 to be charged R & B terms.

10.45 a.m. Mr Palmer paid   £52·95 . on account.

11 a.m. Mr James transferred to Room 7.

11.30 a.m. *Coffee.*

Room 1, 10p   Room 10, 20p
Room 9, 20p   Chance: 70p

11.45 a.m. *Telephone*

Room 3, 75p   Room 10, 8p
Room 9, 3p

2 p.m. *Luncheons.*

Room 1, luncheon, £1·10; coffee, 5p; wine, 85p.
Room 3, two luncheons; coffee, 10p; beer, 15p.
Room 4, one luncheon; minerals, 5p.
Room 7, one luncheon; coffee, 5p; whisky, 20p.

Room 9, luncheon, £1·50; coffee, 5p; wines, 90p; Benedictine, 20p.
Room 10, luncheons, £1·80; whisky, 10p; minerals, 5p.
Chance: luncheons, £15·50; coffee, 60p; wines, £3·50; beers, 40p; cigars and cigarettes, 75p.

2.30 p.m.   *Banquet Room.*
Seabridge Ladies Luncheon Club.
Luncheons, £35·00; coffees, £1·75; wines, £6·65; account transferred to sales ledger folio 152.

2.35 p.m.   *Arrival.*
Miss Hepplewhite given Room 6 to be charged inclusive terms.

2.40 p.m.   *Telephone.*
Room 1, 5p   Room 9, 20p

3 p.m.   *Departure.*
Room 9 (no charge for apartments today). Account paid in cash.

3.30 p.m.   Control disclosed the following:
Afternoon tea 35p on 4 May charged to Room 3 instead of Room 4. Overcharge on dinners on 4 May for Room 10 of 25p. Whisky 25p omitted on 4 May from Room 6.

4.30 p.m.   *Disbursement.*
Flowers for Lady Fairweather, £1·35

5 p.m.   *Afternoon Tea.*
Room 1, 35p   Room 10, 70p
Room 3, two.   Chance: £1·75
Room 4, one and one guest, 35p.

5.25 p.m.   *Arrival.*
Mr and Mrs van Bergman given Room 5, to be charged R & B terms.

5.50 p.m. *Telephone.*
Room 1, 5p   Room 5, 60p

6.10 p.m. *Cigarettes.*
Room 10, 20p

7.15 p.m. *Arrival.*
Lord and Lady Bramshott given Rooms 9 and 12 to be charged R & B terms.

8 p.m. *Garage.*
Room 1, 25p   Room 7, 25p
Room 3, 25p   Room 9, 20p
Room 5, 20p

8.30 p.m. *Dinners.*
Room 1, £1·25; coffee, 5p.
Room 3, two, coffee, 10p.
Room 4, one.
Room 5, £2·50; coffee, 10p; wine, £1·40; liqueurs, 35p.
Room 6, one.
Room 7, one; coffee, 5p; beer, 10p.
Room 10, £7·25; coffee, 20p; wine, £1·95.
Chance: £21·80; coffee, 70p; wines, £3·25; spirits, 25p; beers, 30p; liqueurs, 45p.

9 p.m. Room 9, sandwiches, 35p; whisky, 25p.

9.30 p.m. *Banquet Room.*
Trento Motors Ltd. Dinners, £21·00; coffee, £1·05; wines, £7·50; cigars, £3·15. Account transferred to sales ledger folio 176.

10.30 p.m. *Hotel Bar.*
Liquors and minerals, £42·45; tobacco, £3·40.

15. When you come on duty this morning, the visitors' tabular ledger shows the following:

Room No.	Name	Terms	Balance b/f. £
3	Mr and Mrs Smythe	Inclusive	18·85
4	Major Browne	R & B	2·75
6–7	Mr and Mrs Franklin and two children	Inclusive	98·20
8	Miss Smithson	R & B	9·80
14	Lady Telman	R & B	11·05
15	Mr and Mrs Cavendish	R & B	23·10
19	Mr Smith	R & B	1·80
21	Cmdr Tipson	R & B	4·15
25	Mrs Chippenham	Inclusive	28·55

Tariff:

Room and Breakfast, £1·80 per person, per night (£1·50 for room, and £0·30 for breakfast).

Inclusive terms £3·15 per person, per day (£1·40 for room, and £1·75 for food).

You are now required to post the following charges in the order in which they appear, then complete and balance the 'tab' for the day.

7.30 a.m. *Early morning teas* (5p *per person*).

Room 3, 2 teas.	Room 14, 1 tea
Room 4, 1 tea.	Room 15, 2 teas.
Room 6, 2 teas.	Room 21, 1 tea.
Room 8, 1 tea.	Room 25, 1 tea.

8 a.m. *Disbursements.*
Room 4, postage due, 2p.   Room 19, chemist, 20p.
Room 15, postage stamps, 3p.

8.15 a.m. Major Browne asks for his bill. He pays cash and **leaves.**

8.30 a.m. *Disbursement.*
Room 14, postage stamps, 8p.

9 a.m.   Miss Smithson is leaving. Instructions have been received for her bill to be sent to Chic Modes Ltd.

9.15 a.m.   Mrs Chippenham leaves, and pays by cheque.

9.30 a.m.   *Telephone Calls.*
             Room 3p   Room 19, 68p
             Room 8p

9.45 a.m.   Mr Smith departs, transfer account to ledger.

10.15 a.m.   *Disbursements.*
             Room 14, shoe repairs, 65p; Room 3, postage stamp, 6p.

10.30 a.m.   Control discovers Room 15 was charged 54p instead of 45p for spirits yesterday. Make the necessary adjustment.

11 a.m.   Mr and Mrs Norton arrive and are allocated Room 10 on inclusive terms.

11.30 a.m.   Cmdr Tipson is joined by Mrs Tipson. Adjust rate.

12.15 p.m.   *From Lounge.*
             Room 6, 4 coffees (5p per person); Room 14, 2 coffees (5p per person); Room 21, pot of tea (10p), biscuits (3p), cigarettes, 20p.
             Chance teas and coffees, £1·20, biscuits, etc., 30p; tobacco, £1·90.

12.30 p.m.   *Telephone Calls.*
             Room 14, 18p   Room 21, 3p
             Room 15, 3p

12.45 p.m.   Col and Mrs Priestleigh arrive and are allocated Room 4 on R & B terms.

2.30 p.m.   Restaurant Book shows the following:

Room No.	Luncheons £	Wines £	Spirits £	Beers £	Minerals £	Beverages £	Tobacco £
4	1·60		0·15	0·20		0·10	
6–7		1·00			0·20	0·10	0·15
10				0·20	0·05	0·10	
14	0·75	0·45				0·05	0·20
21	1·90	1·35	0·35			0·10	
Chance	38·70	8·55	1·60	0·90	0·30	1·35	0·60

3.15 p.m. Mr and Mrs Miller arrive and are allocated Room 1 on inclusive terms.
Mr and Mrs Roche arrive and are allocated Room 16 on inclusive terms.
Mr Baird arrives and is allocated Room 5 on R & B terms.

3.30 p.m. *Disbursement.*
45p paid by Hall Porter for Mr Baird (taxi).

4 p.m. Mr and Mrs Cavendish move to Room 22.

5 p.m. *Afternoon Teas (25p) served in the lounge, as follows:*
Room 4, 2 teas; Room 5, 1 tea and cigarettes (20p);
Room 14, 6 teas; Room 22, 2 teas.
Chance: teas, £4·50, and tobacco, £1·20.

6 p.m. *Laundry Charges.*
Room 3, 35p   Room 6, 70p

7 p.m. *Garage Charges.*
Room 3, 35p; Room 6, 35p; Room 14, 35p and petrol,
95p; Room 21, 35p.

7.30 p.m. Mr Franklin gives you a cheque for £100 towards his account.

9 p.m. *Telephone Calls.*
Room 1, 3p   Room 10, 15p
Room 3, 8p   Room 14, 5p
Room 4, 45p   Room 22, 80p
Room 5, 60p   Chance: ££2·15

9.30 p.m. Restaurant Book shows the following:

Room No.	Dinners £	Wines £	Spirits £	Beers £	Minerals £	Beverages £	Tobacco £
3		1·25				0·10	
5	1·95	0·85	0.40			0·10	0·45
10				0·20		0·05	
14	6·85	3·50	1·10			0·30	
22	2·00					0·20	
Chance	55·30	20·75	3·40	0·60	0·20	2·25	2·70

Banquets.
River Room: Tennis Club Annual Dinner – £140·50.
Cash takings: wines, £58·20; spirits, £40·60; beers, £10·10; minerals, £0·95.
Oak Room: Dr Carr's party. Dinner, £95·00; wines, £30·90; spirits, £20·15; minerals, £0·20.

CHAPTER 5 – CASH AND BANKING

1. State the methods by which payments can be made, giving a brief explanation of each method.

2. What is meant by the imprest system of keeping a petty cash book? Illustrate your answer with specimen entries in the petty cash book of the Angel Hotel, Westhampton, for the week ended 21 January 197–.

3. Draw a facsimile of a cheque dated 2 May 197–, making it payable to E. Harwood. The drawer of the cheque is T. Sampson, the amount £7·20, and the bank on which it is drawn is the Central Bank Ltd. Cross the cheque and write the words 'Not negotiable' between the crossing.
You are required:

(a) to explain the effect of the words 'Not negotiable'.

(b) to state, with reasons, whether it is necessary for Harwood to endorse the cheque before:
(i) paying it into his bank account.
(ii) passing it on to A. Peters in payment of a debt.

4. When a bank returns a cheque it is customary for the reason to be noticed on the cheque or on a slip attached thereto. The following are examples of such reasons. You are required to write a brief note on each and explain its meaning and significance.

(*a*) 'Refer to drawer'.
(*b*) 'Drawer deceased'.
(*c*) 'Post-dated'.
(*d*) 'No account'.
(*e*) 'Words and figures differ'..
(*f*) 'Endorsement requires confirmation'.

5. On 30 April 197– the cash book of Greyfriars Hotel showed a credit balance of £43·70 and the bank pass book at the same date was in credit to the extent of £25·73. Prepare a bank reconciliation at that date taking into account:
Cheques entered in cash book but banked on 1 May:

G. Stevens	£23·72
T. Wood	£51·88
W. Jones	£47·66
S. Brown	£61·61

Cheques dispatched but uncleared:

Carlton Butchers	£73·23
Grocery Supplies	£47·33
Seaside Borough Council	£114·89
Hardware Stores	£18·85

6. In a certain hotel it is the practice for deposits received against future bookings to be retained in cash in the hotel safe until the guest arrives, when the cash is credited to his account and banked. Mention the dangers of this practice and outline a satisfactory system.

7. A guest queries the charge shown on his account under the heading 'paid outs'. Explain the action you would take to ascertain its accuracy and, if found to be incorrect, how you would rectify the error.

8. As cashier you are responsible for the receipt and payment of monies at the hotel. You are provided with a floating balance of

£10·00. Describe fully how you would ensure that your float could be accounted for at the end of a day's business.

9. In an hotel where a book-keeper/cashier handles visitors' accounts, list the sequence of events and actions taken by him, from the time a departing guest asks for his bill until he leaves the hotel, and the steps taken by the book-keeper/cashier after the guest has left the desk. Assume cash settlement.

10. What should a receptionist know about travellers' cheques?

CHAPTER 6 – MECHANIZED HOTEL BILLING

1. Explain in outline what points would have to be considered before installing a mechanized system of visitors' accounts in an hotel of eighty bedrooms.

2. What arguments would you advance for a mechanized system of visitors' accounts in an hotel of about 100 bedrooms?

3. Compare the advantages and drawbacks of the tabular ledger system and of a mechanized system of visitors' accounts with reference to a large hotel. State the size of the hotel and the kind of mechanized system to which your comparison applies; you may choose the hotel described in question 5, Chapter 1, as a basis for your comparison.

CHAPTER 7 – SUNDRY GUEST SERVICES

1. List ten reference books of most use to an enquiry clerk in a London hotel and state concisely the principal contents of each.

2. To assist a guest, to what reference books would you turn to supply the following information:

(a) The correct title and/or honours of a nobleman.
(b) The address of a clergyman.
(c) The distance from one town to another.
(d) The name and some particulars of an hotel in another town.
(e) The postal district of a street in London.
(f) The postage on an airmail letter to Tokyo.
(g) The name and address of an interpreter.

3. (*a*) In what reference books would an enquiry clerk in a London hotel find the following information:

(i) The early closing day in a provincial town
(ii) the hours of opening of a museum
(iii) the postal district of a London street
(iv) the charge for an overseas telegram
(v) the address of a particular firm of jewellers?

(*b*) State concisely what information is provided by each of the books under (*a*) above.

4. What methods of safe custody of guests' valuables do you know? Describe each briefly.

5. Outline an efficient system for dealing with guests' registered mail and give a specimen ruling of any special record(s) required in connection with your system.

CHAPTER 8 – COMMUNICATIONS

1. Give some examples showing how the housekeepers can supply information which will assist the reception clerks in their work.

2. Two departments with which the receptionist co-operates a great deal are: (*a*) the uniformed staff, and (*b*) housekeeping.

Give details of the various ways in which each of these departments can assist the reception office to provide an efficient service to the guests.

3. Give a specimen ruling of an arrival notification and describe fully its function and use.

4. At a busy hotel where 'chance' bookings for one night's accommodation account for a large proportion of the daily occupancy it was discovered that a certain number of guests could, and did (after staying one night), depart without paying their bills. What is the common hotel practice for dealing with this situation?

CHAPTER 9 – CONTROL

1. Select five commonly used reception records and explain how you would check in detail the accuracy of each at the end of a day's business in an hotel.

2. What is the purpose of 'control'? Give five examples of its operation in practice.

3. What is meant by 'control'? Describe the duties undertaken by a control clerk.

4. The balancing of the visitors' ledger achieves arithmetical accuracy but some mistakes may remain if no control is applied. What are the types of error which may not be revealed when the visitors' ledger balances?

5. List the steps involved in the night audit of visitors' accounts in an hotel where a billing machine, with which you are familiar, is used.

CHAPTER 10 – REPORTS AND STATISTICS

1. The following is the total accommodation of the A.B.C. Hotel, and the number of rooms vacant on a particular night (all occupied rooms are fully occupied):

Type of room	Single	Twin	Double
Price per room	£2·50	£4·50	£4·00
Total number of rooms	80	35	35
Number of rooms vacant	35	5	5

(*a*) Calculate percentage room and guest occupancy, total room sales, average sales per room occupied, and express the total room sales achieved as a percentage of maximum possible.

(*b*) State from which records you would obtain the information needed for the above calculations in practice, and with what records you would check its correctness.

2. From the information below, relating to September, give in the form of a self-explanatory table room and guest occupancy for each type of room and for the whole hotel, and comment briefly.

	Total	Single	Double
Bedrooms	120	80	40
Room/nights	2,640	1,920	720
Guest/nights	3,240	1,920	1,320

3. You are required to submit a report to the managing director of a new hotel detailing your proposals for the equipping, staffing, and organization of the reception unit.

The hotel is sited in Central London and is planned to cater for the luxury trade. It has 200 twin-bedded rooms and 100 single rooms, a short average length of stay, and the reception unit is concerned neither with visitors' accounts nor guests' inquiries.

SUNDRY QUESTIONS

1. What are the main provisions of the Hotel Proprietors' Act, 1956?

2. Explain briefly the following terms:

(a) alien
(b) chance business
(c) demi-pension
(d) 'en pension'
(e) innkeeper's liability
(f) innkeeper's lien
(g) room occupancy
(h) safe custody
(i) service charge
(j) visitors' disbursement.

3. Describe fully and give the use and purpose of:
(a) Arrival and departure lists.
(b) The reception board.

4. In what ways can the reception office staff co-operate with:
(a) The head waiter
(b) The telephonist
in the performance of their duties?

5. Write briefly on the following:
(a) Arrival list
(b) Visitors' record index
(c) Safe custody receipt book
(d) Record of registered letters.

6. State accurately the meaning of the following abbreviations and write short notes on each:

(a) a/c
(b) A.D.C.
(c) c/o
(d) C.O.D.
(e) MTH
(f) R/D
(g) S.T.D.
(h) V.I.P.
(i) WK
(j) V.P.O.

7. Explain fully the purpose of the necessary files you would recommend for use in the reception office of a large hotel.

8. Give in detail the action a receptionist would take when a guest arrives at an hotel.

9. On 18 February 197– Mr T. Bradley writes to your hotel, booking a room for the period 20–27 May. He encloses a deposit of £5·00. Explain in detail the accounting entries to be made in the relevant books from the time of the receipt of the deposit to the time of Mr Bradley's departure. (N.B. – Actual ledger accounts are not required.)

10. Name five of the most important books or ledgers maintained by the reception office of a large hotel and explain the function of each one.

11. Explain a system for dealing with advance bookings of accommodation received by letter or by telephone.

12. When presenting a guest's account at the end of his stay what procedure would you adopt and what safeguards would you take in each of the following circumstances: he wishes to settle the bill (a) by cash; (b) by cheque; or (c) have it sent to his company for payment at a later date.

13. Explain how the principles of double entry book-keeping apply to the guests' tabular ledger.

14. Give a specimen ruling of a summary book, illustrating your answer with figures for one day's takings.

15. Describe the difference between a current account and a deposit account.

16. Describe in detail a system of dealing with:
(a) Deposits made to secure a reservation.
(b) Deposits for safe custody.

17. Write briefly on the different types of receipt that may be issued to a guest for property or money.

18. Describe the procedure for accepting deposits which are received with advance bookings, and how they are dealt with when the visitor is at the hotel.

19. In an hotel where there is a wide variety of visitors' disbursements, describe a method for obtaining authority for, and recording, paid-outs. (Specimen rulings are not required.)

20. At the end of a day's business the cashier's till contains:
Cash £30·63
Cheques £86·23
$20 U.S. travellers' cheque (exchange rate $2·40 to £).

The travellers' cheque was exchanged for a visitor at the rate of $2·45 to the £.

The books show the following:

	£
Bill sheet receipts	124·27
Visitors' disbursements	0·58
Sales ledger receipts	34·83
Petty cash paid for grocer's bill	10·86
Wages paid	52·84
National Insurance stamps bought and handed to Manager	4·79

Prepare a statement showing the calculation necessary in order to arrive at the cashier's floating balance.

21. Upon being presented with the hotel account prior to his departure, a guest complains that he did not take the dinner for which a charge has been included in the previous day's total. Explain the action you would take.

22. On 20 February, Mr J. Jones sends a cheque for £25·00 to the hotel as a deposit against an advance reservation. On 1 April, at the end of his stay, his account amounts to £21·15.

Describe fully how you would deal with the deposit, and the fact that Mr Jones will require a refund of £3·85.

23. At the end of his first week's stay at an hotel Mr J. Bamberg of New York presents a cheque for $50 on account, drawn on an American bank. Describe how you would ascertain the sterling equivalent of this and how this would be credited to Mr Bamberg's account in the hotel's books.

24. What is a cheque? How many parties are there to a cheque and who are they? What steps can be taken to prevent a cheque from being cashed by an unauthorized person?

25. An hotel cashier starts the day with a £10·00 cash float. At the end of the day she has cash and cheques to the value of £93·24.

During the day she has paid out on behalf of guests (V.P.O.s) a total of £6·42. The total of her duplicate receipts book amounts to £89·84 for the day. You are required:

(*a*) to prepare a statement showing the checking of the cash float, indicating the amount (if any) over or short, (*b*) to state how you would deal with a V.P.O., being £5·00 refund of a deposit.

26. A guest protests that:

(*a*) A cheque that he sent to secure his reservation has not been credited to his account.

(*b*) He has been overcharged on his account for dinner the previous evening.

Describe in full how you would deal with and remedy these two complaints.

27. You are a book-keeper in an hotel and have been provided with a £10·00 float. At the end of each day you are required to account to the head book-keeper for the float and for all moneys which you have received during the day. Describe fully how you would do this.

28. You are a book-keeper in an hotel responsible for the receipt of all moneys and payments of sundry bills, including wages. At the end of the day you try to balance your receipts against cash on hand, but cannot agree. Describe what checks you would carry out to discover the reason for this in order that the mistake can be rectified.

29. Describe in detail the procedure for banking the day's takings consisting of cash and cheques. The latter are made out to the hotel or cash or self or are cheques made out to the guest and endorsed by him at the hotel.

30. Describe how the reception, bill, and cashiers' offices in a large hotel co-operate with each other to create smooth running.

Appendix S

Bibliography

Barrett, T. J.	*Accounting for Hotel Management*	Gee
Boardman, R. D.	*Hotel and Catering Costing and Budgets*	Heinemann
Boni, de G. and Sharles, F.	*Hotel Organisation, Management and Accountancy*	Pitman
Bull, F. and Richardson, C. J.	*Hotel and Catering Law*	Barrie and Rockliff
Dukas, P.	*Hotel Front Office Management and Operation*	Brown
Dunseath, M.	*The Hotel Book-keeper*	Practical Press
Kotas, R.	*Book-keeping in the Hotel and Catering Industry*	Evans
Lewis, A. R.	*Hotel Administration and Accounts*	Jordan
Marshall (ed.)	*The Uniformed Staff*	Barrie and Rockliff
Pitcher, M. E.	*Hotel Book-keeping*	Pitman
Rennie, M.	*Elementary Office Practice*	Heinemann
Taylor, D.	*Hotel and Catering Sales Promotion*	Iliffe
Taylor, H. R.	*Hotel Operation and Control*	Practical Press
White, P. and Beckley, H.	*Hotel Reception*	Arnold
Winslet, V. G.	*Accountancy for Caterers*	Practical Press

Index

Index